D1345216

STATION TO STATION

Also by James Attlee

Isolarion: A Different Oxford Journey
Nocturne: A Journey in Search of Moonlight
Gordon Matta-Clark: The Space Between (with Lisa Le Feuvre)

STATION TO STATION

SEARCHING FOR STORIES
ON THE GREAT WESTERN LINE

JAMES ATTLEE

guardianbooks

Published by Guardian Books 2015

2 4 6 8 10 9 7 5 3 1

First published in Great Britain in 2015 by
Guardian Books
Kings Place, 90 York Way
London N1 9GU
www.guardianbooks.co.uk

A CIP catalogue record for this book is available from the British Library

ISBN 978-0852-65567-2

Cover design by Two Associates
Typeset by seagulls.net

Printed in England by CPI Group (UK) Ltd, Croydon CR0 4YY

For my children

'I felt the sharp nostalgia of train whistles,
piano music down a city street, burning leaves.'
William Burroughs, *Junky: The Definitive Text of Junk*

'Once the search is in progress, something will be found.'
Brian Eno and Peter Schmidt, *Oblique Strategies*

CONTENTS

INTRODUCTION

After all the emails and phone calls and the anxious wait for a response, the meeting itself seems to take no time at all. I receive an invitation to an office above Platform 1 at Paddington, give my name to the security guard at the door and climb the stairs to emerge above the glass panels of the station's curved rooftops, stained nicotine orange by years of smoke and diesel fumes. It feels as if, after attending performances at a great theatre for many years, I have finally slipped behind the curtain.

I pause beside a window in a corridor; this sudden elevation, allowing me to look down from above on the course of so many of my own journeys, seems symbolic of my intentions. The person I have come to speak with, the Director of Communications for this multinational train operator, is herself sliding in from somewhere else, having been detained at another office location along the line. Once we sit down at a table together it is obvious she understands what I need. Yes, I can write what I want, tell it how I find it. She will arrange a letter of authorisation that allows me to talk to staff, which I can produce if I am challenged. Most importantly, a pass is being written that will allow me the freedom to travel the network that runs west from London, starting at a point beneath my feet. Without having to sign anything, or even to kneel and be touched with a sword on each shoulder, I am appointed Writer on the Train.

I leave the meeting in a state that is equal parts shellshock and euphoria. The first thing I decide to do is follow the advice of my benefactors and have my new pass laminated; I want to ensure its permanence, prevent its evaporation back into the realms of possibility and dream. There is a copy shop opposite the station; the man behind the counter tells me he is a little busy, it will take 20 minutes if I am prepared to wait. I walk around the corner to an Italian café to get a coffee. The sky has turned grey, but it is warm enough for diners to be seated outside and I decide to carry my cup out to a table by the door.

The hinterlands of long-distance stations, despite all attempts to smarten them up, remain the stage set for small dramas, just as they were when they were first built. The prostitutes may largely have vanished from Paddington – sex, like other retail offerings, now being freely available on the internet – but the area still attracts those with alternative business strategies in mind. Gangs prowl in search of tourists who they offer to accompany to a bureau de change with favourable rates and then part from their money in a back alley. A constantly shifting population of fresh arrivals is delivered daily, the naive among them matched through the speed-dating mechanism of the street encounter with the unscrupulous operators who will prove their nemesis. In addition to the ripples such incidents produce, a visitor to Paddington, if they are alert, may notice among the bustle of its pavements a faint breeze blowing from another place. Once detected, such a subtle hint remains in the mind, a nagging invitation. This is, after all, the western door marked 'exit' from the city, a way out of the labyrinth, giving access to another world beyond.

My route will follow the railway line laid in the 19th century between London and Bristol, still used by many thousands of passengers each day. It cuts like a blade through the country, linking two great cities, leaping over the space that separates them, its fast trains thundering through small stations on the platforms of which they deposit dust rather than passengers. Now we may think of it chiefly as a commuter line, but it was not always so; its creators had different, more extensive ambitions. Nevertheless, that is how I first encountered it. For 12 years I travelled this steel highway into London every working day. It is hard not to feel that some part of myself is left there, permanently in motion back and forth, a pale reflection in the carriage window overlaid on the fields, skies and buildings rushing past.

But I am not only haunted by the ghost of myself. It is not possible to travel the Great Western route without being aware of the presence of its creator, the Victorian engineer Isambard Kingdom Brunel. There are many lives of the man already and I have no wish to embark on another. What interests me is the way his presence persists, his photographic image as recognisable as the structures he created. In the second decade of the 21st century he is once again at the forefront of our consciousness as we embark on a new age of large-scale rail engineering projects. As I write, his head and shoulders are displayed on a banner hanging from the ceiling of Paddington station (for once he is portrayed without his trademark cigar, this being, after all, a no smoking area). Overprinted across his face in yellow are the words: '£7.5 billion – The greatest investment since Brunel'. Alongside him, on the same heroic scale, hang massively enlarged colour photographs of current workers on the line: Nigel Swan, Engineer; Rosaria Rea, Customer Service; James Cullinane, Customer Service; Bill Mitton, General Operations. Over each portrait, in the same yellow typeface but in capitals this time, is printed the slogan: 'BUILDING A GREATER WEST'. Once again, railways are promising to redraw the map and bring prosperity to the furthest reaches of the kingdom.

Beneath Brunel's iconic station, another is being hollowed out for the new Crossrail route, currently Europe's largest engineering project. Its vast boring machines are eating their way beneath London to join Essex in the east to the Thames valley in the west, the most radical technological realignment of Britain's geography since the railway boom of the 19th century. As Thomas Carlyle wrote of that first great expansion of the rail network, 'Railways are shifting all Towns in Britain into new places; no Town will stand where it did, and nobody can tell for a long while yet where it will stand. This is an unexpected … result. I perceive, railways have set all the Towns of Britain a-dancing'.[1]

A 'cultural place-maker' called Future City has been tasked to oversee an art programme, finding gallery partners who will choose artists to create work for each of the London Crossrail stations. Their website attributes the original idea for the Crossrail route beneath London to an unrealised plan of Brunel's, although whether this is true or apocryphal is a matter of debate. It was Sigmund Freud who compared the workings of human consciousness to an ancient city, its layers of historical accretions, each buried beneath the next, available only to those willing to uncover them. Crossrail, then, burrows beneath the surface of Brunel's documented achievements, into the collective subconscious; almost any engineering endeavour can be given validity, it seems, through association with the great man's name.

Heroic works. Improved connections. Big money. Railways. The message is clear, wherever you look: these elements are lining up today, as they did in Brunel's time. Giants stalk the land once more, treading in the footsteps of the diminutive engineer. Or do they? In an age of increasing wireless and online connection, can these vast hard engineering projects be justified? Who will benefit? Will they truly bring wealth to the regions or merely line the pockets of metropolitan financiers, happy to lend money at profitable rates to projects underwritten by governmental guarantee?

My progress westward, I decide, will be recorded in different forms, summarised under three headings: Locations, Diversions and Digressions. Locations are self-explanatory. Diversions will relate journeys that require taking temporary leave of the main line. Digressions will allow me to expand upon themes arising from my journey. In addition to these there will be the record of the encounters I have along the way. The direction of my journey established, all that remains is to set in motion the engine of my book, leaving its doors unlocked to see who climbs on board.

My seat at the café table is a perfect place from which to observe the theatre of the street, but I have no time to waste. A few yards away, in a copy shop, is a ticket with my name on it that will open up the possibility of travelling thousands of miles around the country by rail. It is a dizzying feeling. For any travel writer – indeed, any traveller – the chief obstacle to movement is the cost of entry. The truth is, the freedom to travel the rail network of the United Kingdom comes at a high price, as anyone who has bought an annual season ticket will know. It is time to collect my ticket and enter the gaping mouth of the station. I must leave before I can return.

II

But before I do – leave that is – I need to step back for a moment in order to remember how I first arrived on the platform. For more than a decade, as I have said, I commuted every day into London, my hour on the train each way bookended with a cycle ride, a period during which, I calculated, I spent more than a year in motion. This is how I formed my relationship with trains: not by going to museums or watching nostalgic TV programmes; not even by standing at the end of platforms jotting serial numbers in a notebook. The sounds and rhythms of trains have entered my body, their timetables are inscribed on my brain. Swiftly the miles I accumulated on the track looped the earth, each day's travel part of an epic but unnoticed journey in which I was joined by countless thousands of others.

One of these was a novelist I knew by sight and whose last book I had read, who boarded the same train as I did each morning. He spent his journey in silence. With him he carried a paperback, a notebook and a pencil. Part of his journey was spent reading; part, it seemed, in noting down his thoughts about what he had read. For the last part of the journey he would alternately look out of the window and write in his notebook. He had, I knew, a young family and a demanding job that he was good at. Yet he found time here to continue his other work; an occupation that came with no guarantees of financial reward or recognition.

The contrast with my own achievements was clear. Various files, drawers and notebooks throughout my own house contained unfinished novels, stories and other failed projects. Now I had been presented with what people call a 'window of time' in which to pursue these ideas to their conclusion. Wasn't this what William Blake spoke of, in his epic poem *Milton*?

There is a Moment in each Day that Satan cannot find
Nor can his Watch Fiends find it, but the Industrious find
This Moment and it multiply, & when once it is found
It renovates every Moment of the Day, if rightly placed.

I knew all about the Watch Fiends already; weren't they the ones marching up and down the platform, blowing their whistles almost as soon as the train had come into the station, creating an atmosphere of urgency and panic? But what if they were the unwitting gatekeepers to another kingdom? Pass this threshold and use the time within it correctly, the poet tells us, and your everyday .

life, however exhausting or humdrum it may be, will be 'renovated' by a sense of purpose and achievement.

I had mourned never having a workroom of my own, or even the time to enter one if I had possessed such a thing. Here it was! Life had delivered it at last. The only significant way it differed from the one I had dreamt of, a difference that could only be seen as a design enhancement, was that it came equipped with wheels. Yet the profession of scribe is universally identified with stasis, immobility, as etymology attests. In Mandarin, a writer is *zuòjiā* – made up of the two characters *zuò*, meaning in one transliteration 'sit' and another 'compose'; and *jiā*, meaning 'home'. A writer is a 'sit-home' – someone who doesn't leave the house. The European tradition provides a more pastoral image. The word 'page' has its origins in the Latin *pagus*, a field of the type that a peasant farmer would plough; the worker on the page is ploughing a furrow, his or her journeys like those of the farmer to the barn or market, all strictly local and very different to the migrations of the modern commuter. I had no desire to be either a farmer or a sit-home. Instead, as a fully mobile writer, I would ride the rails, or *Zuò huǒchē lǚxíng* – literally 'sit fire-car travel', words still bearing the scorch marks of their birth in the age of steam.

In this manner a decade or so un-scrolled outside the carriage window, until I saw an opportunity to change the pattern of my employment and join the freelance army. How much more writing I will get done now, I told myself! Of course the reverse was true; finding space in the stationary world for writing, without the momentum provided by the train, proved harder than I had imagined. Experiments have revealed that divers remember things while deep underwater that they cannot recall on land. In a similar way, in order for a man to recollect where he hid money while he was drunk, he has no choice but to get drunk again. To regain what

I had lost, it became obvious I must re-enter the sealed world of the
railway carriage, a world both noisy, subject to shudders, groans and
vibrations, and at times unnaturally quiet, where a place at a plastic
desk awaited me, a *zuòjiā* in a swiftly moving home.

LOCATION: PADDINGTON
A TEMPLE OF GLASS AND IRON

'Today the city gates are at its centre –
for its real gates are the railway stations.'
Le Corbusier, *Urbanisme* (1925)

Let us consider our surroundings as we stand at the beginning of our journey. The route we are about to travel comes as loaded with symbolism as any of the great pilgrim paths that traverse the Continent. Like them, it begins in a cathedral of sorts, a vast building that enshrines the beliefs and aspiration of the culture that produced it, yet one that conceals itself within a fold in the landscape of the city. Paddington has no monumental exterior, no triumphal approach. It does not pretend to the status of a Greek temple or a Gothic castle. Instead, the passenger entering the station from Praed Street descends a slope along the northern side of the Great Western hotel, arriving like a piece of luggage down a chute, to be dispatched towards the sunset. In the reverse direction, passengers leaving the station to enter the city on foot must move upwards into the light on a winter's morning, temporarily blinded by its rays.

Paddington, for Brunel, was far more than a gateway to London in the sense Le Corbusier understood it almost a century later. This station, connected as it is to Bristol, the city from which his first steam-powered ships set out across the Atlantic, was nothing less than a place of departure for the voyage to North America.

Architecture, Johann Wolfgang von Goethe famously said, is like frozen music. What does the traveller hear as he or she passes beneath the vast arched roofs of Paddington? The drawn-out squeal and explosive sigh of locomotive brakes; the slapping of a thousand feet on stairs; the slamming of carriage doors; the horns of the electric trolleys used to supply the trains; the percussive opening and closing of automated ticket barriers. These sounds alone provide an ambient symphony; but behind and beyond them, is it possible to detect a melody vibrating in the structure of the building itself?

To make Goethe's metaphor relevant in our own century, we need to extend it a little. Perhaps it would be more accurate to compare the effect of architecture today to a film soundtrack, rather than an icebound orchestra. Less directly instructive than the great temples or cathedrals of the past, buildings operate on our moods at a subliminal level, providing a score to the drama of our lives. 'All architecture proposes an effect on the human mind, not merely a service to the human frame,' John Ruskin wrote in *The Seven Lamps of Architecture*. Paradoxically, he felt any attempt to decorate a station was one of the 'strange and evil tendencies' of his day that he most deplored. 'There was never a more flagrant or impertinent folly than the smallest portion of ornament in anything concerned with railroads or near them,' he argued. '... the only charity that the builder [of a station] can extend to us is to show us, plainly as may be, how soonest to escape from it.' But where might the 'effect on the human mind' he spoke of be more keenly felt than at a great metropolitan railway terminus, the stage door to the city, where people arrive each morning to take up their roles or depart for destinations unknown?

Does this London station qualify, in Goethe's terms, as frozen music? Rather than write a tune, at Paddington Brunel freeze-frames a moment in a nation's intellectual and spiritual development, when traditionalists, even of Ruskin's stature, were temporarily pushed aside and astonishing new developments transformed architecture for ever. The original station at Paddington, a simple train shed erected with minimal amenities – local residents complained of male passengers urinating on Bishop's Bridge Road – was swiftly outstripped by demand. Its conception coincided with a revolution in architecture, the moment it broke free from its slavish dependence on stone and brick and learnt to soar in new forms created from iron and glass. Six million Britons had filed through Joseph Paxton's Crystal Palace housing the Great Exhibition in 1851, a building that owed no debt to the past. Instead, Paxton drew on his experience building glass houses in his role as head gardener at Chatsworth House, taking inspiration for their cross-bracing and undergirding from the giant Amazonian water lily he had in his charge, the pads of which could support a human child. For all its modernity, his building had received the royal imprimatur through Prince Albert's close involvement with the Exhibition, helping to bring about a monumental shift in consciousness. Although Brunel's own design for a hall for the Exhibition had been rejected, the engineer immediately saw the potential of this new architecture and the materials it used. Writing to the young architect and critic Matthew Digby Wyatt, whom he hired as an assistant, he was clear in his ambition for the site. 'I am going to design, in a great hurry, and I believe to build, a Station after my own fancy; that is with engineering roofs etc. It is at Paddington, in a cutting, and admitting of no exterior, all interior and all roofed in …'[2]

Brunel was aware that, once thronged with people and filled with smoke and noise, the space beneath his 'engineering roofs' might appear harsh and disorientating to those passing through it. The upper- and middle-class passengers who travelled on the early railway lived insulated from any direct experience of the Industrial Revolution; they consumed the goods it produced without ever stepping inside a factory, had never been surrounded by the sound of machinery in motion and rarely negotiated a space constructed from iron rather than brick or stone. Confident in his ability to design the station, Brunel was less sure of overseeing the decorative scheme he hoped could ease this transition, details for which, he admitted to Wyatt, he had 'neither ... time nor knowledge'. (In this he was being a little disingenuous. Pages from his sketchbooks reveal both his substantial input into the design of ornamentation at Paddington and his legendary inability to delegate.) Alongside Wyatt, Brunel engaged the designer Owen Jones to mastermind the station's colour scheme. As well as being designers, Owen and Wyatt were both theorists of the new aesthetic; Owen's two-volume work on the Moorish architecture of the Alhambra palace in Granada had been published in 1836, providing a rich source of ideas for the decorative work at Paddington. Wyatt had already praised Brunel's lack of ornament for its own sake in *The Journal of Art* in 1850. 'From such beginnings, what glories might be in reserve', he had written, 'when England has systemised ... a vocabulary of its own, in which to speak to the world the language of its power.' The two men's collaboration saw Brunel's industrial train sheds woven through with Wyatt's sinuous ironwork, inspired by Moorish influences, softening Paddington's industrial styling with a touch of the exotic, reassuring those who felt themselves about to be swallowed up in a vast machine.

To best appreciate the fruits of the Brunel–Wyatt collaboration, it is necessary to raise one's eyes to the great end windows over which decorative motifs creep like vine tendrils, or stand beneath them on the footbridge at the point where the roof spans leap from the top of the iron columns. Here, it feels, we are suspended in the canopy of an iron forest, its sheets of foliage replaced by glass, the wild animals of the forest floor by immense, grumbling trains. This, then, is the tune played by the architecture at Paddington; one that reconciles heroic engineering with delicate artistry, ushering in the future with a nod to the exotic past, wrapping itself around its audience and, whether they are aware of it or not, shaping their day.

DIGRESSION
A RAILWAY IS MANY THINGS

To our recent ancestors, train travel was the most exciting revolution brought about by new technology, connecting people and places in unprecedented ways and opening up the possibility of all kinds of human encounters that transcended the barriers of social class or geography. In terms of its transformative effect on society, perhaps the only useful comparison would be with the impact the internet has had in our own time. Messages could be conveyed from one end of the country to the other at previously unimagined speeds. People from all walks met each other in newly constructed social spaces. Previously isolated individuals and communities were connected to the centre of things. Today the miracle of mass transportation is rendered banal through repetition, only the hiccups in our progress remaining cause for comment.

Yet all the possibilities that intrigued early train travellers – of observing humankind en masse, of seeing the world in a different way when travelling at speed, of finding new ways to utilise the time provided by the journey between our homes and places of work – remain accessible. Far from being downtrodden victims of the system, workers who travel thousands of miles a year at high speeds to reach their employment are riding the crest of a wave in human evolution; members of a futuristic elite, able to choose to live remotely from their work for the first time in history.

The new cyber networks we have created don't seem to have replaced the old, forged from sleepers and steel; despite all the recent developments in electronic communication, which send our words running along fibre optic cables underground or weightlessly through the air, the physical presence of human beings is still needed to spark inspiration, forge business relationships and seal deals. The scale of the investments being made in rail both in developed and developing countries – the new monorail bisecting Addis Ababa, for instance, or the high-speed trains connecting cities in the Chinese interior – demonstrates that railways are seen by many as key to a future freed from gridlocked roads and airport check-in queues. Only our thoughts travel faster than the train; disembodied outriders rushing ahead, announcing our imminent arrival.

Yet even as rail points forward to a more efficient future, it connects us to the past. Whereas an autobahn or orbital motorway would be unrecognisable to the Victorian, the visual appearance of the line itself has hardly changed for 150 years. Very often we embark on our journeys from stations constructed before the birth of our grandparents or great-grandparents. Cuttings, bridges, viaducts, containing walls, all take on the patina of ancient relics. As long ago as 1929, Walter Benjamin wrote of how André Breton's novel *Nadja* converts 'everything we have experienced on mournful railway journeys (railways are beginning to age) … into revolutionary experience, if not action. They bring the immense force of "atmosphere" concealed in these things to the point of explosion'.[3] How much more acute has the tension become between the weight of this atmosphere and that of the disembodied, digital present, with the passage of another three-quarters of a century.

A railway is many things. At one level we can think of it in terms of infrastructure, a physical network laid across the surface of the earth, linking together strategic points. In order for it to function correctly, another railway must exist, a virtual railway plotted in planning meetings, held on databases, web servers, manifesting itself on departure boards and in tweeted updates. A third railway exists in the image it projects of itself. Historically, the GWR channelled an extraordinary amount of resources into publishing guides to its routes and other advertising, particularly during the 1920s under the direction of its general manager, Felix J. C. Pole; his name is at the foot of the title page of a number of publications of the period that can be found in second-hand bookshops or perused in the Great Western archives at the Steam Museum in Swindon. It was Pole who realised the importance of promoting the GWR as a holiday line, given the lack of major conurbations along its route. Londoners must be persuaded to leave the city, to see the whole of the kingdom as their playground, its historical riches as an educational opportunity, accessible via the charmed gateway of Paddington. There were literary precedents for this position, not least in an essay entitled 'London' by Henry James, first published in *The Century* magazine in 1888, in which he proposed that much of the richness and interest of the capital derived from the fact that 'all England is a suburban relation to it'. 'Thanks to the … elaboration of the railway service, the frequency and rapidity of trains, and last, but not least, to the fact that much of the loveliest scenery in England lies within a radius of 50 miles,' the American author enthused, 'thanks to all this [the Londoner] has the rural picturesque at his door and may cultivate unlimited vagueness as to the line of division between centre and circumference.'[4] A station like Paddington extended the borders of London, a city James named 'the capital of our race', to 'the remainder of the United Kingdom, or the British Empire in general, or the total of the English speaking territories of the globe'.

Pole's strategy was bold, an exercise in rebranding before the concept had earned itself the name. His writers would rename and reshape the territory through which the railway passed, changing perceptions of places along the route and even the demographics of those who lived there. In doing so, they would play off Romantic ideas about the landscape and provide an easily accessible encounter with the 'other'. At the same time, the minds of readers of GWR publications could be subtly sown with a sense of inferiority, and the corresponding need to improve themselves and their knowledge of history, by the skilful deployment of establishment figures as authors. Take, for instance, the gloriously patrician tone of the letter written on Lambeth Palace notepaper by Randall Davidson, Archbishop of Canterbury, to Viscount Churchill, Chairman of the GWR, and reproduced at the front of the guidebook to the cathedrals on its route.

24th of January 1924

My Dear Churchill

I am delighted to see the proof of your forthcoming Great Western volume … No one can travel much without being struck by the number of people who one meets in a railway carriage who are passing unintelligently through places of the very foremost historic interest or natural beauty or architectural glory. This unintelligence is due simply to lack of opportunity to know better. Any endeavour to promote a truer understanding of the wonders which your Railway brings within the reach of all of us is entitled to our warmest welcome and co-operation. You will be rendering a wonderful service to the English people and to visitors from overseas if you will help them to realise better the sacred heritage which is ours …

Relying perhaps on the 'unintelligence' identified by the archbishop, Pole's team began by ascribing exotic new names to regions of the country, promoting them heavily through both guidebooks and poster campaigns. 'Everyone has dreamt of a land where the sun always shines but is never enervating, where we may bathe in the winter and take active exercise in the summer,' we are told in one publication. 'We had to have a name for this Elysium, so we called it The Cornish Riviera.' In *North Wales: The British Tyrol*, the landscape is praised as 'not a bit less salubrious, invigorating, beautiful or romantic than those bracing uplands of Austria and Switzerland which have hitherto alone borne the name'. Areas too close to the capital to be promoted as holiday destinations had an even more important function, as dormitory towns for the new breed of commuters emerging as the century progressed. Urban dwellers were urged to forsake the grime of the city and relocate to the commutable countryside. 'Within 40 miles of Hyde Park there exist tracts of sylvan country,' we are told in *Rural London: The Chalfont Country and the Thames Valley, Their Historic Landmarks and Residential Advances*; a land of 'luxuriant woods, expansive commons, limpid streams and fruitful cornfields … within easy reach of those who may need a brief period of rest or change, or be in quest of a permanent residence, away from the din and smoke of London, but within a convenient distance of the scene of their labour'.

Thus Pole's team of writers turned the world upside down. The freezing Atlantic waters off the Cornish coast were suddenly warm enough to bathe in during the winter, long before the invention of the wetsuit. Farmland dotted with villages and provincial towns became 'rural London'; and emigrants from the capital, once lured to and trapped in a suburban villa somewhere in the Thames valley, are transformed into guaranteed customers for ever.

ENCOUNTER
JOHATSU AND A GREAT HORNED OWL

In Japan a homeless person is called *Johatsu* – a wandering spirit, one who has lost his identity. This is a useful reminder of the extent to which position in society is dependent on our actual position, a location on the map to call our own. It is not surprising that the homeless have long been attracted to railway stations: places where impermanence is the norm, in which they can take shelter and achieve some kind of invisibility. Electronic barriers and police patrols have made it harder to find a place to rest, part of the creeping privatisation of public space that is such a feature of our time, but great Victorian train sheds at major termini still offer a temporary respite from the streets.

I am buying a cup of tea at a kiosk in Paddington station when I become aware of someone at my elbow, an anxious-looking, bearded figure in a slightly grubby anorak, zipped up to the neck. The man serving me obviously recognises him and shows no surprise when he asks for a cup of hot water, passing one over without comment. Together we go to the counter from which we can help ourselves to milk and sugar. 'Look,' I say, on an impulse, 'do you want my teabag to put in your cup? It's got plenty of strength left in it.' At this moment it does seem ridiculously extravagant to throw it away, as it hangs spinning on the end of its string, bleeding a dark-brown spiral in the tea's milky surface. 'That's a good idea,' the man says. 'But no, I have tea here.' He pats his pocket. 'And coffee.'

All open circulation systems admit elements that are not part of their essential purpose; the presence of my new acquaintance with his pocketful of teabags is evidence of this. However, if such interlopers reach a critical level the service will be compromised, just as arteries in the human body can grow too furred to allow the passage of blood. This explains the groups of policemen who patrol the concourse, some of them carrying guns, on the lookout not just for panhandlers but also more aggressive toxic agents. Such sorting and categorising of human life beneath the roof spans of Paddington is nothing new. William Powell Frith's painting *The Railway Station* was completed in 1862, a decade after work started on Brunel's station and three years after the engineer died. Although derided by some later critics,[5] contemporary audiences loved it, queuing in their droves to stand before it and decode its multiple narratives. Reproduced in its thousands in the form of engravings, the painting became one of the best known and loved of its day. Frith, like many of his contemporaries, was fascinated with phrenology and classifying human 'types' by their physical characteristics. As Henry James observed, railway stations provided perfect opportunities for such analysis. 'The exhibition of variety of type is in general one of the bribes by which London induces you to condone her abominations, and the railway platform is a kind of compendium of that variety,' he wrote, some 30 years after Frith completed his painting. 'I think that nowhere so much as in London do the people wear – to the eye of observation – definite signs of the sort of people they may be ... You recognise that if the English are immensely distinct from other people they are also socially – and that brings with it, in England, a train of moral and intellectual consequences – extremely distinct from each other.'

The station concourse challenged the rigid segregation of social classes James alluded to by allowing people of different backgrounds to share the same public space, a situation that would have been equally thrilling and threatening to Frith's middle- and upper-class audience. The artist cleverly mitigates the threat posed by such a situation by placing the railway carriages in the background, suggesting that those moving through the painting in worrying proximity will be sorted and separated into their correct social groupings once they board the train. The feeling of reassurance is strengthened by a powerful triangular composition in the centre of the painting, in which a dominant father figure shelters and protects his wife and children from the crowd that surrounds them and a porter bends down subserviently to pick up luggage. Frith himself took the role of the father in the painting, enhancing his brand as both artist and family man, which indeed he was; he had 10 children with his wife but a further eight with his mistress, who lived a few minutes away from his home in Paddington. (Despite careful sifting of faces on the canvas by critics down the years it appears Frith's mistress is not in the painting.) Paperboys move through the crowd, representing the passage of time, while to one side an incident unfolds that will make the news the next day as a foreigner is arrested for fraud by a pair of top-hatted policemen, based on two real-life 'celebrity detectives' of the time. As threatening as the crowded platforms of the station may seem, the painter implies, the forces of law, and more importantly order, as represented by these two gentlemen, will ensure that anarchy does not prevail.

However vigilant the armed police officers at major stations today are in attempting to sift legitimate travellers from terrorist infiltrators, they can do little about the non-human inhabitants who regard such places as convenient shelter for breeding colonies. To protect itself from such unwelcome visitors the railway deploys other forces in its defence. I meet one such warrior upstairs beneath the roof of the station concourse, where I am sitting at a café. His arrival is announced by a sudden commotion among the pigeons that have been contentedly hopping between the feet of customers sitting at the tables. His name is Ernie and he is about one and a half feet tall with staring yellow eyes the size of 10 pence coins and powerful talons almost entirely covered with feathers. He is a three-year-old great horned owl – *Bubo virginianus* – and he is perched on the glove of his owner, Mark Dunn. Dunn is an experienced falconer, both a breeder and supplier of hawks, whose business offers pest control through the presence and supervised flight of birds of prey. The pigeons are right to be frightened. Another name for these North American owls is 'winged tiger' and they can swallow a small rabbit whole, although they prefer to pluck and dismember their prey before devouring it. In the wild, turkeys, swans, porcupines, snakes and small alligators are all on the *Bubo* menu: an urban pigeon would be a mere *amuse-bouche* to such a creature.

With so many passengers in the station, Mark is not about to fly the owl; instead, he merely lifts him up like a Gorgon's head, a primal symbol from the night-time of a pigeon's imagination, a single flap of the wings so terrifying they scatter in all directions. Ernie is part of a war fought with both physical and psychic weapons. It is easy to spot the vicious-looking spikes projecting from most perching-surfaces in the station. I also notice yellow disks that have been attached to the metal struts supporting the roof and ask Mark what they are. 'Oh, yes, those,' he says with a smile, one soldier in the war on vermin admiring the equipment of another. 'Pigeons see in UV [ultraviolet]. Those things contain holograms – they look like they are on fire, to a pigeon.'

A few minutes after Mark descends the escalator to patrol elsewhere in the station, a couple of the miscreant birds land on the floor at our feet. I can't help admiring their resilience. At threat of impalement when they come in to roost, haunted by ever-flickering fires that never go out, and terrorised by the sudden appearance of giant predators, they nevertheless make light of whatever disruption life throws at them, returning to their routine apparently unperturbed. In this, of course, they resemble the commuters with whom they share the station. The day after the Paddington rail crash in October 1999, in which 31 people died and over 500 were injured, passengers were back on the train, as they were on the underground – albeit in temporarily reduced numbers – the morning following the Tube bombings of July 2005. It seems the tidal pull of the city is stronger than midnight terrors or waking nightmares; it would take more powerful deterrents than terror attacks or derailments to erase the timetable etched into the bones of the perpetual traveller.

LOCATION: HANWELL

THROUGH ST BERNARD'S GATE

One of the most popular guides published by the GWR, which went through several editions and formats, was *Through the Window: The Great Western Railway from Paddington to Penzance*.[6] The key idea this and similar guides promoted was that the journey itself, rather than a boring interlude between leaving London and reaching one's destination, was something to be anticipated and enjoyed. Above all, they built on the concept of the city station as a stepping-off point to distant and exotic locations. 'Paddington Station is London's great gateway to the West,' the guide explains. 'The fascination of travel begins from the moment one arrives beneath its great glass roof.'

For those taking up their guides as their train rolls out of Paddington, that excitement might have to be momentarily deferred. As the guide explains, 'London has a habit – a very unwise one, considering the kind of first impression it gives to strangers arriving in the capital – of showing her worst side to the railway.' However, once the train has passed West Ealing, notable landmarks begin to appear. 'It must be confessed', the 1924 edition tells us, 'that the most imposing feature of Hanwell is the great LUNATIC ASYLUM of the County of London set above the west bank of the [river] Brent.' I am intrigued by this choice of landmark and decide to investigate it for myself, along with certain other features of the area.

Despite all the technological advances of the present day, it is surprisingly complicated to travel by rail to Hanwell. Although the station is on the main Great Western route, to reach it the passenger must first change trains at Slough and take the stopping train to Hayes & Harlington. There it is necessary to disembark again to catch the Heathrow Connect service, the only train that now stops at the station, before heading off on a branch line to the airport. It is a bright October day and the platform is empty and silent; disembarking feels like stepping on to a stage set. The station buildings and even the signage are largely unchanged. At first sight, Hanwell appears a peaceful but otherwise unremarkable suburb. In fact, it is the location of at least three astonishing architectural monuments, the most famous of which is the Wharncliffe viaduct that carries the Great Western line over the valley of the river Brent, one of the first construction projects completed for the Great Western Railway. But there is another site I want to visit before I reach the viaduct.

I set out on foot from the station, passing the town's modernist clock tower erected to commemorate the coronation of George VI in 1937, and the Viaduct public house. At the road bridge over the river Brent I drop down on to a footpath, beginning the long circuit of the exterior wall of what was originally the Middlesex County asylum. Still a mental-health facility today, it has reverted to a name it had in the 1930s, St Bernard's Hospital. Walking beneath the overhanging trees, on a path strewn with yellow and golden leaves, it is hard to believe I am a few minutes by train from inner London in one direction and the bustling streets of Southall in the other. A woman has loosed a dog – or, it appears, some kind of domesticated wolf – from its lead and it bounds towards me, shaking the river from its coat. I continue to the point where I join the canal and turn west along the boundary wall of the hospital. This brings me to one of the unmissable attractions of Hanwell, its flight of six locks, which, in an extraordinary feat of engineering, raise the level of the canal some 53 feet (over 16 metres) in a few hundred yards. At the top of this ascent is the 'Three Bridges', designed by Brunel in 1859, the last year of his life. A branch line of the Great Western Railway to Brentford Dock needed to cross the Grand Junction Canal at the point where a road bridge already carried Windmill Bridge Lane. With typical flair, Brunel made a cast-iron trough to contain the canal, carrying it over the railway and beneath the road, connecting the transport systems of three different eras at a stroke.

Hanwell, then, is the site of one of the great engineer's first and one of his last structural projects, his life bookended neatly in this often-overlooked corner of west London. But it is the hospital's monumental wall running alongside the canal that makes this place doubly impressive. Opened in 1831, it was the first purpose-built pauper lunatic asylum in England, and was originally designed to house 500 patients. By the 1880s, it held nearly 2,000 patients and was the largest such institution in Europe. The author of *Through the Window* was not the first to comment on its commanding presence when seen from the train. 'As a traveller by the Great Western Railway dashes through Hanwell,' wrote 'Sylvanus Urban' in *The Gentleman's Magazine* in 1858, 'his attention is arrested for a moment by a large building on the southern side of the railway, a plain but handsome structure, which stands cheerfully in an open country, and discloses even to the hasty glimpse of the traveller, as he hurries past, evident indications of careful and attentive management. It is the LUNATIC ASYLUM for the county of Middlesex, one of the most interesting buildings in the kingdom; a temple sacred to benevolence, a monument and memorial of the philanthropy of our times.'

The asylum was renowned for its progressive regime. Its first medical superintendent, Dr William Ellis, introduced the idea of the 'therapy of employment', encouraging inmates to continue with

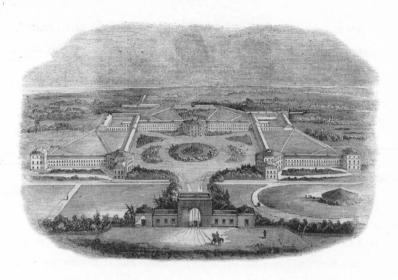

the trades they had pursued before they had fallen ill, helping them maintain their self-respect and a connection with their former lives outside. They grew much of their own food and took part in musical concerts and other entertainments. Funding requirements most probably led to a degree of exploitation of this captive workforce, but at least they had meaningful activities with which to fill their days, as well as contact with local craftsmen who set up workshops within the hospital walls. The third medical superintendent of the hospital, Dr John Connolly, had equally revolutionary ideas. Under his direction, Hanwell was the first asylum in the capital to abandon the use of mechanical restraints. Connolly found that keeping the patients busy following Ellis's plan, with the occasional deployment of sedatives or of padded cells for violent or disruptive inmates, did away with the need for straitjackets or ties. Over 100 patients attended classes in various subjects. Aprons, shoes, caps, gowns and other garments were made and those who worked in these occupations or in the gardens were rewarded with extra beer or tea. As Connolly wrote in his report:

The great and only real substitute for restraint is invariable kindness. This feeling must animate every person employed in every duty to be performed. Constant superintendence and care, constant forbearance and command of temper, and a never-failing attention to the comfort of the patients, to their clothing, their personal cleanliness, their occupations, their recreations – these are but so many different ways in which such kindness shows itself; and these will be found to produce results beyond the general expectation of those who persevere in their application.

Visitors eager to see this philosophy in action were commonplace at the hospital and the influence of Hanwell shaped the future of the nation's mental health services. The hospital had its own well, brewery and laundry, and a port on the canal called 'Asylum Dock', where coal was unloaded and produce from the gardens shipped out for sale. The opening in the wall where such imports and exports passed between the outside and the enclosed world within, although long since bricked up, is still clearly visible.

What came to mind as I looked upon these relics was the way this ingenious age managed and channelled two elemental forces: water and madness. As if to confirm this connection the observant will notice, spaced along the wall at ground level, much too small to allow a human passage to the outside, a series of openings. These 'fire doors' were designed, in case of a conflagration within, to allow firemen from the hospital's dedicated fire brigade to pass their hoses through the wall from the canal without breaching the asylum's security. Water can enter, but madness must remain confined, at whatever risk from fire.

I leave the dock behind and continue the lengthy journey around the hospital's perimeter wall, climbing up to join Windmill Lane

at Brunel's 'Three Bridges'. I have seen an original plan of the
asylum as it was in the 19th century, and am particularly interested
to discover whether any of the three octagonal panopticon towers,
from which staff watched over the inmates, survive. The idea of the
panopticon had been developed by the philosopher and reformer
Jeremy Bentham, along with his brother Samuel, as a model for the
design of prisons and published in book form 40 years before the
opening of the asylum at Hanwell. A tower in a central position
would allow a viewpoint over the entire prison, while the guards
within it remained invisible. Prisoners would not know at any given
moment whether they were being watched; they would have to
assume that they were, and regulate their behaviour accordingly. In
this way they would become their own jailers, cutting down on the
numbers of staff required. The present-day equivalent of Bentham's
idea is everywhere to be seen; our streets, buildings and public spaces
bristle with cameras, our movements are monitored by an invisible
army of observers. Above the door on the inside of the carriage I
had ridden as far as Slough that morning was a sticker proclaiming
'Smile! You're on CCTV!'

Those parts of the original asylum buildings visible from Navigator
Drive – presumably named after the navigators, or navvies, who dug
the canals it borders – have been smartly renovated, their windows
mirrored out. Off Windmill Lane, on an impulse, I enter a gate that
has opened automatically for a car. The hospital is in transition: parts
are awaiting renovation and stand empty; parts are being sold off as
private luxury accommodation. At certain points these borders are
clearly visible, and at others less so. Turning back I find that the gate
has closed behind me and I feel a momentary panic, but a quick
search reveals a green release button and I continue on my way to
Uxbridge Road. Here I have no difficulty in finding the original
entrance to the hospital, via St Bernard's Gate, a triumphal arch

dressed in ivy, against which a member of staff is leaning, smoking a cigarette while speaking on a phone. No one challenges me as I enter. A few of the institution's residents are gathered in the autumn sunshine, some sitting on a wall, others standing on the pavement, smoking profusely and conversing with animation. A middle-aged woman sits on a bench on the grass in front of the chapel, her head in her hands, in need perhaps of a dose of Dr Connolly's prescription of 'invariable kindness', accompanied by a large suitcase that looks as though it never leaves her side. A perpetual traveller, she waits on a platform for a train that may never come.

I locate two of the original panopticons, standing at the end of the east and west wings, one still with windows and recently restored, the other blinded with brickwork. From these, warders would have been able to survey what the *Illustrated London News* of 1843 described as 'the large front airing-grounds, to which the patients have access daily, the shrubberies, gravel-walks, sun-shades, fountain and bowling-green, and other requisites ... all indicative of comfort and order within'. A large proportion of these grounds have subsequently been sold off to house Ealing hospital, but the great wall around St Bernard's maintains the sense of a protected space; an asylum in the true sense of the word, as a place of safety from the world outside. Most of the great Victorian mental hospitals have been swept away in the health reforms of the last 30 years, and now even the security of incapacity benefit is being removed from those leading precarious lives beyond their walls. We can only hope the pioneering spirit of the early superintendents of this hospital survives our apparent desire to return to a time that preceded its foundation.

As I have no wish to intrude, I take my leave. It is time to seek out one of the most remarkable survivors of the early years of the Great Western Railway, the Wharncliffe viaduct. To walk beneath its brick arches, in many places dripping with water and high enough to accommodate the fully grown trees that have seeded themselves in their shadow, is to experience a sequence of spaces worthy of Piranesi. Isambard worked on the design for the viaduct with his father, Marc, supporting the structure with tapered, Egyptian-styled columns reminiscent of those designed for the Clifton Suspension Bridge. They are hollow, now home to a large, protected colony of bats. The bats' entrances into the pillars remind me of the fire doors in the asylum wall. Looking up at the great brick arches is dizzying, like gazing up into the cupola of a Renaissance cathedral.

Even as I think this, standing in the remains of a tramp's fireplace among the trees, another thought enters my mind: of course, stupid, this *was* the Renaissance, for England at least. Emerging at last into the light, I turn back to take a final shot of the viaduct as a walker approaches. For a moment, time appears to slip …

LOCATION: SOUTHALL
OF JALEBIS AND DRAGONS

23 October 2014. It is the final night of Diwali, the Hindu festival of lights, also sacred in the Sikh and Jain traditions, which falls each year between mid-October and mid-November; where better to celebrate than Southall, the west London suburb on the GWR line colloquially known as Little India? This is where I go when I get nostalgic for Indian street food, or south Indian delicacies like *iddli* or *dosa* – for a few pounds you can be transported 5,000 miles; but I have never been in Southall at Diwali. By mid-afternoon the streets near the station are full of people buying all they need for the festival in neighbourhood shops, while the reports of the first firecrackers echo from the facades of the buildings. A large billboard at the roundabout on South Road wishes the community 'Happy Diwali' from TRS, Asia's Finest Foods.

It seems as though every shop, including, I notice, a wedding planner, a vegetable wholesaler and a dry-cleaner, is offering special buy-one-get-one-free, or even buy-one-get-two-free deals on fireworks. Ultra, Devco, TNT, CAT, Olympica – the rival firework brands compete for the attention of passers-by, along with particular favourites from their ranges: Magnum Series, Happy Dragon, Colourful Dragon. As the afternoon progresses towards evening, more and more people I pass are hurrying home with large boxes of explosives under their arms, while children appear to be licensed by their indulgent parents to throw firecrackers at the feet of passers-by, so that progress along the pavement is punctuated with snaps and bangs. *Diwas,* the small clay lamps that are filled with mustard oil and lit at Diwali, are on display at three for a pound, along with brightly coloured decorations and religious images. My favourite restaurant, where I had hoped to eat, has turned its tables over to stacks of gift-wrapped boxes of sweets, while at the counter customers select from multi-coloured piles of confections including *ladoo, peda, barfi, jalebi* and *gulab jamoon.* I cross the road to Jalebi Junction instead and pre-pay for the smallest amount of *jalebi* I can buy – 250 grams for £2 – taking my ticket to the growing queue in front of the booth on the pavement, where a woman is coiling strands of sticky-sweet dough into bubbling fat.

This is Southall today: a vibrant community with a strong sense of its own identity, numbering around 700,000 people. Four decades ago the position was somewhat different. The 1970s saw a high-water mark in openly racist politics in Britain, with the National Front and the British National Party determined both to win council seats at the ballot box and to control the streets through thuggery and intimidation. The murder of the Sikh schoolboy Gurdip Singh Chaggar in Southall in 1976 led to the formation of the Southall Youth Movement, an alliance between young people of South Asian and African-Caribbean ancestry determined to protect their neighbourhood. Then, on 23 April 1979, the National Front announced they would hold a public meeting in Southall town hall. Because 23 April was St George's Day, the Union Jack would be flying from the town hall flagpole, making it look like a National Front stronghold (the Front had largely co-opted the flag as their own personal symbol at this time). Over 3,000 police arrived to usher the 30 or so National Front supporters into the town hall, in defiance of the massed protesters outside. Predictably, and exactly as the Front had hoped, a battle ensued. Blair Peach, a schoolteacher and anti-fascist campaigner from New Zealand, was with his friends some distance from the front of the town hall when police from the riot squad known as the Special Patrol Group pursued fleeing protesters down the back street where he was standing. Local resident Parminder Atwal described what happened next:

> As the police rushed past him one of them hit him on the head with a stick. I was in my garden and I saw this quite clearly. He was left sitting against the wall. He had tried to get up but he was shivering and looked very strange. He couldn't stand. Then the police came back and told him like this, 'Move! Come on, move!' They were very rough with him and I was shocked because it was clear he was seriously hurt. His tongue seemed stuck in the top of his mouth and his eyes were rolled up to the top of his head. But they started pushing him and told him to move, and he managed to get to his feet. He staggered across the road and came to where I was in the garden. I tried to sit him down. He was in a very bad state and he couldn't speak. Then he just dropped down. I got a glass of water for him, but he couldn't hold it and it dropped out of his hand.[7]

An ambulance was called but Peach was fitting, and slipping in and out of consciousness. He died the next day. No policeman was ever prosecuted, either for the murder or for conspiring to pervert the course of justice when fellow officers closed ranks to prevent his killer being identified. The internal report on the incident drawn up by Commander John Cass, suppressed for a decade, stated it could 'reasonably be concluded that a police officer struck the fatal blow' with something other than an official truncheon, possibly a lead-filled cosh or a police radio. (Illegal weapons, including baseball bats, crowbars and sledgehammers, as well as Nazi regalia, were found at the Special Patrol Group's base when lockers were searched following Peach's death.) Commander Cass was obviously uncomfortable about the unavoidable conclusions of his report; in mitigation, he included the following statement: 'Without condoning the death I refer to Archbold 38th edition para 2528: "In case of riot or rebellious assembly the officers endeavouring to disperse the riot are justified in killing them at common law if the riot cannot be suppressed".' Words not chosen, presumably, to offer comfort to Blair Peach's wife and daughter, or to the many children whose lives he touched through his work as a teacher in the East End of London.

At the beginning of the 19th century, the population of Southall was around 700; by the beginning of the 21st, it had grown a thousand-fold. This expansion was accompanied by a shift in occupation for its inhabitants from agriculture to light industry, enabled by the arrival firstly of the Paddington and Grand Union canals and, in 1839, by the Great Western Railway, with its station on the main London to Bristol line and, some years later, the branch line to the docks at Brentford. Windmills, like the one painted by J. M. W. Turner at Southall Lock, were gradually replaced with brickworks, gasworks and manufacturing. Southall's inhabitants ceased grazing livestock and growing grain, fruit, beans, turnips, potatoes, mangel-wurzels, clover and peas, as they had in the 1830s, and began instead to be employed making jam, marmalade, chemicals, wallpaper, braille apparatus, processed foods, radios, televisions, paints, telephones, margarine and London buses, among the many other products manufactured in the town.

Among all this varied industry there is one family business whose products are for ever linked to the borough in which they were made. In 1887 Robert Wallace Martin arrived in Southall from London on a barge loaded with equipment, to set up R. W. Martin pottery in a disused soap works on the bank of the Grand Union Canal, along with his brothers Walter, Edwin and Charles. (Legend has it the drunken bargees mutinied at Brentford, refusing to go further unless they were paid more money.) Together they built a kiln, establishing a pottery the reputation of which is still revered around the world. The Martin brothers' pottery burnt down in the 1930s but their work is held in many major museums and private collections. Southall library houses a remarkable selection of Martinware, together with an exhibition about their lives, within walking distance of where their business was sited on Havelock Road.

In the closeness of their working lives the brothers somewhat resembled a medieval guild, and their refusal to embrace mass production sat well with the guiding principles of the Arts and Crafts movement. In reality, the unity suggested by the 'Martin Brothers' heading on their notepaper concealed a whirlpool of jealousies, suspicions, rivalry and arguments over money and the direction of the business. Robert Wallace Martin gave the pottery its name and at least initially was its driving force, and many of its products bore the clear imprint of his artistic personality; nevertheless, each of the four brothers brought his own interests and abilities to bear on its output. As a teenager, Wallace worked at a candle factory in Vauxhall and began modelling figures in wax in his spare time. At 15, he was apprenticed to a stonemason at the Houses of Parliament. He studied at Lambeth School of Art in the evenings, eventually winning a place at the Royal Academy. His fascination with sculptural form and his interest in the grotesque gave rise to some of the pottery's best known and most collectible pieces: the tobacco jars named 'Wally' birds after their creator, each fantastical bird with its own individual expression, as well as face-jugs and figural jars that enabled further outlet for the humorous and outlandish characterisation he enjoyed.

Wallace's brother Walter had worked at Doulton's pottery in Lambeth as a teenager and, as well as being a fine potter, was an expert in glazes. Salt glaze stoneware of the kind the brothers made at Southall is technically demanding, especially using a wood-fired kiln. A mix of clay and sand is fired at a very high temperature; salt is thrown in during the firing, which vaporises, causing the soda to combine with silicate in the clay, resulting in a hard glaze. Judging the temperature and also the amount of salt to add was a crucial part of Walter's role. He experimented continually with colour, translucency and texture. When he died in 1912 of a cerebral haemorrhage, it was discovered he had recorded the details of how to make his glazes in code, and his surviving brother Edwin, who was in charge of decorating the pots, was unable to achieve the same stunning effects.

Charles Martin's role in the business was less direct but no less important than that of his brothers. He ran the family shop in Holborn, in central London, and returned by train with cash to pay the wages at the end of the week. He also brought first-hand reports on the popularity of particular wares, thus influencing the direction of the company. He styled himself the art director of the pottery and made it his job to source botanical and biological illustrations, providing a rich source of inspiration for designs. So nervous was he of spies coming to the shop to steal the brothers' ideas that he kept the finest examples of their craft hidden in a back room wrapped in tissue paper, only showing them to his 'best' customers. In 1909 there was a fire at the shop that destroyed a large amount of stock and resulted in the death of three people living above the premises, plunging Charles into a depression from which he never recovered. He died of tuberculosis in 1910.

In 1913 Edwin was diagnosed with cancer and grew increasingly desperate to secure some share in the business, in order to provide for his family in the case of his death. His relationship with Wallace deteriorated. In 1914 the two brothers had a row in London, where Wallace had closed the shop without consultation. Edwin asked Wallace how he was returning to Southall. 'By train,' Wallace replied. 'Good,' said Edwin, 'then I shall go by bus.' He died in April 1915.

Robert Wallace's 'Wally' jars and face-jugs remain highly sought-after, fetching high prices at auction, but to me their grotesqueries are not the aspect of the pottery's production that has travelled best through time. Instead, it is Walter's extraordinary luminous glazes and the 'experimental pots' inspired by Charles's findings – based on seeds and pods, sea creatures and the shells of crustaceans, often the work of Edwin – that retain their fascination. The economy and simplicity of their organic forms and the way they emphasise the material of their own manufacture would not look out of place in a contemporary design studio.

Another aspect of the work on display at the library that reaches out towards the present is its Orientalism; the brothers, like so many of their contemporaries, were inspired by prints, porcelain and ceramics from China and Japan and were great collectors of Japanese wood-block prints. Walter emulated the dark blue glazes of Chinese pots on the large urn-shaped vases the pottery produced towards the end of the 19th century and his interest is reflected in some of the most striking motifs with which they are decorated: Chinese dragons with clawed feet, long, serpentine tails and extended tongues, battling each other in the deep blue of an imagined Oriental sky.

Back out on the street I meet the dragons again, this time as terracotta decorations on the red-tiled roof of the Himalaya Palace,

the imposing structure that was built as a cinema in 1929 and is currently an indoor market. The work of architect George Coles, the Palace is the only one of the 90 or so cinemas he designed that takes the form of an art-deco Chinese pagoda, with a tiled exterior and large stained-glass windows – another example of the enduring role Orientalist fantasies played in British culture for a century or more.

As recently as 2010 the Palace was still in use after a major restoration had returned it to its original glory, showing the latest Bollywood movies: doubtless Coles would have been astonished by the somewhat different way in which the Orient he evoked in its architecture had arrived in reality, both as the source of images on the screen in his cinema and in the streets that surround its location.

Those streets continue to get busier as the light fades. I follow the current of the crowds, from shops on the Broadway where bhangra tunes are blaring from the famous ABC music store and bargains are promoted via loudspeakers, to the Vishwa Hindu Mandir temple on Lady Margaret Road, where worshippers are already lighting *diwas*.

By the stall selling cups of hot corn and pink Kashmiri tea, a woman thrusts a flier into my hand. 'ARE YOU DISAPPOINTED MEETING INDIAN ASTROLOGER?', it asks. 'Then once meet our World Famous Astrologer Devi Ram, to get permanent solution to all your problem either personal life or professional life in just 9–11 days. We are here to let you understand your strength and weaknesses based on the planetary configuration of your birth chart.' At the bottom of the densely worded sheet there is a personal message from the pandit himself. 'Helping other is what I enjoy & clear's problem from the root work. IT'S MY CHALLENGE!'

Setting aside this opportunity to sort my life out, I walk back down through the area of Southall Green known as Little Mogadishu, populated with stores catering to the area's Somalian residents, on to the largest Sikh gurdwara outside India, Sri Guru Singh Sabha on Havelock Road, with its impressive golden dome floating in the twilight. The moonless sky begins both to look and sound like a war zone. There may be official firework displays somewhere but I do not find one: the detonations going off all originate in back gardens and informal spaces, patches of grass outside blocks of flats, or even the car parks of large shops (still containing a number of cars) bordering the main street. No one seems in the least perturbed when a couple of youths launch a fusillade from outside the Iceland store, a few feet from the crowded pavement. This is, after all, a festival of light. For Hindus, lamps guide the goddess Lakshmi into homes and businesses, bringing prosperity for the year ahead; I notice one shop owner pulling down the shutters on his premises and lighting a small candle in a saucer that he leaves burning on the pavement as he walks away. They also commemorate the slaying by Rama of the 10-headed demon Ravana and the end of his 14-year exile. He and his consort Sita returned to Ayodhya on a moonless night like this one, and the people guided them to their palace by setting out lanterns. For

Sikhs, the festival is known as Bandi Chhor Divas, the Prisoners' Release Day, and marks the release of their sixth guru, Guru Har Gobind, from captivity, along with 52 Hindu princes imprisoned by Emperor Jahangir whose freedom he also won; he arrived in Amritsar at Diwali and residents lit up the city with hundreds of lamps and candles in welcome.

At the gurdwaras on South Road and Havelock Road, crowds are flowing in and out of the main entrances and gathering outside around long troughs of sand in which hundreds of lamps and candles flicker. As the darkness deepens it is strangely moving to watch people squat down quietly to light candles or pour mustard oil into the lamps to keep them burning. Occasionally, a pool of oil ignites, shooting a flame upward, illuminating the faces of those bent over the soft glow: women with elaborately made-up eyes dressed in their best new saris, children being helped by their fathers to light a candle, young men capturing the scene on their phones.

The combination of fire and ritual is timeless, far older than the Victorian technologies that brought prosperity to this area of Britain. However, in the first decade of the 21st century it was the railway that returned Southall to national attention; specifically the high number of rail suicides that took place on the stretch of line running through the town. An internal report by a manager at rail operator First Great Western in 2007 claimed that 80 out of the 240 rail suicides – one-third – that had been recorded nationally during the previous year had occurred on the short stretch of line passing through Southall, and that a disproportionately high percentage of these were Sikh women.

One incident in particular, the death of Navjeet Sidhu, who jumped in front of a Heathrow Express train in August 2005 together with her son and daughter, was covered by national press and TV, and was picked up by the media in India. Six months later, her mother

41

Satwant Kaur Sodhi, killed herself at the same location. In his study of suicide, written in the last years of the 19th century, French sociologist Émile Durkheim stated that the means people choose to end their lives are dependent on opportunities offered by the location they find themselves in. 'That, for example, is why suicides by throwing one's self from a high place are oftener committed in great cities than in the country,' he wrote. 'The buildings are higher. Likewise, the more the land is covered with railroads the more general becomes the habit of seeking death by throwing one's self under a train.'[8] Yet why should the station at Southall, more than any other, have such a powerful attraction for the distressed? Arranged marriages and domestic violence seem to figure large in the tragedies played out here. Young, middle-class Sikh women from the Punjab who believe they are marrying wealthy businessmen in Britain can find themselves trapped in marriages with partners from very different backgrounds, subject to domestic violence, isolated from social contact and treated as slaves by their new mothers-in-law. 'There are very few girls from Punjab who are not graduates. I have seen girls come here who have masters degrees in English, in economics,' Southall MP Virendra Sharma told a reporter on a visit to India. 'Their families arrange marriages with boys here who are not professional, not educated.' They are aware of how much money their parents have spent on their wedding and do not want to dishonour them by returning, to 'bring a stain to their father's turban'. They have no one to turn to. It is at such times 'the permanent solution to all their problems' mentioned in the astrologer's leaflet begins to beckon. 'This is the woeful template', as the newspaper put it, 'that sees brides flying out of Delhi and Amritsar, dreaming of a new life in England, but whose dreams and hopes end tragically under a fast train in an alien land.'[9]

Tonight such dark shadows seem far away. For Sikhs, as for Hindus, this is a time of new beginnings and fresh hope for the future. Every back garden in Southall, it appears, is hurling fireworks upward that explode in cascades of sparks; one house behind the small hotel on the Broadway I am staying in keeps up a continual barrage for two hours, making sleep impossible. Particularly popular is a rocket that fizzes and twists, trailing a corkscrew of sparks, surely one of the Happy Dragons I have seen advertised, and thus a descendant of those battling each other with intertwined tails on the Martin brothers' jars. Southall, it seems, is a place that can help us 'understand our strengths and weaknesses', as the astrologer promised. Just as the death of Blair Peach led to political awakening and eventually to reforms in the police force, perhaps the equally tragic deaths at the station can play their own small part in ending the culture of violence against women that remains endemic in our century.

LOCATION: SLOUGH
AN URBAN HEART TRANSPLANT

Rarely has the reputation of a place been struggled over as publicly as that of the Berkshire town of Slough. This Thames valley town is in the process of becoming one of the best-connected places on the planet. Close to the M40, M4 and M25 motorways, it will soon be joined to central London by Crossrail and, if plans go ahead, by a new rail link to Heathrow. From Slough to central London will take 17 minutes; Slough to Heathrow will be a mere six minutes. Already site of the headquarters of some of the world's largest multinationals, the town is also one of the most ethnically and religiously diverse communities in Europe. The first wave of immigration to Slough came in the 1920s as workers from the Welsh valleys travelled east to escape the effects of the Depression; the next after the second world war, when Polish ex-soldiers who had been stationed in the area chose to settle there. Today, 65 per cent of its population class themselves as being from the black and minority ethnic communities. Stepping off the train at Slough, then, is in many ways like stepping into the future; a future that began when the town was first connected to London by the railway.

Yet in national consciousness Slough remains stubbornly linked to the past, most notably through the eponymous poem John Betjeman published about the town in 1937, the opening lines of which invite 'friendly bombs' to come and fall on Slough, as it 'isn't fit for humans now'. It seems Betjeman was irritated by the appearance of the Slough Trading Estate, founded in the 1920s and the first of its kind in Britain. When he wrote the poem the estate was already a powerful economic engine in the locality, its activities apparently as beyond his ken as the lives of the double-chinned businessmen and 'bald young clerks' he satirised. In terms of the potential of bombing to alter the architectural landscape and in advance of the arrival of the Luftwaffe over Britain, perhaps he took inspiration from events unfolding in Spain, where the German air force had come to the aid of the Nationalist side, most famously carrying out an aerial attack on the town of Guernica and in the process inspiring another, more substantial work of art. A mere three years after its publication the poem had achieved its stated aim; bombs did indeed fall here. A cabinet minute by a military spokesman is headed 'Bomb dropped on Aluminium Factory at Slough' and is dated 15 July 1940. 'I was told today that one of our pilots, on returning to his aerodrome, had said that one of his bombs dropped out by mistake,' the minute reports. 'It is very unfortunate that this casual bomb should have been the only one which had done any serious damage to one of our factories.'[10] In the terminology of bombs, 'casual' and 'friendly' read like synonyms. The poet's invitation had been answered.

I know, I know: Betjeman would maintain that he was joking, and it seems he later regretted the fame the poem achieved. (In 1947 he wrote to a friend: 'I am not a satirist and dislike the few satirical poems I have written ... e.g. "Westminster Abbey" and "Slough", both poems of which I am now ashamed as they are cheap [illegible].') A further threatening formation of comedians appeared in the skies above Slough some 65 years later, when Ricky Gervais and his writing partner Stephen Merchant devised the television series *The Office*, set in a fictional paper merchant on the trading estate ruled over by the nightmarish figure of manager David Brent. In the opening credits, it is once again architecture that sets the mood. A panorama of concrete office blocks and multistorey car parks gives way to a bus emerging from the brutalist concrete edifice of the Brunel bus station; the scene shifts to traffic flowing round a roundabout and a sign showing the route for lorries to the Slough Trading Estate, before arriving, as the title credit rolls, at a forbidding office building where the action supposedly takes place. Gervais and Merchant use Slough as filmic shorthand for ugliness and provincial small-mindedness, the backdrop to the dramatic themes explored in the series of self-delusion, embarrassment and (a long-standing British favourite) the idiocy of those in charge. What would it mean to those who live in such a place to feel so ridiculed? To many, apparently very little; the population of Slough has grown by 10 per cent since the first episode of the series was broadcast. To those engaged in what was known in North America at the turn of the 20th century as 'boosterism' – talking up their town to encourage inward investment, a practice often associated with the arrival of the railroad – it is possible the other two 'B's, Betjeman and Brent, remain a problem.

The first sign that things are changing at Slough is visible to commuters passing through the station from the train. To the south of the line an extraordinary silver building has appeared, looking, in the desolate landscape that surrounds it, as if it has landed from another planet. The ground floor of the frontage facing the line is closed off behind metallic doors but the first floor, supported on pillars, is all glass, its ribbed oval window revealing figures moving about in a mysterious and apparently leisurely manner. It is only when the train moves to reveal the building in profile that the viewer becomes aware of its most distinct features: two long, undulating canopies that float above a forecourt, extending behind it as if the structure were an aquatic life form of some kind, swimming towards the track. This is Slough's new bus station, designed by Matthew Bedward of Bblur Architecture, selected as one of the top 10 best designed bus stations in the world by architectural magazine *DesignCurial*. Slough, one of the first towns to benefit from rail connection to the capital, is still defining and redefining itself through the infrastructure of public transport. Passengers passing through the bus station will not only be making local journeys to the shops or the town centre but embarking for the other side of the planet, via rail links both long-established and still imaginary, their route yet to be fought through the congested topography of 21st-century Britain.

Arriving on a morning in late June to meet Matthew Bedward, I can't help being conscious that the train station itself has also been contested territory. In the 1830s, the provost and headmaster of Eton College strongly opposed the first Great Western Railway bill, as they feared a station at Slough would 'encourage the boys to seek the doubtful dissipations of London town' (the college lies a mere two miles away by road). The bill was redrafted, including an enactment that 'preclude[d] the Directors from constructing any Station or Depot within three miles of Eton College without the consent of the Provost and Fellows of that Establishment'.[11] As a result of the dispute, the railway opened on 4 June 1838 without a station at Slough, the train merely halting for three minutes to allow people to board from beside the tracks. On the railway's first day it carried 1,479 passengers; by the end of its first week of operation, over 10,000. Within a month, the objectors appeared to be wavering. 'It appears likely that even Eton will allow us to have a station at Slough,' George Henry Gibbs, one of the directors of the company, recorded in his diary in early July, 'and, strange to say, a train was provided on Thursday at the request of the Masters to convey the Eton boys up to town.'[12] (They attended the coronation of Queen Victoria on 28 June.) Their official opposition wasn't withdrawn until the end of the following year, however, when the construction of a station became paramount.

Unfortunately, the opening of the railway at its eastern end had brought more, rather than less work for Brunel, and he found himself pulled in many directions, required in several locations at once. The ride provided by the trains at the opening of the line had proved bumpy and uneven, partly due to the springs in the carriages but largely down to mistakes Brunel had made in selecting ballast for the laying of the line itself. Reports of the discomfort experienced by passengers led to a fall in share prices and the public questioning of Brunel's judgement in choosing broad gauge for the Great Western line over the narrow gauge used elsewhere.

As Gibbs reported in his diary, solutions had to be found urgently to these problems. 'Brunel's character and reputation … as well as our own peace and comfort, demand our best attention at this moment to the repacking of the line … as much as Brunel is wanted in Bristol, it seems impossible to part with him at present.' Although the engineer worked himself famously hard, he was fond of his children and tried to make time to play games with them, as well as instruct them, as a proper Victorian father should. Generally, however onerous his workload, he took Christmas Day off. Among his papers, though, there is one drawing dated 25 December 1839.[13] It shows the front elevation of a station building for Slough, sketched in pencil on the squared paper of his notebook in his usual elegant manner, its details picked out in brown wash.

Around 170 Christmases will have passed before Bblur's very different vision of a transport hub for Slough is unveiled. Doubtless its appearance would have been startling to the Victorian engineer, although he would have been fascinated by its use of materials. The controversy it has caused would have been entirely familiar, the accompaniment to innovation in any age.

Equally familiar would have been Bblur's involvement in the wider infrastructure of the town, fanning out from the bus station

itself. In readiness for the arrival of Crossrail and the mooted fast rail link to Heathrow from the west, Slough is undergoing radical surgery. Thanks to a vast public and private investment of almost half a billion pounds, the Heart of Slough project is clearing space for landmark buildings, offices, public amenities and housing to create a new centre to the municipality, almost from scratch. Already, a substantial area of land adjoining the main through road stands empty behind hoardings, in readiness for the construction of eight and 14-storey office towers, with publicly accessible space beneath them creating a 'linear park'. Along with the bus station, Bblur have been commissioned to create a new library and cultural centre, to be known as The Curve; I have already been sent a link and taken a dizzying virtual tour of its interior. As I begin the short stroll from the rail station to the bus station with Matthew and his colleague Richard Fairhead, he draws my attention to the space immediately outside. 'As well as the station and The Curve, we have taken on all the public realm,' he explains. 'We started by creating space around the rail station and pushing back the roadway so we could create some usable space. Previously, the taxis pulled right up to the station. We wanted to clear the sightlines to the station entrance as it is one of the older and more interesting buildings in Slough. We had hoped to have a row of mature trees here, but they got lost in a cost-cutting exercise.'

It is true that the train station is a handsome building, its French-style roof with scalloped tiles and porthole windows crowned with distinctive decorative ironwork. It is not, however, the station that Brunel drew on Christmas Day. It often happens that any 19th-century railway building still standing along the route of the Great Western line is assumed to have taken shape in the brain lodged beneath the famous stovepipe hat, and the Brunel brand is freely applied to roads, pubs, shopping centres and civil amenities. However, the drawing that took him away from his family on one of the precious occasions when they could be together was for a station formed from two adjacent platforms on the same side of the track; it was replaced within 30 years. The urgency he attributed to the task of designing it may have had to do with a different family, resident a few miles away at Windsor. Prince Albert had already ridden on the line in 1839, boarding the train at Slough from the trackside. Queen Victoria was more reluctant to try the new mode of transport, but eventually announced she would travel on 13 June 1842, by which time a suitable station had been constructed from which she could embark.

'At Slough the Royal Party, on their arrival at the station a few minutes before 12 o'clock in six carriages, were received by Mr. C. Russell the Chairman, Mr. F. P. Barlow one of its Directors, and Mr. C. A. Saunders the Secretary of the Company' a contemporary report records, 'and conducted to the splendid apartments at the station designed for the reception of Royalty. Her Majesty ... Proceeded to examine the line and the Royal Saloon, enquiring very minutely into the whole of the arrangements. Precisely at 12 o'clock the train left Slough for Paddington, Mr Gooch, the Superintendent of the Locomotive Department, accompanied by Mr Brunel, the Engineer, driving the Engine.'[14]

The journey took 25 minutes. It is not certain for how long Brunel, rather than Gooch, would have taken the controls; on another occasion he claimed: 'I never dare drive an engine ... because if I go upon a bit of the line without anything to attract my attention I begin thinking of something else.' Such dreaminess, well suited to an artist-engineer, would clearly be detrimental to the supervision of a train. However, he may have found the grandness of the moment irresistible, as he did on at least one other occasion when a train he boarded was carrying a royal passenger. At Paddington, a red carpet was laid the length of the platform to receive the newly mobile monarch. Having arrived safely and suffered no apparent ill effects from the speed of her passage, Victoria was converted to the railway and became a regular traveller, a branch line to Windsor later being constructed for her additional convenience.

It is appropriate that Daniel Gooch should make an appearance alongside Brunel at the controls of such an important train. His job title – Superintendent of the Locomotive Department – doesn't fully cover his role, which was to convert Brunel's vision for the line into a working reality. The first locomotives constructed for the GWR to Brunel's exacting specifications were underpowered and performed miserably. Brunel was determined to prove he knew better than his rivals in the north how to design a steam-engine, but his ambition exceeded his abilities. It was only when the company's directors appointed the 21-year-old Gooch, who had trained with Robert Stephenson, over Brunel's head to design and build their engines that matters were rectified. The two men became inseparable in the public mind. Brunel's critics in the press, ever keen to accuse him of tilting at windmills, christened them Don Quixote and Sancho Panza.

Until the Windsor branch opened, Slough was a royal station, its approach broad enough to accommodate the queen's carriages. The Royal Hotel, which stood nearby to accommodate the better class of traveller, has long since disappeared. Today, almost opposite the place from where Victoria took her maiden train journey, looms an empty and semi-derelict block of the type featured in the opening credits of *The Office*. It is scheduled for demolition and I struggle to imagine the space without it, my eyes unschooled in the architect's ability to project a future dreamscape.

The shape of the new bus station, and in particular its undulating roof canopies, was partially inspired by the work of one of the town's most famous former inhabitants, the astronomer William Herschel, who came to live in Slough in 1786. 'We wanted a story to connect the building to the place where it is sited,' Matthew explains. 'Herschel was an immigrant yet he made a huge contribution and went on to become the astronomer royal. Slough is very ethnically diverse, a place where many immigrants have made their homes. The shape of the canopies is inspired by Herschel's experiments on light waves, carried out in Slough. We had originally thought of using string theory and the idea of the universe as we know it coming from Herschel, but it got too complicated. We simplified the concept to make the bus station look like two light waves.'

Herschel, a musician and composer originally from Hanover in Germany, had already come to the attention of the Royal Society when resident in Bath, through various eccentric papers in which he argued the likelihood of forests and even extraterrestrial life on the moon. The Society's misgivings about his seriousness were confounded when he correctly identified Uranus, long thought to be a star because of its dimness, as a new planet, redrawing the map of the solar system for the first time in a thousand years. His achievement was the result of acute observation combined with technological innovation. In Bath he cast his own speculum in moulds constructed from pounded horse dung and spent hours polishing the metal mirrors, first by hand and then with a machine of his own devising, obtaining powers of magnification that exceeded those available to leading astronomers in London.

Assisted by his sister Caroline, an accomplished astronomer in her own right, Herschel continued to 'peruse the great volume of the Author of Nature' when he moved to Datchet, near Slough, to be close to his new patron and fellow Hanoverian, King George III. His experience convinced him that the larger the mirror used and the more light it could capture, the further a telescope would allow him to see into space. Once he had secured funding from the king all he needed was a dwelling large enough to construct the instrument he had in mind. He found it at The Grove, later renamed Observatory House, on the east side of Windsor Road in Slough. The house and surrounding outbuildings stood on a spur of land that provided the perfect observational platform, once Herschel, to the chagrin of his neighbours, had felled a line of mature elm trees that stood at the edge of the property. The telescope was the biggest and most powerful anywhere in the world, with a seven-foot mirror and a tube that was 40 feet long; during a party held to celebrate its near-completion, the more usually self-effacing Caroline led a group of revellers in dancing through it as it lay on the ground.

The vast telescope, manipulated by assistants using a system of pulleys, proved cumbersome to operate, its metal mirror, weighing half a ton, easily tarnished by moisture. Towering above the skyline in its elaborate wooden housing, it perhaps functioned more as a magnificent advertisement for the science of astronomy than a practical tool; classed as one of the wonders of the world, it even appeared on the Ordnance Survey map of the area. A stream of discoveries continued to emerge from Slough, galvanising the world of science and astronomy.

Undertaking her own sweeps of the night sky, Caroline found eight comets, earning her international fame as a scientist of note. William, meanwhile, was on an unending journey in his own mind, sending back reports that continued to shift previous conceptions of 'the construction of the Heavens' and humanity's position within them. Ranging further and further, he identified nebulae situated outside our galaxy. Rather than being fixed in the heavens, they were in an active state of evolution, forming new stars from condensing gas and acting as what he described as 'laboratories for the universe'. Far from being at the centre of all this activity, he pointed out, humanity existed at its fringes, inhabitants of the planet of an insignificant star (the sun) in a solar system that was in itself a mere footnote in the Author of Nature's treatise.

Attracted by these revelations, by the opportunity of seeing the giant telescope and of meeting the venerable astronomer and his remarkable sister, visitors arrived in the town from throughout Europe and as far afield as North America. Caroline dutifully wrote the names of those who called in a leather-bound visitors' book now held in the Herschel Museum of Astronomy in Bath. On the day I visit, the book is on display, open at pages 10 and 11, covering dates between July 1789 and October 1790. In France, during the same period, the Bastille was stormed and the Ancien Régime overthrown; visitors to Slough were bearing witness to an equally far-reaching revolution in the skies overhead. On 28 August and 17 September 1789, as feudalism was abolished in France and the National Constituent Assembly published the Declaration of the Rights of Man and of the Citizen, Herschel discovered two further moons of Saturn, through 'the great light of my 40-foot telescope'. In October, an armed mob of 7,000 women marched on Versailles, storming the palace and killing several guards, forcing King Louis XVI to acquiesce to their demand that the royal court be moved to Paris. In Slough, the world's first female astronomer of note discovered two comets, in January and April 1790, the third and fourth of her final tally of eight that made her the leading comet-hunter of her day. During the 14 months covered by the visitors' book, pilgrims to Observatory House included the secretary to the prime minister; the president of the Academy of Sciences at Rotterdam and his sister; a French envoy; a professor of philosophy from Germany and a professor of mathematics from Glasgow; Polish, Portuguese and Russian ambassadors; various counts, lords, ladies, duchesses and clerics; and the former astronomer royal, Nevil Maskelyne and his wife. Others who visited the sage of Slough and his talented sister included Lord Byron and the composer Joseph Haydn, who credited the experience with inspiring the composition of *The Creation*.

It wasn't the discovery of moons or comets that was to provide the key motif for the design of the bus station I have come to see over two centuries later, but an entirely different one, made in 1800. Herschel was making direct observations of the sun, splitting its light through a prism into the spectrum of different colours discovered years before by Sir Isaac Newton. He was interested in the different temperatures of colours and had placed thermometers inside each colour provided by the prism, with others positioned outside to record the ambient temperature of the room as a control. The temperature increased, he observed, as he moved from the violet to the red end of the spectrum. To his surprise, he noticed that a thermometer placed just beyond the end of the red spectrum, where no colours were visible, showed a higher temperature than one placed anywhere within the spectrum that could be seen. Something was producing heat; after further experiments he decided it must be a spectrum of light invisible to the naked eye. He had discovered infrared.

Bblur's appropriation of this momentous event as a visual metaphor does not seem to have won over all the local residents.

During my research I come across a website, calling itself 'The Slough Times', which appears determined to harpoon the ambitions of the council to regenerate the town. The bus station is singled out for particular opprobrium. 'While it rained for several hours on a cold and wet Saturday afternoon, 18 February, I visited Slough Borough Council's much criticised Slug bus station,' writes one correspondent. 'Passengers say it is a very expensive silver-coloured monstrosity looking like a quashed [sic] onion with the top sliced-off.' The news that his building has been compared to a sliced onion and a shell-less gastropod mollusc leaves Matthew apparently unfazed.

'A slug? I don't mind that. Feedback from the public has ranged from the extraordinarily positive from the vast majority of people to those who have questions about it being windy and wet and not covered over. What they perhaps don't appreciate is that the brief for the bus station was for an open, glorious shelter. It is the complete opposite to what was here before. The old Brunel bus station made famous through *The Office* was dark, dank, full of rats and smelt of urine. Lots of people are saying it's great, but you'll always get other opinions. One person told us, "Slough has always been a shithole and you can't polish a turd." What can you say to that?'

Walking along the partially cleared boulevard, past people making their way to catch buses beneath the sheltering wings of the canopies, we look up at the sides of the building, which are gleaming in the sun. The aluminium cladding is softened with a satin lacquer, Matthew explains, to avoid it creating too harsh a light. 'What I'm particularly pleased about is that the building reads as an urban sculpture from every direction. Its tail will extend further towards the town and what we call the "torch ends" will draw people through from the town to the railway station. We can just unbolt the first section and extend the waveforms further.' Those arriving in Slough, then, either by train or bus, will be able to walk, accompanied by these aerial messengers, to and from the town centre. Once they have been guided to this destination, what will such visitors find? On previous visits I have explored these streets. The immediate vicinity is shaped by the dual carriageway of the A4. Alongside it stands the largest branch of Tesco Extra I have ever seen, stretching for several blocks, already a monument to a past age of economic confidence. Everything in the environment facing the road has been designed for the sightlines of those moving through the space at driving speed, including the large advertisements that border the cliff face of the supermarket building. On the other side of this barrier, which feels more like a Los Angeles freeway than a local road, is the pedestrianised high street, which follows the route of the old coaching road to London. Within a two-minute walk I count five betting shops, two or three payday loan outlets, pawnbrokers, a Poundland with, opposite it – evidence of competitive spirit among local retailers – a 99p emporium, as well as the usual fried chicken outlets and run-down malls. There is no visible sign here of wealth flowing from the multinationals who have their headquarters on the trading estate; indeed, there is no real sense that this space comprises a centre to the town at all. Open-heart surgery suddenly seems an urgent priority.

Once Crossrail and the Heathrow rail link arrive, Slough's orientation will shift away from the car and towards public transport, a reverse in emphasis to that of the mid-20th-century town planners who did so much to shape the town's present-day layout. The Brunel roundabout, with its dank and dangerous underpasses, has gone. Traffic lights have been resequenced to shorten journey times. Bblur have reshaped the edges of the highway, widening pavements and introducing high kerbs to discourage jaywalkers from crossing the road other than at designated spots, while avoiding penning them in behind railings. The planting of mature, 25-year-old trees brings a touch of elegance and shade. As we stand looking across the road at the church, next to which the futuristic outline of The Curve will rise in coming months, Richard points out that workmen are unloading panels bearing computer images of the building from a truck and carrying them along the pavement. 'Slough regen' reads one panel, as its fragmentary message proceeds down the road on its side. It must be a surreal moment for the architects, watching an image of something they have designed, but which does not yet exist, being assembled, piece by piece. This is its first three-dimensional entry into the world, a significant step beyond a computer screen in an architect's office. Across four lanes of traffic we find ourselves addressing the men: 'No, mate, you've got that upside down. No, that doesn't go there, they're in the wrong order ...' As Matthew resumes talking about the Heart of Slough project, Richard remains alert, watching the progress on the other side of the road. 'Look!' he says. 'They've cut it in half!' Sure enough, a large image of The Curve has taken shape but the building has been cropped, almost through its centre. Have they left a panel back at the depot, we wonder? 'No, I bet they just trimmed all the images we gave them square,' Richard says, shaking his head in disbelief.

It is time to part company with the two architects, who have a meeting to go to. I too have one scheduled, with the chief executive of Slough borough council, Ruth Bagley. It has been a little difficult to secure, but that is no surprise. Bagley is the very visible figurehead of the council, overseeing the Heart of Slough project and also heading up the campaign to secure funding for WRAtH (the somewhat unfortunate acronym for the Western Rail Access to Heathrow). It is she who has to convince the voters of Slough that the way towards prosperity lies with visionary projects rather than a more mundane focus on finding solutions to local problems. This is not an altogether easy argument to make in the face of the statistics. Slough is experiencing serious pressure in terms of housing, with a waiting list for accommodation roughly equivalent to its entire stock of properties. In 2013, a 'spy plane' equipped with heat detection cameras was hired by the council to overfly the town, in an effort to locate garden sheds and outbuildings let out by unscrupulous landlords for illegal occupation. Six thousand suspicious dwellings were identified, and the phenomenon of the 'Slough Shed' featured in the national press. The borough has levels of diabetes, TB and childhood obesity above the national average, as well as challengingly high rates of problem drug use. A strong and vocal opposition has grown up to the direction of council policy. Bagley herself has been subjected to a campaign of harassment, both online and through abusive emails; on one occasion, she had to hide in the footwell of a car as she left a public engagement. This is local politics for real, played for high stakes.

As I wait in the foyer of the borough council building to be summoned, I notice that the space I have entered is organised along planetary lines: the East Wing houses suites named after Saturn and Venus, and the West Wing after Pluto, Jupiter and Mercury. The moons of Saturn discovered by Herschel through his monster telescope were named Mimas and Enceladus by Herschel's son John, after his father's death. The chief feature of Mimas, the closest moon to Saturn, is the vast impact crater, named after Herschel, which takes up nearly a third of its surface area. As the *Cassini* spacecraft revealed in 2005, the highly reflective moon Enceladus has an atmosphere and is geologically active, spouting plumes of water vapour and solid matter into space. It is thought to contain an ocean beneath its surface that may include organic molecules, warmed by a tidal mechanism through its nearness to Saturn, making it one of the sites most likely to harbour extraterrestrial life. (Of course such close observation from space of the satellite's surface, like the spy plane's aerial survey of illegally occupied sheds in the borough, depends on

infrared technology derived from Herschel's researches in Slough.)
The astronomer, who found it absurd anyone could think the earth
might be unique in supporting life, would have been delighted that
one of 'his' moons might eventually prove him right.

It is clear Bagley feels passionate about Slough and the way it is
perceived, and she begins, with recourse to a map pinned above her
desk, by giving me a history lesson. We speak of the way the town
has been a magnet for light industry since the arrival of the Horlicks
company in 1908 – their red-brick, castellated factory is still a
landmark visible from the train – and the establishment of the trading
estate in the 1920s on land requisitioned for the repair of army vehicles
during the first world war. Over the last 20 years the emphasis of
the estate has shifted from manufacturing to providing a site for the
headquarters of businesses in fields including information technology,
pharmaceuticals, automotives and precision engineering, as well as for
a new breed of creative media companies who have moved into the
borough. The route from the station to the council offices takes me
past the headquarters of Burger King, proudly announcing itself, with
no apparent concerns about the current epidemic of obesity, as 'The
Home of the Whopper', while a swift exploration of the surrounding
area reveals buildings occupied by Amazon (relocating as I write·to
central London), ICI and Dell, among others. 'At the moment on
a good day by road it is 20 minutes from Heathrow airport,' Ruth
Bagley informs me. 'I was telling one of our international CEOs the
other day about the planned Western Rail Access to Heathrow, saying
that when we get it built it will take seven minutes to get to Heathrow
from Slough – since then we have got it down to six, but at the time
it was seven, which is important to the story. He told me their global
headquarters is seven minutes from Schiphol airport in Holland, so
having a seven-minute train journey at each end of the flight, aside
from being incredibly convenient, has a neat symmetry to it.'

Later that day I walk to the trading estate; its appearance has changed considerably since Betjeman's day. Vast, inscrutable buildings extend horizontally along the Bath Road. Their design is entirely devoid of vernacular touches or local references; we could be anywhere, from California to Bangalore. Their architecture demonstrates how real power is no longer a matter of ramparts or battlements or even of fame and visibility. Instead, it is measured in anonymity. Only the truly powerful are unseen, while the most private thoughts of the rest of us are catalogued and stored as data for future mining in the interests of commercial exploitation. No one seems to be around, at least not on foot, as traffic swishes past on the A4. A block or so beyond BlackBerry's regional headquarters I find the offices of SEGRO, the owners of the estate, emblazoned with its new brand: 'IQ Slough – Where Business Works'. The visitor centre, adjacent to the front entrance of the building, is locked. I go into the foyer, which is empty apart from a terminally bored man on reception, who is lying with his cheek to the desk, watching something on his phone. He tells me the woman looking after the visitor centre has gone to post a letter, which seems an impossibly antiquated activity in an environment indistinguishable from a computer simulation.

When she returns she is momentarily flustered to see me, but turns on the lights in the exhibition area. I watch a black and white film of an American CEO in the 1930s cutting the first sod on the site of a new factory building. American and other international flags flutter over the estate's impressive entrance. The sense that this place has long constituted a republic in its own right is added to by the fact that it generates its own electricity, from a power station that now runs on recycled waste. Like that other closed community, the asylum at Hanwell, it also has its own source of fresh water, taken directly from an underground aquifer and pure enough to be used in the laboratories it houses. If the world beyond its perimeter descends into chaos, the estate will still have heat, water and light. This was the original home of the Mars bar, I learn from the displays, of Milky Ways, Maltesers and Galaxy; the headquarters of Citroën in the UK and the place where the Ford GT40 racing car was built. It was also the home of the studio where the futuristic television puppet series *Thunderbirds* was filmed in the 1960s, granting the nation a foretaste of the year 2065; footage playing on a screen shows earnest young men aiming hairdryers at the ground beneath a model spacecraft to create an authentic-looking dust cloud as it ascends skywards. Will the equally futuristic transport system provided by Crossrail lift Slough into a new era of prosperity as effectively as the puppeteers' wires?

Slough may already have excellent transport links with other areas of the country, yet within itself it remains fragmented. A 10-minute walk across a park from the Bath Road brings me to the centre of Chalvey, one of the borough's most impoverished wards. On the edge of a housing estate brightly painted signs promise '4 Nans for £1 from the Roti and Curry Hut'. A glance at my watch confirms it is lunchtime, but when I follow the direction of the arrows on the signs into a small arcade I find it abandoned, the shutters drawn on all the shops. Only the barber's shop in Chalvey Road seems busy. Through the window I glimpse young men with set jaws having their hair precisely sculpted, while others wait their turn. As local politicians squabble over the future of their town and developers and architects vie to reshape it, they can at least exert control over this most immediate part of their environment. Back on the main road I find myself outside the headquarters of Reckitt Benckiser. The name means nothing to me but a brief look at their website reveals they are the creators of a multitude of domestic products, many of them household names. In an idle moment I begin to martial them into a capitalist ABC in my notebook. I fantasise that perhaps it could be used in the local primary school, where pupils share 40 languages between them and 75 per cent of those arriving are new to England. The familiarity of the brands might be an aid to learning:

Airwick

Brasso

Calgon

Durex

E45

Finish

Gaviscon

Harpic ...

Crossing the road to a newsagent's directly opposite the headquarters from which the advance of this army of products is controlled, my eye is caught by a headline from the local paper, the *Slough and South Bucks Observer*, taped in the window: 'POVERTY FORCING PEOPLE TO STEAL FOOD'. 'The number of people "entrenched in poverty" and forced into crime just to put food on their table has risen by 40 per cent in three years,' its author, the appropriately named John Dickens claims, based on an increase in recorded incidents of food theft.[15] An article on the same page laments the fact that none of 253 two-bedroom homes advertised for sale in the town are affordable to a family on an average income. This, then, is the paradox of Slough: the presence of huge multinational corporations with inestimable wealth, certain of whom make every effort to avoid paying tax in the UK, in a town where some are forced to live in garden sheds through a lack of affordable accommodation. The bill for the increased connectivity from which these businesses will benefit, enabling their senior staff to flit effortlessly in and out of Heathrow and central London, will largely fall to the British taxpayer. Even virtual businesses use real infrastructure: trains, roads, trucks, feet on pavements, as well as a workforce educated at the expense of the state. How, then, can they justify spiriting sales away elsewhere in order to avoid paying a fair contribution to its upkeep? In some ways, Slough's connectedness brings its own problems, a microcosm of those arising from the unrestricted ebb and flow of capital in a global economy. Many highly skilled workers in the surrounding area commute into the town, leaving again at the end of the day without setting foot beyond the trading estate, while its inhabitants, many of them unskilled and low-paid, travel in the other direction to work at Heathrow airport. A dam has to be built in this river of wealth, allowing it to collect in Slough, otherwise all that those who actually live in the town will gain from its transport connections is the air and noise pollution generated by three motorways and the world's fifth busiest airport.

Ruth Bagley has spread a map on the meeting table in her office, the better to outline the kingdom she is creating. She appears, at this moment, some combination of a chef and a scientist, a mathematician and a Faustian dreamer, attempting to corral the primal forces of capital for the benefit of the people she represents. The philosophy behind the project, she explains, is that if you put 1,000 housing units over *there*, introduce new office space *here*, put up a hotel *there*, then you will 'generate' a lot of people and a lot of footfall through the town. To people and footfall you add the Crossrail link and, she argues, you have created a set of factors that will result in greater prosperity. Does her equation add up? There is little doubt that dramatic architectural interventions into run-down neighbourhoods can bring regeneration – few would deny that the opening of Tate Modern transformed the London borough of Southwark, for instance – but unless such institutions cater for the local community as well as the influx of visitors they attract they can further exacerbate social division. Despite its diversity, Slough prides itself on the fact that its different ethnic communities live alongside each other rather than in separate ghettoes. Regeneration could change all that; money divides even more effectively than class, politics or religion. Whether the new heart being grafted into the town will 'take' – and whether such an operation is the right course to follow in the face of the social challenges the borough faces – only time will reveal. What is certain is that, far from being an amusing provincial backwater, Slough is closer to one of the 'laboratories of the universe' her former son William Herschel described, in which the most pressing challenges of 21st-century urban living are being worked through.

Five minutes' walk from the council offices and a stone's throw from the skating rink lies a feature in the landscape that divides opinion just as effectively as the planned future of the town. Some historians claim the Montem Mound is a Norman motte, others that it is a Saxon or even Iron Age tumulus, while still others conjecture it may have been a gathering place for Druids or been formed naturally by the nearby brook and road. For almost three centuries the mound was associated with the Eton College festival of 'Montem', first recorded as taking place in 1561. Scholars from the school would parade in military or fancy dress from the college to the mound, where they would demand money for 'salt' from passers-by, funds received being put towards the celebration as well as to the expenses of the head boy when he went to Cambridge. Beginning as a fairly small affair, the festival developed over the years into a military-style parade that attracted onlookers, including royalty from nearby Windsor Castle. The arrival of the railway changed the character of the event. Montem began to draw large and unruly crowds that arrived by train from London. Thus the effect of the station at Slough was just as the headmaster and provost had feared: from a localised, aristocratic ritual, Montem mutated into a spectacle for the vulgar. While they could not cancel the railway, they could cancel the festivities. Montem ceased forthwith.

LOCATION: SLOUGH AND PADDINGTON

MURDER ON THE GREAT WESTERN EXPRESS

'It is quite a just remark that the Devil,
if he travelled, would go by train.'
Lord Shaftesbury, *Journal* (9 August 1839)

'Few things impress the traveller more when leaving the metropolis by this route than the extraordinary extent to which "wireless" has captured suburban London,' we are informed in the 1924 edition of *Through the Window*. 'Practically every back garden has its aerial.' It would have been impossible for the author of these words to imagine rail travellers today, idly toying with hand-held devices that allow them to communicate instantly with contacts around the world, uploading personal photos and enjoying 'face time' without the need for aerials in the garden or wired connection of any sort.

The section of the line between Slough and Paddington was the proving ground for another revolutionary new technology in the 19th century, laid alongside the track – William Fothergill Cooke and Charles Wheatstone's electric telegraph. This innovation, originally intended for railway communications only, might have gone largely unnoticed by the public had it not been used to dramatic effect in the capture of a murderer.

In January 1845 a Quaker businessman named John Tawell bought a bottle of Scheele's prussic acid – a treatment for varicose veins – in a chemist's shop. Tawell had trained as a pharmacist, but on this occasion he did not intend to use the medicine for its prescribed purpose. Instead, he travelled to Salt Hill, then at the edge of Slough, where he forced his mistress, Sarah Hart, to drink it. His efforts met with some resistance and, by the time he had prevailed, the woman's cries of distress had alerted her neighbours that something was amiss. Tawell was observed leaving the house in a great hurry.

Tawell had already led an eventful life. As a young man he had been deported to Australia for forging a £10 note. Such a crime against the currency usually carried the death penalty; it was only commuted to deportation on account of his religious beliefs – Quakers had long campaigned against capital punishment. In Australia he appeared to turn his life around. Freed on a pardon, he trained as a chemist and opened a successful pharmacy business, summoning his family to join him. Shortly after they returned to England, his wife and children died, and he sought comfort in the arms of Sarah Hart. When he remarried a Quaker widow some years later, the expense of maintaining his mistress and the pressure of keeping up his double life appear to have become too much of a burden.

Tawell did not make a clean getaway. The local vicar gave chase, but lost him at Slough station, where he boarded a train to London. However, the quick-thinking reverend was not ready to admit defeat. He suggested that the stationmaster telegraph ahead to the police at Paddington. This he did, in words that have become famous; the limitations of the early four-needle telegraphic system, which had no facility for transmitting the letters 'J' or 'Q' or for marking punctuation, are inscribed into the text.

A MURDER HAS GUST BEEN COMMITTED AT SALT HILL AND
THE SUSPECTED MURDERER WAS SEEN TO TAKE A FIRST CLASS
TICKET TO LONDON BY THE TRAIN WHICH LEFT SLOUGH AT
742 PM HE IS IN THE GARB OF A KWAKER WITH A GREAT COAT
ON WHICH REACHES NEARLY DOWN TO HIS FEET HE IS IN THE
LAST COMPARTMENT OF THE SECOND CLASS COMPARTMENT

The telegraph did its work, sending its tapped accusations down the line faster than a train could travel. Tawell was spotted among the crowds on the platform at Paddington on account of his Quaker-style coat (the telegraph operator receiving the message had balked at 'Kwaker', asking for it to be retransmitted for clarification more than once). A police sergeant, William Williams, tailed the suspect, following him on to an omnibus and eventually to a coffee shop, where he was arrested. It is impossible to guess where Tawell thought he was going. He must have realised his identity as the killer would already be known. As he sat and drank his coffee, was he dreaming of another future, readying himself to leave the country and start life again, one more time?

The murder trial caused great excitement. There is nothing quite as fascinating to the public imagination as someone who has acquired knowledge for the service of humanity but who uses it to take, rather than preserve, life. There was also the delicious irony of Tawell's Quaker beliefs: they had saved him from the hangman's noose once before, but on this occasion only served to identify him to his captors. Despite his sudden celebrity, the murderer's role in the story was almost eclipsed by that of the technology that played such a decisive part in his undoing; the telegraph received the sort of publicity its manufacturers could not have dreamt of. The drama was, as the *Illustrated London News* reported, 'an extraordinary instance of the working of the newly applied power of electro-magnetism ...

by which any communication can be made from one point to the other in an almost inappreciably short space of time'. Tawell's life ended at the end of a rope in Aylesbury on 28 March 1845, before an audience of 10,000. From that moment on, he became known as 'the man hanged by the electric telegraph'.

While murder retains its power to shock and astonish, the telegraph did not. By the mid-19th century, the speed with which the latest technological innovations pass into the realm of the mundane had begun its exponential acceleration. Queen Victoria had already announced the birth of a son at Windsor by telegraph in 1844. Large towns began to open 'telegraph news rooms', to which those wishing to keep up with the latest events could gain access by paying a subscription. A decade after Tawell's execution, what had so recently seemed extraordinary had become ubiquitous. The *Railway Traveller's Handy Book*, published in 1862, noted it was a common occurrence for a passenger to forget some important item or instruction when setting off on a journey. 'For such emergencies', it instructed, 'the telegraphic wires are ever ready to obey the behests of their employers. All that a traveller has to do is write his message on a slip of paper, and at any station deliver it to the guard, together with the fee, and everything is then done.' From a murder and a royal baby to the minutiae of personal communication, our interconnected age had truly begun.

Cooke and Wheatstone's ambition was not confined to running their telegraph along railway lines. Although their relationship soured over arguments about credit for the original invention of the telegraph, both continued to be involved in the communication revolution that shaped the modern world. The same year that Tawell swung, Wheatstone was working on plans for a cable beneath the English Channel. He subsequently served on the scientific committee of the Atlantic Telegraph Company, of which Cooke was a director. Brunel had dreamt of connecting London to North America, but his interest was primarily in transporting people and goods between Old World and New. In this he betrayed his origins in the industrial age. His three transatlantic ships – the SS *Great Western*, the SS *Great Britain* and the SS *Great Eastern* – were each larger and more revolutionary in design than their predecessor. There is a story that Brunel took Cyrus Field, the American businessman and prime mover behind the Atlantic cable, to the Millwall dock where the SS *Great Eastern* was being constructed and told him, 'There is the ship to lay the Atlantic cable!' In all probability apocryphal, the story most likely arises from the desire of those working on the cable to benefit from association with the engineer's name after his death; at the time, the ship was being fitted out for passengers and would have been completely unsuitable for the task. It took Brunel's faithful Sancho Panza, Daniel Gooch, to envision how the vast ship could deliver a connected world in a manner Brunel could not have imagined: linking stock markets, putting governments in instant communication with one another, ushering in, Cyrus Field believed, a world not only better for business but one in which universal peace was inevitable. The huge vessel had bankrupted a succession of owners before Gooch bought her for a minimal amount and had her refitted as a cable-laying ship. Five times larger than anything else afloat, she proved magnificently suited to the task, as Henry Field, Cyrus Field's brother, poetically recorded in his memoir of the enterprise.

> Throughout the voyage the behaviour of the ship was the admiration of all on board. While her consorts on either side were pitched about at the mercy of the waves, she moved forward with a grave demeanour, as if conscious of her mission, or as if eager to unburden her mighty heart, to throw overboard the great mystery that was coiled up within her, and to cast her burden on the sea.[16]

DIGRESSION
TRAVELLING HOPEFULLY

'The life of a person is the sum of his tracks,
the total inscription of his movements, something
that can be traced along the ground.'
Roy Wagner, *Symbols that Stand for Themselves* (1986)

Once they get free of us, words take on a life of their own. Nowhere do we see this more clearly than in the use, and misuse, of quotations, whether they are stolen from the mouths of prophets or the jottings of humble scribes. *It is better to travel than arrive. Travelling hopefully is better than arriving. The journey is more important than the destination.* We have all heard a version of this saying, without, for the most part, knowing where it originates. In one or other of its permutations, it is a mantra for those who consider themselves 'real' travellers. For anyone contemplating the subject of commuting it takes on a new significance.

In fact, it was the 19th-century writer Robert Louis Stevenson who coined the phrase in his essay 'El Dorado', published in the collection *Virginibus Puerisque* in 1881. 'Little do ye know your own blessedness', he wrote, 'for to travel hopefully is a better thing than to arrive …' What a surprise: he isn't writing about travelling at all, at least not in the literal sense. His subject is the art of living; more specifically, the function curiosity and desire play in keeping mankind interested and engaged in the world. It is the very impermanence of satisfaction, he argues, the need to constantly feed our appetite for food, knowledge, love or wealth, while all the time maintaining the illusion that eventually we will possess all that we desire, that gives colour and meaning to our lives. Arriving at the end of such a journey is dangerous. As an example of such peril, he cites the young man reading through the complete works of Thomas Carlyle, who, on reaching the final page, cries in consternation, 'What? Is there no more Carlyle? Am I left to the daily papers?' Authors themselves are not immune to such feelings of desolation and despair. Edward Gibbon, Stevenson reports, on finishing *The History of the Decline and Fall of the Roman Empire,* 'had only a few moments of joy; and it was with a "sober melancholy" that he parted from his labours'. Happiness is derived from the pursuit of happiness; it is no more achievable in itself than arriving at El Dorado. The trick seems to be to keep occupied, to remain curious. The full version of Stevenson's often misquoted statement is: 'Little do ye know your own blessedness; for to travel hopefully is a better thing than to arrive, and the true success is to labour.'

If Robert Louis Stevenson is not writing about travel but instead about living, how has he found his way into this book? The journey, or quest, provides one of the oldest tropes in storytelling and has survived in the form of travel writing. The author leaves home, bound for a destination already known to the reader, his onward progress towards his goal the central spine of the book. Eventually he returns, having attained the goal of the journey but changed by the experience. It is hard to see how this redemptive model applies to the commuter. He is endlessly travelling, yes; but where is the sense of narrative progression in journeys that are undertaken each morning and then undone again as he retraces his steps at the end of the day?

Stevenson has the answer. All literature is artifice, of course, whether it claims to be fiction or non-fiction, but in the case of the quest narrative, he demonstrates, we are dealing with an illusion based on an illusion. In life, despite the fact that we keep 'ceaselessly marching, grudging ourselves the time for rest; indefatigable, adventurous pioneers', none of us really arrive anywhere, or have any hope of attaining what we strive for. 'There is only one wish realisable on the earth,' Stevenson tells us, 'only one thing that can be perfectly attained: Death. And from a variety of circumstances we have no one to tell us if it is worth attaining.' This might sound gloomy; but for Stevenson it is the justification for channelling all one's energy into the pursuit of interests and enthusiasms, whether or not they will ever be brought to fruition. It doesn't matter that the journeys forming the backdrop to this book also take their voyagers nowhere, other than places they have been many times before. If none of us really get anywhere anyway, commuting is a far more fitting metaphor for life than any great linear journey. Indeed, so much of our time does it occupy, it might better be thought of as *living* than *travelling*. Why would so many describe it as 'a way of life' if this was not the case? Stevenson goes further in his metaphorical appropriation of the unending journey, comparing physical travel with progress across the page by deploying a playful quote from Ecclesiastes.

'Of making books there is no end,' complained the Preacher; and did not perceive how highly he was praising letters as an occupation. There is no end, indeed, to making books or experiments, or to travel, or to gathering wealth. Problem gives rise to problem. We may study for ever, and we are never as learned as we would.

Work, writing, travel – for Stevenson there is essentially no difference between the three. Each is an activity with no final destination, and this, he argues, is something to be celebrated.

LOCATION: SLOUGH

STATION JIM

Slough station is unique as a place of pilgrimage for the curious. Those who make a search of Platform 5 will find a glass case, in which the stuffed body of a departed railway worker is displayed for all to see. I refer, of course, to Station Jim, the dog that lived at Slough in the last years of the 19th century and worked as canine collector for the Great Western Railway Widows and Orphans Fund. Dog Jim (as he was also known) suffered poor health and died in harness after serving in his post for only a couple of years. However, he made a great impression in his brief career, winning the public's affection by barking whenever a coin was placed in his collection box and performing a number of other tricks, including 'playing dead'.

Now of course, at permanent attention in his transparent sentry box, he plays alive.

He certainly looks real enough; a demonstration of the fact that it is perfectly possible to be scooped out from the inside while keeping up external appearances. Jim didn't choose to prolong his presence on earth in this manner, unlike another famously preserved figure, known as the Auto-Icon, which resides in its own glass-fronted box a mile or so from Paddington station at University College London. The inventor of the panopticon, Jeremy Bentham, had made his desires for the treatment of his mortal remains clear on his deathbed in 1832 and they were enshrined in his will. After his body had been dissected in front of an invited audience, his head and skeleton should be preserved and reassembled for public display, 'in the attitude in which I am sitting when engaged in thought and writing'. So important to him was this ambition that he is said to have carried the glass eyes he had selected for the purpose in his waistcoat pocket for a decade before his death. For Bentham, power was inextricably linked to both seeing and being seen. His body would stand like one of his famous octagonal towers at the heart of the university, his gaze unblinking. Could any future students or administrators be sure he wasn't present among them, keeping a watchful gaze through those carefully selected eyes? Unfortunately, the methods used in the preservation of his head gave it a rather discoloured and disturbing appearance and it was replaced with a more 'lifelike' wax portrait. For many years, the rejected head rested between the feet of Bentham's fully dressed skeleton. Its presence became too much of a provocation for student pranksters, who kidnapped it more than once, demanding a ransom. According to one story, it was taken for a lengthy excursion through the United Kingdom by train, by an unknown route, finally ending up in a left-luggage locker at Aberdeen station.

Would Station Jim have been moved to bark as a train bearing Bentham's mummified head passed by? It is telling that the dutiful dog's continued presence among us, over a century after his death, was enabled through public subscription and the contributions of his fellow members of staff at Slough. Frozen in position, he stares glassily across the platform, his expression one of infinite, long-suffering patience. Meeting his gaze, I wonder if this might not be a model for memorialising the departed. Why consign them to graveyards where they moulder forgotten? How much more appropriate that the worthy live on where they made the greatest impression during their lives: at their places of work. Friendly station staff, missed by the travelling public when they disappear from service, would surely be a popular choice for mummification, as would the long-term commuter who shocks his fellow travellers by dying in harness. Among the jostle and flow of the crowd on our rush-hour platforms these figures would not move, frozen in attitudes and gestures once familiar, their continued presence a reassuring reminder of values that endure.

LOCATION: MAIDENHEAD

THE GHOST OF A BRIDGE AND A DEPOSED KING

Today, I am travelling to a point on the railway that epitomises something of the spirit of the time of its construction, when the world appeared to be careering into the future, every week bringing news of some novel invention or technological innovation. A time in this sense, then, not unlike our own. My journey is a kind of pilgrimage, to one of the earliest monuments of the genius of Isambard Kingdom Brunel, an architectural masterpiece itself immortalised by a genius of a different kind, the painter J. M. W. Turner. I speak, of course, of the railway bridge at Maidenhead.

I am in no hurry to arrive, which is just as well, as I am on board the stopping train. No city-bound commuter ever takes this service; by definition, such people want to proceed from A to B as fast as possible. Lifting their eyes momentarily from an e-reader or pausing in their perusal of a newspaper to stir a cup of coffee, they may notice a town flashing past that they will never visit and wonder what happens there. Is there a vegetable market? Do people go fishing? What do they make in that silver factory by the canal? This service is to an inter-city express what a ruminating cow, ambling towards the milking parlour, is to a racehorse at full stretch. From Oxford, we trundle through the landscape at a pleasant speed that allows the traveller to fully appreciate its shifting gradations of colour, contour and light beneath the heavy sky. The river plain is planted with fields of wheat and oilseed, bordered with strips of wild flowers; at Radley station, grasses, wild camomile, purple loosestrife and poppies reach through the fence, where a lone figure dressed in orange protective overalls is spraying the weeds growing up through the platform. After Didcot, the view opens out further, with the Chilterns in the distance studded with purple clumps of trees. Overhead, red kites, nature's drones, wheel on their endless circuit of inspection. A view of the 12th century St Mary's church at Cholsey where Agatha Christie, the author of the Miss Marple mystery *4.50 from Paddington*, lies buried, makes an almost impossibly idyllic vista, especially when passed at 35 miles an hour. This is the England some would die to protect; a place to never leave, to retreat to when old, or to buy into after achieving a level of success in business or the City.

Platform 3 of Maidenhead station bears a reminder that however rural or tranquil an area might appear, it never exists in isolation from conflicts elsewhere. A bronze statue forming part of a bench portrays an elderly man with distinctive, square-framed glasses reading from a large book, his head tilted to one side in appraisal. It is a portrait of one of Maidenhead's most famous residents, Sir Nicholas Winton, the organiser of the *kindertransport* trains that ferried Jewish children to safety in Britain from German-occupied Czechoslovakia; the book he is portrayed reading is supposed to contain photographs of the children he saved, whose direct descendants number some 5,000 people. Statues commemorating the exodus exist in other stations: at Liverpool Street in London, where trains carrying the children arrived from the port of Harwich and were met by Winton, who had organised families to sponsor and take in each refugee; and at Praha Hlavní nádraží, the station in Prague from which the trains departed.

Winton's 105th birthday fell in May 2014, during the writing of this book; it was marked by celebrations in the UK and the announcement he was to be awarded the Order of The White Lion, the highest civilian honour in the Czech Republic. In October 2014 he travelled with his family to receive the award from the Czech President at a ceremony at Prague Castle. 'England was the only country at that time willing to accept unaccompanied minors,' Winton explained in his acceptance speech. 'I thank the British people for making room to accept them, and of course the enormous help given by so many of the Czechs who were at that time doing what they could to fight the Germans and to try to get the children out.' The same day the ceremony was reported in the British press the newspapers carried the announcement by Foreign Office minister Lady Annelay that the British government would not be supporting search and rescue operations in the Mediterranean to save refugees from drowning, as such activities would provide 'an unintended pull factor' encouraging further migration. During the previous 12 months, in response to what the British Refugee Council has called 'the greatest refugee crisis since the second world war', Italian Naval vessels mounted Operation Mare Nostrum rescuing 150,000 migrants from overcrowded boats, while at least a further 2,500 were known to have perished. Unsurprisingly the Italian state felt unable to finance and man the operation indefinitely and their European allies have not stepped into the breach. Platform 3 at Maidenhead provides a space in which to contemplate the contradictions of a world that, while giving accolades to those that saved refugees from a previous war, prefers to leave those fleeing equally terrible conflicts today to their fate.

Emerging from Maidenhead station my eyes fall on one of the town's principal architectural attractions, its clock tower, built in 1897. It is constructed from red brick faced in white stone in the Gothic Revival style, a less flamboyant, miniature version of Gilbert

Scott's clock tower at St Pancras station in London, completed some 30 years earlier. Thanks to a postwar redesign of the town that prioritises vehicles over pedestrians, it now stands stranded in the central reservation of a dual carriageway, flanked by malls and the office of a mobile phone network provider. After waiting some time for a convenient gap in the traffic, I cross the road and step over the barrier to better appreciate its charms, wondering as I do how many others make the same perilous journey. The tower was erected, I learn from its inscription, 'To commemorate the Diamond Jubilee of her Most Gracious Majesty Queen Victoria, who on June 20th 1897 completed the Sixtieth Year of a Reign Unparalleled for Progress in All that Makes for The Happiness of the Human Race'. This is quite a claim – one that might have been disputed, I can't help feeling, in parts of her empire far from the Thames valley. But Maidenhead is a royal borough, designated as such because of its twinning with Windsor, the home of Windsor Castle, so a royalist perspective is to be expected. Indeed, such loyalties stretch back well before the Saxe-Coburg and Gotha dynasty, to the time of the English Civil War.

No visit to Maidenhead High Street would be complete without a brief halt at the National Westminster bank – not to use its ATM, but instead to look at the plaque that decorates the wall above the hatch to its night safe. It records that this was once the site of the Greyhound Inn, where in July 1647 the recently defeated King Charles I was brought by Thomas Fairfax, commander-in-chief of the New Model Army, for what turned out to be his last meeting with his younger children before his execution. Banks, of course, have replaced monarchs as our real contemporary rulers; yet they too have had their ascendancy challenged in recent times. While their leaders have not, so far, been taken to a public place and executed, their powers, long comparable to those associated with the divine right of kings, have come under scrutiny in courts and in the wider arena of public opinion. Fitting, then, that a bank memorialises this ultimate fall from grace. Yet all such moments have their human and tragic aspects. While Fairfax remained loyal to the Parliamentary cause, he appears to have lost any enthusiasm he may have had for regicide, failing to attend the royal trial and arguing for a postponement in the mortal sentence it meted out. He was not alone. Despite the deposition of the monarch, a considerable element of the population failed to shake off its quasi-mystical attitude to royalty. 'The local people', the plaque records, 'decked the King's route with green boughs and strewed it with flowers.'

Wandering away from this melancholy spot, a memorial to the severing of a man from his family as much as to the severing of his head from his shoulders, I spot a pedestrian in his early 60s, who is achieving a feat of balance and decorum that characterises contemporary life, walking briskly down the high street while holding a canned drink and eating his lunch from a paper bag. I ask him the way to the river. 'Oh, that's a hell of a long way,' he says. 'Have you got a car? No? Well, it's an ambitious walk. I wouldn't walk it. But a fit chap like you might be all right.' In fact, it takes a matter of minutes, but much of the route is along the side of a busy main road – perhaps this is what he means by 'ambitious'. It is instructive to be a tourist in your own country, walking while looking into the grills of advancing cars, climbing over twisted metal traffic barriers and gulping down fumes. Risking life and limb at a roundabout I buy coffee at a service station, squirted into a paper cup by a machine. I feel as out of place as a pedestrian in Los Angeles, but my goal is within reach. Once I gain access to Maidenhead Bridge, which carries the road across the river, I am able to get a first glimpse of what has drawn me here.

Brunel's design at Maidenhead was revolutionary. His railway bridge cleared the river in two brick arches 128 feet long and a mere

24 feet high, supported by a single pier sunk on a mid-river island, today overgrown with trees. Spans of such length and shallowness had only ever previously been constructed of stone, rather than brick, and many predicted the bridge would collapse.

As he did elsewhere on the line, Brunel had to battle various demons in the achievement of his goal. The first took the shape of the Thames Navigation Commissioners, who insisted his bridge should obstruct neither the navigable river, plied by the barges that before the advent of the railway were the chief transporters of heavy goods, or the footpaths along its banks. The second was one of his eternal foes: gradient. For locomotives of the mid-19th century to achieve reasonable speeds, it was imperative they were forced to climb as little as possible, even in the distance required when approaching a bridge. Many of the engineer's most extraordinary feats were undertaken in the cause of achieving flatness; not for nothing was the GWR known as 'Brunel's billiard table'.

At first it seemed the doubters might be right. Chadwick, the contractor undertaking the work for Brunel, ignored instructions and eased the wooden centring supporting the arches before the cement was sufficiently dry. The lowest three courses of bricks in the eastern arch separated from each other by a matter of one and a half inches. In the popular mind this was soon exaggerated into a gap large enough to allow insertion of a man's arm. Chadwick admitted responsibility and undertook repairs at his own cost.

Brunel ordered that the supporting structure be restored and that it should remain in place – naturally, his public critics thought he didn't dare remove it. On 8 October 1838 the centrings were eased slightly on Brunel's instructions, without being removed. Effectively, they were no longer directly supporting the bridge, but the clear air between wood and brick was indiscernible to the naked eye. This gave rise to the first of two persistent myths about Brunel's bridge – that this was a playful 'duping' of the public, who could not be expected to understand the genius of his design and should therefore be pacified with the display of impractical scaffolding. His biographer, L. T. C. Rolt, maintained he acted out of an 'impish sense of humour'. In fact, he had no such mischief in mind; he was just allowing for any natural settling of the bridge.

The second fable, recorded by E. T. MacDermot, the 'official' historian of the Great Western Railway, was that 'one night in the autumn of 1839 a storm blew the centring down' and, to the astonishment of the public, the bridge stayed up. This story enhances Brunel's status as a playful magician, adept at sleight of hand, the sort of man who whisks the tablecloth from a table while leaving the crockery in place. Its mythic qualities are intensified by the presence in the account of the Romantic archetype of a storm, representing the forces of an all-powerful Nature. Traditionally, such events expose hubris, humbling mankind; in Brunel's case it merely demonstrated the inviolability of his powers. Disappointingly for those wishing to believe in the story, Brunel's correspondence indicates the centring was in place long after the turbulent autumn weather had subsided, in the spring of 1840.

I drop down on to the Thames towpath by the corrugated iron sheds of Marlow Boat Services and walk along the bank of the river until I am at Brunel's bridge. A barge, the subject of so much dispute between Brunel and the Thames commissioners, its function today purely one of leisure, nudges the bank as a train rumbles overhead. In fact, what I am seeing is not his bridge at all – or, at least, when the bridge was widened in the 1890s to carry four lines, two extra bridges were built, on either side of and encasing Brunel's design. Looking up from the towpath you can see the shape of Brunel's structure in the brickwork, although its outline is disguised by water stains; even these central bricks may not be original. In effect, what we are seeking is the trace left by a revolutionary idea, the ghost of a bridge.

This spot on the towpath beneath the bridge has long been known as the 'Sounding Arch', because of its superb echoes. Generations of local children, visiting sightseers and drunks walking home from the pub have tested its acoustic potential. On my own visit I cannot resist sending whistled notes bouncing around its interior. What is it that has always attracted human beings to places that have an echo? Is it connected to our propensity for mimicry? On the internet I find the blog of a French horn player named Carly Lake, who has made a special journey to Maidenhead, drawn by the acoustic properties of the bridge, to play and record the solo horn movement from Olivier Messiaen's *Des Canyons aux Étoiles* (From the Canyons to the Stars) beneath its arch. The piece is called *Appel Interstellaire* (Interstellar Call) and does indeed at moments sound like a cry sent out across the vast empty reaches of space. I listen to her performance on headphones. The piece has an extraordinary tonal and emotional range and is something of a showcase for a horn player's virtuosity. In loud interludes of brief staccato notes, as many as seven repeats bounce back from the arch; gentler passages are soaked in a deep, sustaining reverb. She pauses for a barge to make its way upriver, its engine gurgling, water slapping at the brickwork of the bridge, and again as a high-speed train passes overhead, sufficiently distracted to repeat a passage twice. The French composer's appropriation of birdsong within his compositions has become one of the best-known features of his work, capturing nature's greatest mimics in a musical feedback loop. This piece includes passages that evoke the distinctive whistling calls of the Chinese thrush and the canyon wren. Of course, hearing the sound of the train accidentally included on the recording, I cannot help thinking of the vast number of musical compositions inspired by trains, their sounds, rhythm and mournful calls fulfilling for many musicians the role birds did for Messiaen. Through Lake's intervention, Messiaen's music is itself captured by the Sounding Arch and repeated back, in a waterfall of echoes as complex as a dawn chorus.

This combination of music and architecture is only two sides of a triangular exchange between art forms taking place here, bridging time and distance. Messiaen himself was a synaesthete for whom sound and colour were intimately connected; perhaps he would have understood these overlapping conversations. Brunel's bridge inspired what has been called 'the first impressionist painting', J. M. W. Turner's *Rain, Steam and Speed,* completed some six years after the bridge was built. A day or two after my visit to Maidenhead I decide to pay it a visit at the National Gallery in London. Our great museums are not mere repositories but more like countries in themselves, with their own ecosystems, politics and dramas created by those who work in them. When I go to the cloakroom to deposit my bag, I can't help overhearing the conversation of the two attendants behind the counter, a man and a woman in their 20s. Its subject matter is so strange, I feel compelled to interrupt. Excuse me, I say, are you speaking about a dream?

'Yes,' the man replies, 'I always write my dreams down. I was just telling her about one I had last night.' He continues, apparently unperturbed that his audience has grown. 'I dreamt I had lost a two-year-old sister. I was very upset about it and I was singing a song dedicated to her on the guitar in front of lots of people. I was singing like this' – he mimes for a moment, with his head back and his eyes closed – 'and tears were rolling down my face. When I woke up I could remember the words, the melody, everything.'

'Did you lose a sister in real life?' I ask.

'No, not that I know of,' he said, 'but I am going to ask my parents about it now.'

His female co-worker is sitting on a stool, twirling her hair around a finger. I can't help noticing she is looking a little sceptical. Perhaps she has heard this kind of thing before.

'Maybe you lost something else, not a sister,' she says, in a strong Italian accent. 'Maybe your mind. Perhaps life is telling you to get out of the cloakroom. Go get a proper job.'

Spurred on by her comment, I go to seek out Turner's painting. Its viewpoint is very different from the one to be had in Slough, either from the road bridge or at river level – the artist has imagined himself into a position on the bridge itself as the train comes rushing towards him from the direction of London. The pastoral Thames valley has been transformed into a scenic gorge, complete with a sightseeing couple in a boat on the river, one of them sheltering from the rain under an umbrella. Maidenhead road bridge takes on the dimensions of an impressive viaduct in the distance. All is insubstantial, wreathed in mist. Despite the weather, the scene is one of rural tranquillity, a showcase for Turner's atmospheric effects. This peaceful and timeless scene is shattered by the steam engine pulling an open-topped train across Brunel's bridge. In the words of Kenneth Grahame, author of *The Wind in the Willows*, who knew this stretch of the Thames well, the artist 'did his best to seize the spirit of the thing, its kinship with the elements, and to blend furnace-glare and rush of iron with the storm-shower, the wind and the thwart-flashing sun-rays, and to make the whole a single expression of irresoluble force'.[17] In the foreground, what is little more than a gesture in brown paint resolves itself on close inspection into a hare, running away full tilt from the train along the tracks – a champion of speed from the natural world pursued by a newly arrived mechanical rival. The focus of the painting, the one solid body in this sea of mists and rain, is the train itself and the plume of steam and smoke it emits, whipped back along its extent by its own velocity, its boiler glowing red and even white-hot as it hurtles forward towards the viewer. It is as if our vision is at one with that of the passengers, unprotected from the elements, faces whipped by rain, eyes blurred and watering from the unaccustomed speed. Is the artist celebrating technology and innovation, or lamenting the passing of a rural idyll? Or is he perhaps pointing to a fundamental shift in power from the old, landed classes, represented by the pastoral backdrop, to the newly powerful industrialists? Interpretations are as diffuse and hard to grasp today as the swirling vapours that surround the train. What is certain is the future has arrived.

DIGRESSION

'FOR GOD'S SAKE TAKE TO WORKING LIKE A SLAVE'

All commuters by rail must come to terms with the fact that in order to make a living they will spend a significant proportion of their waking life on the train. One way they deal with this reality is to rage against it; another is to slip its grip by turning it to their own ends. This second strategy served me pretty well for a decade or so, although I would never pretend there weren't days when I cursed my fate as much as any perpetual traveller is bound, on occasion, to do. When circumstances left the carriage door open, I stepped through. The challenges of the freelance life are well known and not worth rehearsing here, except perhaps in this respect. Released captives lose more than a prison: they also lose the structure provided by an externally imposed routine. The Czech poet Miroslav Holub held down a full-time job as a research scientist alongside his literary career. The Czech writers' union offered him a grant equivalent to his salary to allow him to concentrate for two years exclusively on his poetry, he told Stephen Stepanchev of the *New Leader*. 'But I like science. Anyway, I'm afraid that, if I had all the time in the world to write my poems, I would write nothing at all.'

This, then, is the paradox: escape from one kind of imprisonment and you can find yourself confined by another. The creator of the Great Western Railway was well aware of such dangers. In around

1848, Brunel heard that his brother-in-law, the artist John Callcott Horsley, was about to leave a teaching post, at which he earned a small but regular salary, to concentrate on his painting. The letter he sent in response to this news was written at a time when the engineer was beset with financial problems himself and forced to lay off large numbers of staff, which seemed (in this instance at least) to prey on his mind.[18] 'Imagine', he wrote, 'the extent of disappointment pain and misery I have had to inflict and you will easily understand the anxiety I must feel for anybody who has to give up <u>any certainty</u> however small.' Brunel was acutely aware that the vast edifices he was building could come crashing down at any moment through lack of funds; after all, his own similarly ambitious father, Marc Brunel, had been declared insolvent and, along with his wife, spent time in Marshalsea, the infamous prison in Southwark, during 1821. Three years later, in 1824, a naval clerk, the father of another great fashioner of the 19th century, Charles Dickens, was imprisoned in the same gaol for a debt to a baker. Dickens was 12 years old when his father went to prison; Brunel, apprenticed to a clockmaker in Paris, was 15. Arguably, Marshalsea was a cog in the relentless engine that drove both men, who, in their turn, did so much to shift Britain's image of itself. Fear of the debtor's prison is not easily erased.[19]

'Do you feel confident that you will <u>slavishly</u> occupy the time you thus gain?' Brunel wrote to his brother-in-law. 'If you give up the school let me entreat you to <u>slave</u>. To compel yourself to certain things by certain times … What I dread is the effect of your being left without any irksome compulsory duty – nothing induces a more <u>time spending</u> (I must not call it idle) habit than the absence of compulsion. I feel it strongly because I believe I am naturally idle but – all my life is one of <u>slaving</u> and <u>compulsion</u> you and many others may think my life a pleasant one – I am of a happy disposition and therefore it is a pleasant one – I am never my own master and I have an overwhelming quantity of work which must be done by certain days and hours – knowing the effect of this – and how artificially industrous it makes a man – I confess I dread a man's being left always his own master. As I said before though if you give up the school for God's sake take to working not industriously but like a slave.'

So, for all his achievements and despite his apparent self-confidence, Brunel saw his life as one of servitude. This seems to have been little short of the truth. In the early days of the GWR he confessed to a correspondent that his working day was a little longer than he would have liked as it rarely lasted less than 20 hours at a stretch. While surveying the route or inspecting works between London and Bristol, he took what sleep he could in draughty inns, or on the move in a black britzka carriage he designed himself, complete with plans, papers and folding bed; its approach struck dread into the hearts of surveyors and construction gangs along the route, earning it the nickname the 'Flying Hearse'. Horses collapsed beneath him; employees were pursued and run to ground at all hours of the day and night. It was particularly fitting that he had chosen the French motto, as a young man, *En Avant* – Let's Get Going.

But there is a much deeper link between slavery and the Great Western Railway than the working routines of its chief engineer. The line was born out of the imagination and ambitions of those Brunel referred to as 'the spirited merchants of Bristol', along with their trading partners in London. These men came from families whose wealth, like that of the elegant city they inhabited, was founded on the triangular trade between Britain, West Africa, North America and the West Indies. The commodities they traded included sugar, tobacco, cotton, rum – and slaves. So how closely did the 'slave' Brunel associate himself with those who profited from enslaving their fellow human beings?

It would have been impossible to remain unaware of the debate raging around slavery during these years, especially in Bristol, a city that had built its prosperity on the trade. When he arrived in 1829, Brunel would have found opinion bitterly divided, with the merchant class, with certain notable exceptions, strongly against abolition. If he harboured liberal views on the subject, he doubtless considered it wise to hold his tongue among those from whom he hoped to gain employment. When owning a slave, rather than the trade in slaves, was made illegal in Britain's colonies in 1833, the government paid out £20m in compensation to plantation owners for the loss of their 'property'. A sum of £500,000 was paid to Bristol merchants alone, equivalent to around £25m today. Naturally enough, the city's venture capitalists, with funds to invest, were looking around for places to profitably put their money. Of the 12 men on the original Bristol committee of the Great Western Railway in 1833, five – Robert Bright, John Cave, George Gibbs, Thomas Richard Guppy and John Harford – have easily established links with families or companies directly associated with the slave trade. Henry Bright and Company organised slaving expeditions and owned Caribbean plantations. John Cave represented the Bristol Corporation on the committee and himself received compensation as a slave owner. George Gibbs was a member of the Society of Merchant Venturers, the organisation that had challenged the slaving monopoly of the Africa Society in the 17th century, winning the right of Bristol merchants to enter the trade. Gibbs was an important investor in the GWR as well as in the Great Western Steamship Company. He was a senior partner of Gibbs, Bright and Co, a shipping company heavily involved in the African slave trade. His cousin, George Henry Gibbs, convened the London Committee of the Railway and became a director.

Thomas Guppy was the son of a prominent Bristol merchant; his mother came from a family made wealthy through estates in the

West Indies. A sugar refiner, as well as an engineer, an inventor and a trained architect, he was one of the few men Brunel would have encountered in Bristol whose breadth of experience and ambition matched his own. Another of Brunel's closest business associates, Christopher Claxton, was a leading figure in the anti-abolition movement in Bristol and came from a plantation-owning family. A former slaving agent in Antigua, he acted as election agent for James Evan Baillie, the MP for Bristol who personally received over £90,000 in compensation for the loss of his 3,100 slaves. Because of his political work in campaigning for Baillie, Claxton's views on race are accessible to us in a way that those of other men of his time are not. Documents that have survived are marked by anti-Semitic and openly racist rhetoric; one pamphlet that circulated in Bristol in 1830 claimed that 'Negroes' were a 'barbarous race', the poisoners of their rightful masters, cruel to animals and therefore unworthy of emancipation. Just how shocking such language was to his contemporaries is hard to judge; it does not seem to have threatened his relationship with Brunel. Claxton's house in Queen Square was attacked during the Bristol riots of 1831, during which, in a surprising historical footnote, his black servant threw an intruder out of a window. Claxton proved a loyal supporter of Brunel, closely involved in various of his schemes for the rest of the engineer's life.

Brunel's own thinking on the slavery question is unknown and it would be unjust to surmise too much. What we do know is that he believed in the right of business to regulate its own relations with its workforce, without interference from government. If the abolition of slavery and the technological advances of the Industrial Revolution saw a shift in capitalism's dependence on human effort to more dependable machines, at the same time, as E. P. Thompson has pointed out, it threw thousands out of work, swelling 'the limitless supply of cheap labour for the arduous work of sheer human muscle in which the times were so spendthrift'.[20] In mining, the docks, porterage, in brickworks and the building trade, as in the construction of the railway, there was virtually no mechanisation. Like many who do not spare themselves, Brunel generally wasted little time on sympathy for the workers engaged on his projects. Conditions for the navvies who built the Great Western line from London to Bristol were in some ways little better than those on the plantations owned by some of the railway's principal funders. 'Society rests on the existence of a vast population ... born to perform the rudest labour, and engaged in nothing else from birth to death,' wrote a journalist in 1864, in an article comparing Southern slavery with the condition of the poor in England. 'England is the government of a minority, resting on the subjection of a majority forced by circumstances to fulfil all the coarser tasks and more repulsive duties of the human race.'[21]

The old Victorian nickname for the railway, the Iron Road, situates it perfectly in history as the ultimate product of the Industrial Revolution. As school students studying the period will know, it was the fact that Britain had coal and iron deposits in relatively close geographical proximity, enabling coke to be used for higher-temperature smelting of iron ore, which propelled the nation into the future ahead of many of its rivals. Iron, of course, features in the most famous image of Brunel to have come down to us, taken by the photographer Robert Howlett.

Brunel is standing in front of the massive launching chains of the SS *Great Eastern*, in Millwall Dock; he is, a casual observer would doubtless say, 'dwarfed by them', yet somehow the exact opposite is true. Brunel was, he readily admits in his diaries, acutely aware of his size; his tall hat and fat cigar, clenched between his teeth in the corner of his mouth in a manner later made popular by North American gangsters, are doubtless attempts to make up for his lack of stature. This is a supremely self-conscious portrait, its subject as

skilled an image-maker as the man who took it. With his hands thrust jauntily in his pockets and his suit trousers smeared with dockside mud, Brunel's figure suggests not so much smallness as a hugely compressed energy and readiness for action. The vast links of the chains, each the size of his waistcoated torso, tumble down behind him, a frozen waterfall of iron. Brunel has grown tired of railways; sickened by the frenzied speculation of the railway boom. There would never, he knew, be another opportunity to build a line entirely to his own design in this crowded island. Only the open ocean now gave scope for the imagination. Standing as he does, apparently bursting with confidence (although, in reality, he was gravely concerned about finance at the time) on the deck of a ship larger than any the world had yet seen, an indirect beneficiary of slavery through the inward flow of compensation money into his earlier projects, it is hard not to see a visual echo in the chains behind him of the leg irons and collars that played such a part in the capture and transportation of African slaves. 'And this also', as Marlow says at the beginning of Conrad's *Heart of Darkness*, speaking of the Thames estuary down which the *Great Eastern* would make its way from Millwall, 'has been one of the dark places of the earth'. It seems an unavoidable fact that the great deeds of the past have often involved the conquest and enslavement of others. Perhaps the greatest of all are achieved by those who also enslave themselves.

LOCATION: TAPLOW AND MAIDENHEAD

HAUNTOLOGY ON THE HILL

Certain points in the landscape emit a magnetic attraction for the rich and powerful, becoming the places they hold court, erect temples and parade their wealth. Much has been written about the occult forces that link such spots. I would suggest their positions are dictated by two factors that have remained constant throughout the centuries – topography and transport. A dramatically positioned or supposedly sacred site grants status, setting its occupants apart from the masses; at the same time, those wishing to maintain their grip on power have to be able to return to the centre of things as swiftly as possible, making fast transport links a vital element in the choice of location.

A particular spur of the Chiltern Hills, near Maidenhead, has long fulfilled these contrasting needs. Below it stands Taplow station, bypassed by the fast London trains and now used by a relatively small local community, including a high proportion of London commuters. For a year, the western terminus of the Great Western Railway lay at Taplow, during which time the station was known as Taplow and Maidenhead, as it also served the nearby town on the other side of the river. Yet even the current station, built after the railway reached Maidenhead itself, seems to have pretensions beyond its status. This is partly, it is said, because of the senior officials from the Great Western Railway who lived nearby during the Victorian era; but it was also undoubtedly because of the number of important houses in the area and the influential people who made the journey down from London to disembark at this rural station. A covered metal bridge between the impressively long platforms protects those travellers who need to cross the line from the elements; today it is much favoured by trainspotters and rail photographers because of the view it affords in both directions: west towards Reading, and east to Slough, where the cooling towers of the power station on Slough Trading Estate stand out against the horizon.

Two great houses, Taplow Court and Cliveden, stand neighbouring one another at the top of the long climb from the station; the red-brick bulk of Taplow Court is clearly visible from the train as it approaches from the west. Politicians, poets and kings have all ascended Berry Hill to pay their respects over the centuries, but its history goes back further than this. By the end of the Bronze Age a large fort commanded the hilltop and the valley below, protected by a timber palisade, ditches and ramparts. Hilltops become less important during times of peace. Under Roman occupation the Thames valley ceased to be a battleground between warring tribes and became rich agricultural land, the breadbasket of Roman Britain. When the Romans left, the area regained its frontier status at the border of different Saxon kingdoms.

To help us gain a glimpse of their culture, the sixth-century inhabitants of the hilltop left us a time capsule in the form of the Taplow Mound, or Taeppa's Hlaw in Anglo-Saxon, a large barrow that lies within the grounds of Taplow Court. It was first excavated, very inexpertly, by local enthusiasts in 1883, after an ancient yew tree that grew on its summit fell down. No proper records were made of the excavation and much of the mound's contents were damaged. What survived the attention of these amateur historians remains

the most significant hoard of Anglo-Saxon treasure to emerge from British soil until the discovery of Sutton Hoo, half a century later.

It seems clear that the occupant of the mound, of whom only a few bones remain, was buried facing west, on a bier in a large oak-lined chamber. If he was, as some historians have conjectured, of the Kentish royal line, he lay at the western edge of his lands, with his feet pointing towards the setting sun, dressed in a tunic trimmed with gold braid and a cloak fastened with gold clasps, surrounded by everything necessary to stage a lavish feast for his warriors. Objects that survive, now held in the British Museum, include silver-mounted drinking vessels, made from the long and twisted horns of now-extinct aurochs; silver- and bronze-mounted wooden cups; a cauldron, glasses and a Coptic bowl and stand; an elaborate sword welded from twisted iron and steel, denoting high status; a lyre to accompany the recitation of poetry; and a gaming board, complete with pieces. Around this chieftain, men would have gathered in a feasting hall, eating and drinking together to further bind the ties of loyalty between them, and listening to the epic poems that contained the foundational myths of their tribe, in a way we can guess was not hugely dissimilar to that in which Celtic warriors gathered here a thousand years before.

A stone's throw from the mound lies another feature that played its part in making this a unique site. Bapsey Pond stands at the edge of the escarpment; immediately beyond it the ground falls away, granting dramatic views of the Thames valley. Fed by a spring higher up the hill, the pool would have been a ready supply of fresh water for those defending the hilltop, the rarity of a clay-lined reservoir at such an altitude making the spot even more desirable. On the day I visit, the pond is a dark, polished mirror, reflecting the sky and touched by the drooping branches of surrounding trees – a suitably mysterious setting for events that caused an historic shift in the power alignments of the surrounding tribes. Around 50 years after Taeppa's death, a messenger of a new dispensation arrived in Taplow: St Birinus had been sent by St Augustine to preach the gospel to the Mercians, but had been diverted when he encountered the pagan Saxons in the Thames valley. He preached here, in the shadow of the burial mound, leading those who accepted his message to wash away their sins in waters they already revered. A church, now removed to the village of Taplow, was built next to the mound, as if to neutralise its power. After his conquest of Taplow, Birinus went on to convert Cynegils, King of Wessex. Nevertheless, some of the area's inhabitants retained a connection to the spirit that prevailed in the place before Birinus's arrival. In the early 19th century, the stream feeding the pond was diverted into a brick-lined channel. Local witches, for whom the waters remained sacred, were said to have placed a curse on the Grenfell family, owners of Taplow Court, which some would argue came to fruition at the beginning of the next century.

Today the hill has fallen under the sway of another philosophical order, again working to change the minds and hearts of the populace. A lay Buddhist society called SGI-UK, followers of the 13th-century Japanese monk Nichiren Daishōnin, bought Taplow Court in 1988. Their presence here is one more example of the increasing influence of Buddhist teaching in western societies, although beyond the walls surrounding Taplow Court it often takes the watered-down form of 'mindfulness', a kind of Buddhism-lite, to be found in everything from diet and self-help books to mental health programmes and the patter of fitness instructors who urge us to 'find our Zen' at the gym. Today's mindfulness trainers might be surprised to find that Brunel also advocated paying attention to the present moment. In his entry in his private journal for 17 August 1828, he wrote: 'Time present seems to me <u>allways alike</u> to a person who only looks at the future or the past the present situation is quite often disregarded like a traveller enjoying a beautyfull landscape or admiring a fine view the mere spot on which he stands never enters into the picture.'[22]

After a member of the society, an ex-ballet dancer, has given me a tour of the house we sit in the library and she tells me something of the particular interpretation of the Gautama's thought being promulgated in the shadow of Taeppa's mound. Daily chanting to deliver 'internal cleansing', as well as energy and rhythm, is apparently fundamental, providing a structure to life the Christian monks who inhabited the hilltop during the middle ages might have recognised. Once again this place is the stage for a battle between worldviews originating far away. Northern California was the area of the western world most receptive to eastern philosophies in the 1960s and 1970s. In what writer and academic Blakey Vermeule has described as 'a bittersweet historical irony', the same area on the west coast has created the currently endemic condition known as 'monkey-mind', characterised by constant hopping from one device, screen or idea to another. 'Since the 1980s,' she writes, 'Silicon Valley has spawned an industry that is waging total war on the human attention span. No Yin without its go-to Yang. Or as a friend of mine likes to say: *Namaste*, motherfucker'.[23]

There is a small Buddhist temple in my neighbourhood in Oxford and I often bump into the Tibetan monk who officiates there striding briskly down the street in his robes, always with a friendly smile on his face. On one such occasion, when I was researching a previous book, I took the opportunity of asking him about a particular aspect of his beliefs. When we finished talking he looked keenly in my face and said, 'Are you interested in Buddhism?' And then, as though seeing something there that answered his question, said, 'No, no, you are not ready.' An assessment I accepted with equanimity. Attachment, no doubt, is suffering, but at least it provides material on which to report, the problems it throws up a stimulus to human ingenuity and invention. Brunel was addicted, he admitted elsewhere in his journal, to 'castle-building' – dreaming up plans and schemes for the future – an activity he worried that without control might lead to 'a kind of madness'. What is writing but another kind of castle-building? On the other hand, I am reminded of the constant travelling undertaken in certain schools of Buddhism; of the Zen monks in Japan who run repeatedly around a hill near their temple, with the aim of eventually running far enough to encompass the world. Perhaps taking the train again and again along the valley past the hilltop temple at Taplow has been part of my preparation. As the Buddha is reputed to have said, you cannot travel the path until you have become the path itself.

II

It is true that the owners of the great houses around Taplow were male, yet at the centre of their miniature kingdoms lay women, wielding their own powerful influence, albeit in the way the times dictated. Charles Pascoe Grenfell, made rich through his family's Cornish mining interests, bought Taplow Court from the Duke of Sutherland in 1852. His grandson, William Grenfell, was one of the foremost athletes of the age; a champion rower, he twice swam across the pool below Niagara Falls and went on to organise the London Olympics in 1908. He inherited the house, along with 3,000 acres, when he was 11 years old. Willie married Ethel 'Ettie' Fane in London in February 1887 and they honeymooned in Paris, Cannes, Rome and Egypt. On their return they were met from the train by a group of Grenfell's retainers, who in an extraordinary, feudal gesture of loyalty pulled their carriage from Taplow station all the way up Berry Hill to the house, so the young couple stepped down from what was then the most modern form of transport to complete their journey by the most ancient. The hill is long and in places steep, as anyone who has climbed it will tell you. However heavy the drag of gravity these dutiful servants felt as they hauled their new mistress up the slope, it was as nothing to the pull she would later exert on society as she gathered the brightest and most powerful around her at Taplow Court.

Ettie was elegant and charming, an expert at calculating her effect on the opposite sex, a large number of whom, from schoolboys to eminent writers and half a dozen prime ministers, counted her as an intimate friend. Many professed to be in love with her and she encouraged such flirtations with the occasional stolen kiss or hand held beneath the dinner table, her influence over hearts maintained across distance through her extensive correspondence. The group that gathered around her became known as The Souls. The secret of her technique as queen of her realm was, it seems, to flatter her chosen favourites with her exclusive attention on walks through the woods or in private conversations in the library, giving personal advice and encouraging confidences she swore never to disclose. Such soft power brought real power in its wake; it is very possible that Willie Grenfell's ascension to the baronetcy as Lord Desborough was through Ettie's friendship with the then prime minister, Arthur Balfour. To her combined amusement and embarrassment she was the clearly recognisable model for society hostesses in fictions written by H. G. Wells, John Buchan and Max Beerbohm, all guests at Taplow. Oscar Wilde wrote to her in 1891, in a note enclosed with a copy of *Lord Arthur Savile's Crime and Other Stories*: 'I am sending you a little book that contains a story, two stories in fact, that I told you at Taplow.'[24] Her aim was to make her house a place where the best minds of her generation could meet and where young and old could mingle and take inspiration from one another. Few others could say they had hosted guests as varied as Winston Churchill and Wilde; Edith Wharton and George Curzon. (Curzon, who was later to become viceroy of India, despaired of the vulgarisation of The Souls, writing to a friend that 'I am disposed to draw the line at Oscar Wilde, about whom everyone has known for years'.)

The multiple tragedies that befell the family during and following the Great War, the fulfilment perhaps of the curse of Bapsey Pond, gave Ettie Grenfell's allure added dignity. Her son Julian, a poet, came to epitomise a generation of doomed young aristocrats who would drown in the mud of Flanders. His poem 'Into Battle', for a brief period one of the most celebrated in the English language, is revealing of the mind-set that led Britain to war, a mix of sentimentality towards animals, an ancient Greek bloodlust learnt through the study of classics at Eton and a mystical, quasi-Christian belief in fate. Reared from an early age to stalk and kill animals, he became a sniper at the front and was unambiguous about enjoying the work. 'I adore war,' he wrote to his mother. 'It's like a big picnic without the objectlessness of a picnic ... One loves one's fellow-man so much more when one is bent on killing him.' Ettie was at Julian's bedside in a military hospital in Boulogne when he died, having, as he put it in a letter, 'stopped a Jack Johnson [a splinter from an artillery shell] with my head'. (Johnson had become the first African American to win the world heavyweight boxing title in 1908.) Julian's brother Billy fell within weeks in a pointless manoeuvre that took the lives of almost his entire battalion; his body was never recovered. A decade later Ettie was again keeping vigil at a hospital after the steering wheel of the car her son Ivo was driving came off in his hands and he ploughed into a wall. She resided at Taplow like a Penelope besieged by suitors, waiting for her departed to return. Or, more prosaically, like someone waiting for a train. The railway played a vital part in the life of the family she married into; Riversdale William Grenfell, Willie's uncle, was one of the original board of directors of the GWR. The Desboroughs relied on the service to orchestrate their social life, regularly reserving a carriage on the 5.05 from Paddington, from which their colourful array of guests spilled on to the platform at Taplow station, to be met by carriages and a luggage wagon to carry them up the hill.

While the engine of social life on top of the hill at Taplow Court was fuelled by connections, politics, privilege and the female magnetism of its hostess, Maidenhead, the town in the river valley below, offered somewhat different attractions.

If the great elevated houses were places to parade social status, where every encounter was planned and every appearance recorded in the visitors' book, Maidenhead's inns, clubs and hotels offered the opposite: anonymity when required and the opportunity to fraternise outside the strict gradations of English society. The Orkney Arms was acquired by William Skindle in 1833 and renamed Skindles hotel; his timing, seven years before the arrival of the railway, was perfect, and in various incarnations his establishment would play a central role in the life of the town for the next century and a half. Boating was an increasingly popular pastime in the mid-19th century and, in 1865, officers of the Brigade of Guards decided they needed a boathouse of their own. Maidenhead was chosen as a location because of its easy access by rail from London, and Skindles became their unofficial headquarters. The presence of the Guards in the town galvanised its social life. Admission to the balls they held during Ascot week was sought as eagerly by the mothers of aspiring debutantes as by young actresses looking for suitable partners. By the 1920s the hotel had earned a reputation as the location of choice for those wishing to arrange a discreet rendezvous with a less than official partner. Those in search of the exit from an unhappy marriage could arrange to be seen here in a compromising situation by helpful detectives, kitted out with cameras and correspondent shoes.

On the opposite bank of the river to Skindles was another focal point in the town's social life – Murray's nightclub. With its white-clad orchestra and its glass dance floor, Murray's was the epitome of glamour. It was owned by Jack May, an American who had served as a medic in the US army before settling in Britain. The pharmaceutical knowledge he gained in the military proved useful; he swiftly became the principal drug dealer to the fast set. Cocaine was readily available at the club, as were more voyeuristic thrills; a few coins placed in the right palm gave access to the space beneath the transparent dance floor, from which to gain a different view of the twirling dancers above.

A psychiatrist and his aristocratic patient Sir Richmond, the protagonists of H. G. Wells's novel *The Secret Places of the Heart*, published in 1922, are on a therapeutic motoring tour when their car breaks down at Maidenhead. The hotel they put up in is called the 'Radiant', but it is clearly based on Skindles, with its 'pleasant lawns and … graceful landing stage at the bend towards the bridge'.

'A resort of honeymoon couples,' said the doctor, and then rather knowingly: 'Temporary honeymoons, I fancy, in one or two of the cases.'

'Decidedly temporary,' said Sir Richmond, considering the company – 'in most of the cases anyhow. The two in the corner might be married. You never know nowadays.'

Locals were annoyed by Wells's portrayal; however, his aspersions were hardly overstated. This was the era during which the town established itself as a playground, particularly for those working in the film industry in studios at nearby Pinewood and Beaconsfield. Stars who stayed at Skindles between 1950 and 1966, and doubtless enjoyed the discretion of its staff, included Bette Davis, Boris Karloff, the Marx Brothers and Alfred Hitchcock. 'Are you married, or do you live in Maidenhead', went the saying of the time. Chorus girls congregated in a street nicknamed 'Gaiety Lane', after the theatre in the West End at which many of them were employed; the last train back from London was known as the 'Greasepaint Special' in their honour. Ivor Novello bought a villa called Redroofs on the river outside Maidenhead in 1926, which was the regular haunt of chorus boys and actresses, near which he was often seen walking his dog in full theatrical make-up. He was rumoured to enjoy lying naked in a glass coffin at Redroofs while his friends paraded past him, rehearsing their mourning lines. Meanwhile, downriver at Bray, his friend, the American actress Tallulah Bankhead, was under investigation by MI5 over a story invented by a newspaper that she had indulged in 'indecent and unnatural practices' with five underage Eton schoolboys, the sons of eminent aristocrats among them, in her hotel room at the Hotel de Paris. (In fact, she and her boyfriend had merely taken his nephew, a pupil at the school, out to tea along with some friends, but this was hardly a story.) 'The charge against Miss Tallulah Bankhead (an

American aged 26)', a confidential MI5 report from 1928 states, 'is quite simply (a) that she is an extremely immoral woman and (b) that in consequence of her association with some Eton boys last term, the latter have had to leave Eton. As regards (a) according to informant, she is both a Lesbian and immoral with men … As regards her more natural proclivities, informant tells me that she bestows her favours "generously" without payment. Informant added that her "circle" is a centre of vice patronised by at least one of the most prominent sodomites in London.'

Bankhead was saved from deportation by the Thames valley *omertà* that seemed to operate at all levels, protecting the confidences whispered in Ettie Grenfell's ear at Taplow Court and sealing the lips of the doormen of the nightclubs along the river. The MI5 agent, identified only as 'FHM' in documents released by the public records office in March 2000, noted that 'the headmaster is obviously not prepared to assist the home office – he wants to do everything possible to keep Eton out of the scandal'.

In spring 1971, Skindles played host to the most potent cultural symbols of the age. The Rolling Stones had decided to leave the country to take up tax exile in France and were looking for a place to play a farewell gig to an invited audience that included Eric Clapton, John Lennon and Yoko Ono. Their roots lay further downriver, on a different line. Mick Jagger and Keith Richards had first met on the platform of Dartford station on the Thames estuary, when Keith spotted Mick carrying a couple of sought-after albums under his arm. By the time their train pulled into Waterloo, the seeds of a writing partnership that would last half a century were sown. It is possible that Skindles, with its waterfront location, reminded the band of the Eel Pie Island Hotel at Twickenham, the legendary blues venue on the river where they played some of their earliest gigs and honed their sound. If so, it was the perfect place to bring the first part of their career to a close.

The wish to pay less tax, it could be argued, is not generally the hallmark of a 'Street Fighting Man'. Nevertheless, the Stones in 1971 were a different animal to the corporate entertainers who have periodically taken to the road in the 21st century. Whip-thin, drugged up and dangerous, they could tear the place up live. *Sticky Fingers*, their new album, was the first to be released on their own Rolling Stones Records following their separation from their manager, Allen Klein. Mick Jagger had taken the precaution of buying flowers and champagne for neighbours likely to be affected by the noise. These offerings were not sufficient to neutralise local bylaws; at 2 a.m., a time when Keith was presumably beginning to wake up and Mick was in mid-pirouette, channelling a combination of James Brown, Rudolf Nureyev and Tina Turner, they were told they had to switch their amplifiers off. In a rage, Jagger threw a table through a plate-glass window. A surviving window from the club now stands in the Maidenhead Heritage Centre, its stained-glass design bearing a coat of arms featuring two heraldic beasts. A document I come across in a file records their proper designation in the cryptic language of the heraldic code. 'The dexter Supporter is an Antelope Argent, armed, ducally gorged, chained and unglued Or. The sinister Supporter a stag proper attired, unglued, ducally gorged and chained Or.' Today, Skindles is closed, the long building boarded up, all its windows blind. Perhaps anyone wishing to refurbish it should commission a new window and a new coat of arms, of which the dexter supporter could be Mick Jagger, the sinister Keith Richards.

III

While the presence of near-legendary figures like the Rolling Stones in Maidenhead was as transitory as the pleasure steamers that plied the river, one regular visitor to Skindles took up residence in the vicinity, becoming, for a period, its queen. Diana Dors was born Diana Fluck in Swindon in 1931, the daughter of a GWR clerk and an ambitious mother who allowed her daughter to change her name – in case it was written up outside a movie theatre and one bulb blew, as the actress explained later. By the time she was a precocious 12 years old, Dors was dancing with American GIs at a local airbase, claiming to be 17, and posing for art classes at an American college on the edge of town. Before long she was taking the train to London to attend the London Academy of Music and Dramatic Art, walking into a contract at Rank aged 16. Along with the change of name came the shift in hair to a shade of blonde impossible in nature, the classic signifier of the postwar actress on the make. In the Hollywood-centred universe, the behaviour of its deities and demigods was as strictly coded as that of Greek mythology; blonde hair and a silhouette that stopped traffic meant you were one of two things: dumb or mean. In either case, you were dangerous to the stability of the male-ordered universe; the phrase 'blonde bombshell' was a cliché which spoke its own truth. Britain's film studios were engaged in a desperate search to find a native Marilyn Monroe and Dors's first husband and 'publicity manager' Dennis Hamilton was keen that she took up the role; but while Dors could approximate Monroe's vital statistics, she never convincingly exuded the air of unwitting innocence the male audience found so irresistible in the American star. Perhaps life had already taught her too much. Hamilton beat her when he was drunk, on occasion throwing her down stairs, and forced her into the second of two abortions she had by the time she left her teens. She may have leased her first Rolls-Royce at 21, but she came of age with few of her dreams intact.

The artistic high point of Dors's acting career was probably the film *Yield to the Night*, nominated for a Palme d'Or at Cannes in 1956, in which she played a woman condemned to the scaffold in the last days before her execution. Although it was made before she came to trial, the film had eerie resonances with the case of Ruth Ellis, the last woman to be hanged in Britain, another blonde who believed she deserved better than the cards life had dealt her. Parallels between art and life were made stranger by the fact that Ellis had taken a minor role as a beauty queen in a previous film by Dors, *Lady Godiva Rides Again*, and the two women had socialised on set. In 1958 Dors followed up with a film noir, *Tread Softly Stranger*, in which she perfected the combination of lip-curling sneer and pouting seduction that entrapped the film's male leads into committing murder. As the daughter of a railway town she must have felt at home on set. From the opening credits playing on a carriage window as the hero boards a northbound express from London to evade his debtors, to the tracks that run alongside the factory, the call of steam whistles and the station that is the scene of a crucial showdown, the whole movie is shaped by trains. Dors plays Calico, a nightclub waitress desperate to escape her provincial prison; perhaps it is this echo of her own origins that gives her performance its power.

Dors died of cancer aged 52 in 1984 and was buried in her favourite gold lamé dress. If her only legacy had been her films, perhaps she would now be largely forgotten. However, the invention for which she is best known was the British sex party; first pioneered with Hamilton in London and Kent, and later perfected at her mansion on the river near Boulter's Lock in Maidenhead and a few miles away with her third husband Alan Lake in Sunningdale. The recipe for such occasions required a celebrity guest list, a sprinkling of aspiring actresses and prostitutes, the occasional East End gangster, two-way mirrors, concealed cameras, pornographic films and a multitude of beds. Woodhurst, the house the couple bought in Maidenhead, had 89 bedrooms, a riverfront equivalent of the aristocratic piles that overlooked it on the hill. They swiftly converted it, dividing it up into flats and retaining a suite for themselves they called Bel Air.

The house has long since been demolished and replaced with anodyne apartments; only the curves in a red-brick wall bordering Ray Mead Road mark the place where statues were inset overlooking the Hollywood-style pool, a key social signifier of the period. What Hollywood had, the upwardly mobile among the British wanted, despite their inclement climate. If the starlets at Ray Mead Road came out in goose bumps and had to rush screaming from the water to rub themselves briskly with towels, that fitted the way sex was portrayed in the mainstream British films of the time, in which occasional nudity was situated alongside slapstick comedy and high camp. For Dors, owning her own pool had added significance. Her attempts to break the American film industry had foundered after a humiliating scuffle by a pool at a mansion off Sunset Boulevard, during which Hamilton slugged a photographer and Dors fell into the water, the resulting catastrophic publicity changing the course of her career. Those of a psychogeographical turn of mind will note that the swimming pool on Ray Mead Road lies in direct line with Bapsey Pond on top of the hill on the other side of the Thames, forming the base of a triangle extending west to another hilltop pool at Cliveden Court, a feng shui configuration within which many of the shifts in power that have taken place in this river valley have been contained.

'There were no half measures at my parties,' Dors boasted to readers of the *News of the World* on 31 January 1960. 'Off came the sweaters, bras and panties. In fact it was a case of off with everything – except the lights.' As the years passed, the gatherings evolved to combine sex with domesticity in a way that was very British. According to an interview her son Jason Lake gave after her death, Dors was known to interrupt people while they were coupling in order to offer them tea and scones. She rarely drank herself and while she enjoyed watching the footage from her hidden cameras, her chief pleasure was gossip about the celebrities she had crossed paths with during her career. She shared an interest in surveillance techniques with Auto-Icon Jeremy Bentham; she would most probably also have subscribed to his call for 'an all-comprehensive liberty for all modes of sexual gratification', agreeing that such an attitude would add incalculably to 'the aggregate mass of pleasure' for all humankind. (Unlike Dors, Bentham was unable to publish his thoughts on the matter during his lifetime, and much of his extensive writing on sexuality remains buried in the archive.) Even after she had skilfully transformed herself from femme fatale to national treasure with the onset of middle age, making ironic cameo appearances in pop videos and fronting a TV slimming show in which she 'lost weight' by removing her heavy jewellery before stepping on the scales, the parties she had perfected continued until shortly before she died.

In March 2014, almost exactly 30 years after her death, my eye is caught by a newspaper on a newsstand as I am about to board a train. An image of Dors in her late 20s dominates the front page of the *Daily Telegraph*; she is wearing a pink diamante-encrusted dress and trailing pink scarf, her platinum hair perfectly coiffed, hands on hips and bright red lips parted in a smile, beneath a headline that could have been written half a century before: 'Diana Dors and the Swinging Sex Parties'. Inside, an older and decidedly homely version of the actress in a sensible nightdress is draped across a bed beside a collection of teddy bears. This is the Dors I see in a photograph in a copy of the *Maidenhead Advertiser* from the late 1970s, sitting at a table with her third husband Alan Lake and Louis Brown, the owner of the newly refurbished Skindles, rechristened the Valbonne. Dors enjoyed the ambiance of the club where, a flier of the period promises, 'members and guests can enjoy the exciting atmosphere of discotheque dancing together with live entertainment on selected evenings'. The Valbonne attracted up to 10,000 visitors a week, travelling by train from as far afield as London, Bristol, Oxford and Southampton, and its no-photography policy guaranteed that what happened in the club stayed in the club. It had a pool, of course, indoors this time. It was opened by the comedian Jim Davidson, accompanied by three topless models, the first to volunteer for a chlorinated baptism; water sprites whose game and slightly weary smiles are captured in black and white in the cuttings file at the Maidenhead Heritage Centre.

In youth, Dors had the figure and attributes of a fertility goddess; in middle age, her image shifted from international siren to the attractive housewife next door with a place in the nation's heart. She was seen, in the words of the ad slogan coined by a young Salman Rushdie in the 1960s to promote fresh cream cakes, as 'naughty but nice'. Times have changed since her death; revelations about the entertainer Jimmy Savile's predation on the underaged and vulnerable have shifted the public mood and launched a series of celebrity show trials, in which those who believed themselves immune to investigation are forced to account for their activities. In 2014, the publicist Max Clifford found himself facing 11 historic charges of indecent assault against women and girls. During his examination Clifford admitted having attended sex parties hosted by Diana Dors, excuse enough to return her to the front pages of the newspapers of middle England. His invocation of the Thames valley deity was not enough to protect him from punishment and he went to prison. (Another Maidenhead resident and showbusiness personality, Rolf Harris, was sent to prison for similar offences a month or two later.) From the front page of the newspaper, the actress reaches out across time, her wicked grin intact, safe from the judgment of a different age.

IV

Despite her social mobility, Diana Dors never made it from water level to the top of the hill. Others, even more adept at social climbing than she was, did. Cliveden, the palatial estate neighbouring Taplow Court, had been styled to arouse feelings of amazement and awe in visitors since the 17th century. As John Evelyn described in his diary in 1679, the setting provided a 'stupendous natural rock, wood, and prospect' while the house itself was 'a romantic object'. The intention was to create a state of mind as much as a house, somewhere that 'answers the most poetical description that can be made of a solitude, precipice, prospect, or whatever can contribute to a thing so very like their imaginations'. Despite the impact the location had on him, Evelyn was careful to report to the king that evening that the hillside retreat of the Buckingham family 'did not please [him] so well as Windsor, for the prospect and park, which is without compare'. It would not be wise to outdo the sovereign in sublimity.

Various incarnations of the house have been built, burnt down and rebuilt over the centuries, each time on a grander and more palatial scale. In the mid-17th century George Villiers, 2nd Duke of Buckingham, lived at Cliveden with his wife Mary, when the couple were not in their London home, Wallingford House; at the latter residence Villiers also installed his mistress Anna Maria Talbot, who bore him an illegitimate son. These were unusual domestic arrangements, even in those different times, but caution was not in Buckingham's nature when it came to this particular woman. He had already fought a duel with her husband, the Earl of Shrewsbury, at Barn Elms in London. Anna was present, disguised as a pageboy holding the head of her lover's horse: a true femme fatale, the kind of woman to turn any man's head, What her thoughts were as the two men and their attendants fought over her with swords, soaking the ground with blood, and her husband was 'run through the body from the right breast to the shoulder', as Samuel Pepys recorded in his diary the next day, is not known. (He died two months later.) Duelling was frowned on at court, not least because of the unfavourable light it threw on the king himself. As Pepys succinctly put it, 'This will make the world think that the King hath good councillors … when the Duke of Buckingham, the greatest man about him, is a fellow of no more sobriety than to fight about a whore.' Despite the damage to his standing, Buckingham was far from shy about the affair; the area of ground known as the Duke's Garden at Cliveden still bears the design he caused to be set into the lawn in flint in the shape of a rapier, along with the date 1668, commemorating the event.

However bold the gestures lovers make, they cannot hold back time. In less than a decade Buckingham was dead, his mistress fled to France and his estate purchased by William, Earl of Orkney. As lord of a significant estate, the Earl needed a bride at his side and in 1695 he married his cousin, Elizabeth Villiers. Elizabeth was another woman who had led a colourful life before arriving at Cliveden. A year before her marriage, she too had been fought over in a duel in which Beau Wilson was killed by a young Scottish gambler named John Law, who escaped justice to become one of the leading economic theorists of his day. The backstory of the chatelaine of Cliveden does not end with a duel. For 15 years Elizabeth had been the mistress of King William III, who valued her not for her looks – Jonathan Swift said of her that 'the poor lady, you know, squints like a dragon' – but for the acuity of her judgment (in a kinder mood, Swift also called her 'the wisest woman I ever saw'). Her relationship with the king was openly acknowledged; the only scandal that touched the monarch arose from the fact that William had one mistress rather than several, as his father had done, leading to rumours about the nature of his friendships with male courtiers. Despite her retirement from London to her hilltop stronghold once she had been dropped by the king, her influence endured. During her reign, the house attracted many of the leading figures of the age.

Despite its wooded walks, sublime views and rural seclusion, Cliveden was rarely far from the mechanics of power. For a time it was home to Frederick, Prince of Wales who rented the house in 1738, living there with his family until he died in 1751 from being hit in the chest by a cricket ball. The Orkney family sold the house in the early 19th century. Twice Cliveden burnt down and was rebuilt, the second time only months after the Duke of Sutherland bought it in 1849. He lost no time in commissioning the architect Charles Barry to build the Italianate villa that stands on the site today. At the end of the 19th century the house and estate were purchased by a man reputed to be the wealthiest in North America, William Waldorf Astor. Having failed in politics and lost his wife, the increasingly embittered old man gave Cliveden to his eldest son Waldorf and his wife Nancy as a wedding present.

Nancy Astor was a very different hostess to Ettie Grenfell. An American divorcée, teetotaller and devoted Christian Scientist, she had come to national prominence in 1919 when she stood for the Plymouth seat previously held by her husband, and was elected as the first woman to take her seat as an MP in the House of Commons. Despite the current imbalance in the representation of women in parliament the isolation they experience is nothing to the resistance Astor had to overcome. Her former guest at Cliveden, J. M. Barrie, author of *Peter Pan*, wrote a personal letter to her to dissuade her from her 'presumptuous ambitions' in standing, asking 'what can you know about politics? These things require a man's brains, a man's knowledge, a man's fairness, a man's eloquence. Woman's true sphere in life is to be a (respectful) helpmeet ...' Once elected she was routinely ignored by male MPs of all stripes, who on meeting her in the corridor of the house would look through her as if she didn't exist. She showed the same courage in the face of this rejection as she did, dressed in her designer clothes, on the poorest streets of Plymouth, where her way with hecklers was legendary and where she once pursued a would-be burglar through streets, alleys and the bar of a pub until he surrendered, only to let him off with a stern lecture. Her performance on the floor of the house, although powerful, was eccentric. Increasingly she was prone to wander, both verbally and physically, losing her thread and leaving her seat to hold private conversations, gesturing with exasperation and calling out remarks during the speeches of others. Author and politician Harold Nicolson caught one such occasion in a diary entry for 23 April 1945. 'Then Nancy got up. For once she had some notes in her hand, but each note suggested an idea and each idea some other idea, and then that reminded her of a story her nurse had once told her in Virginia and how little, now she came to think about it, the British Press knew about Virginia although Sir Walter Raleigh had colonised it and how odd Raleigh was less known in England than in the United States though we knew all about Philip Sidney not the V. C. of course [a reference to an MP who had won the Victoria Cross] such a nice young man and the best type of Conservative although she was not a conservative really although her husband was and nor was Winston really since he had been a liberal once and oh yes she must tell them about Winston ...' and so on, concluding: 'I suppose her rambling is amusing, but it rather saddens me, as I like her, and I wish that she would not make such an idiot of herself in public.'

On the question of universal suffrage for women she was implacable. Why were men so frightened, she asked? 'You need not fear women ... because we are going to give you what is best for you.' To further her efforts in doing so, she turned both her London residence in St James's Square and Cliveden into places where she could engineer meetings between those who would never normally encounter each other on neutral ground. The king and queen mingled with members of the cabinet of the first Labour government, led by Ramsay MacDonald. The Irish playwright Sean O'Casey, a communist, was a house guest for several weeks. At Cliveden, foreign ambassadors and admirals mixed with politicians, painters and writers. George Bernard Shaw was a visitor, accompanying Nancy on a trip to Russia where they met Stalin. Nancy believed the Germans had suffered unfairly through the lack of a just settlement after the Great War and that peace in Europe depended on entering into a frank and open dialogue with Britain's former enemies. At a single Sunday lunch in 1937, during which British relations with Germany were the chief topic of conversation, guests included the British ambassador to Berlin, the top official at the foreign office, the editor of *The Times* and the foreign secretary and his wife, as well as Lord Lothian, who had publicly stated his belief in 1936 that Germany should be allowed to annex the Sudetenland in the cause of peace. The image created by reports of such machinations behind the closed doors of a palatial country house did not sit well with the British public. A news sheet called *The Week*, edited by Claud Cockburn, which had campaigned consistently on the dangers of German expansionism, now turned its attention to the Astors, portraying the Cliveden set as a cabal of anti-Semites and appeasers of fascism. Another leftwing publication, *Reynold's News*, claimed the house was a 'second foreign office'.

Nancy and her husband had misread history, causing damage to their reputations from which they never fully recovered. When, in October 1938, Churchill questioned in the House of Commons the prevailing view that Neville Chamberlain's mission to Munich had been a success, Nancy was unable to resist calling out, 'Nonsense!' Churchill's response would have stung a woman who had spoken so often on moral issues, campaigning to restrict the availability of alcohol and tobacco and for the protection of children. 'When the noble lady cries "Nonsense!",' he told the house, 'she could not have heard the Chancellor of the Exchequer admit in his illuminating and comprehensive speech just now that Herr Hitler has gained in this particular leap forward in substance all he set out to gain … This is only the first taste of a bitter cup which will be proffered to us year by year unless, by a supreme recovery of moral health, we rise again …'

If events at Cliveden during the 1930s undermined the British public's belief that the aristocracy and their politician friends were the best arbiters of their moral health, the spirit of egalitarianism that followed the second world war shifted opinion inexorably further. In 1960, a new chatelaine was installed at Cliveden. Bill Astor, Nancy's recently divorced son, took as his third wife Bronwen Pugh, a Welsh model whose elongated figure, cat-like eyes and dramatic ability on the catwalk had made her the muse of Parisian fashion designer Pierre Balmain. Before her marriage, Pugh was the cover star of numerous magazines and the darling of the tabloids – 'our' Bronwen, they called her, filled with patriotic pride in her success in the world capital of fashion. What the journalists who wrote about her didn't know was that she was undergoing a personal crisis, probably the result of the relentless routine of the model's life, the drugs she took to keep her awake and maintain her weight and the interminable boredom of waiting on photographers and designers. A year before her marriage she had an intense and apparently life-changing religious experience, similar to those recorded by the Spanish mystics; she felt herself falling from a great height into a pit, experiencing intense pain, eventually emerging into the light upon which she recalled 'every cell of my body went into orgasm' and she was filled with an overwhelming love. Afterwards, although she was very fond of Bill, marriage to one person seemed something of an irrelevance, as she loved everybody.

Nevertheless, she felt her duty lay in helping the man who so obviously needed her, even though the running of a vast country house with its endless succession of guests and social occasions, she cheerfully admitted, was completely outside her experience.

How far outside was demonstrated on the weekend of 8–9 July 1961, the hottest of the year so far. Bronwen was five months pregnant. Once again events that would cause a major upheaval in the power structures of the day unfolded beside a pool. Despite the fact they took place some 14 centuries closer to our own time than the ritual conducted at Bapsey Pond, their detail remains unclear; money, power and social position hung on the different versions their protagonists subsequently related. What is beyond doubt is the official guest list at Cliveden over Saturday and Sunday. The most important visitor, around whom social events were constructed, was the president of Pakistan, Field Marshal Ayub Khan. John Profumo, secretary of state for war, along with his wife Valerie, was spending the whole weekend at the house, while Earl Mountbatten, who had been viceroy of imperial India and therefore the former colonial ruler of what was now Pakistan, was joining the party on Saturday for luncheon, along with his wife and daughter. Other guests included members of the Astor family, an economist, a contact from the racing world (Ayub Khan was keen on horses), and a sprinkling of artists, interior designers, social reformers and philanthropists. These were the official inhabitants of the hilltop that weekend, their relationship to each other clearly defined.

There was also another, smaller house party going on in the grounds. Spring Cottage was made available at a peppercorn rent to the osteopath Stephen Ward in return for treating Bill Astor, who had a long-term back problem, and his guests. Ward, while holding what passed for leftwing views in his circle, enjoyed the entrée this arrangement gave him to high society. At the same time he sought

out women from very different backgrounds as his friends and occasional lovers, women who were 'on the make' just as he was, with none of the inhibitions of the debutante set. The cottage, while still on the estate, was situated on the banks of the river at a spot where a mineral spring flows from the chalk cliff above. This was the chink in Bill Astor's social armour, the door left open to infiltrators from the world represented in the gatherings held at the court of Diana Dors. Those visiting Ward that Saturday included a male law student, a model named Christine Keeler and another attractive young woman he had picked up hitchhiking near Slough.

In the evening, Bill Astor led his guests out for a little promenade through the grounds to inspect a statue of his son William riding a dolphin, which had recently been installed next to the pool. He walked ahead of the main party, in conversation with John Profumo. On opening the door in the tall brick wall that separated the pool from the main garden, he realised it was in use. Stepping through that door, he entered a parallel dimension of story and counter-story that would explode in the press over the next two years, once again embroiling the Astor name in scandal and almost bringing down a government in the process. What did he see? Ward was there, certainly, with around five others. One of them, Christine Keeler, had somehow lost her costume, or part of her costume. According to Astor, she was at the other end of the pool and had swiftly covered up in a towel so that when the other guests arrived they noticed nothing amiss. Keeler, in an account paid for by the *News of the World*, claimed Astor and Profumo chased her around the pool while she was still naked, as Bronwen, wearing a tiara, looked on in shock. Profumo, recalling the incident many years later, claimed Astor slapped Keeler's behind and greeted her by name.

Perhaps the continued and unaccustomed hot weather on Sunday introduced a hint of madness into the air, as it often does among the English; a sense that a day of hot sunshine in such a setting might never be repeated and that therefore all the opportunities it offered were there to be seized. The pool was busy; another of Ward's guests had joined the party. Yevgeny Ivanov was officially a naval attaché to the Soviet embassy in London, but was widely known to be working for Russian intelligence and under observation by MI5. Again, the picture Keeler painted for the press of what happened that day at the pool seems wildly improbable. The newspaper stories that depicted the Pakistani president cavorting in the water with a girl on his shoulders had to be retracted, with apologies, to avoid a diplomatic incident. What was doubtless true was that the alpha males present were galvanised by the presence of young and apparently 'game' women from outside their social class. Witnesses agree that John

Profumo had a swimming race with Ivanov, a symbolic duel for Christine Keeler's attention that linked her across time with two other female residents of Cliveden, Anna, Countess of Shrewsbury and Elizabeth Villiers. (Two of Keeler's other lovers, Aloysius 'Lucky' Gordon and Johnny Edgecombe, fought over her for real outside the Flamingo Club in Wardour Street the following year, a contest that ended with Edgecombe cutting Gordon's face with a knife while Keeler looked on, just as Anna had done on the duelling ground by the river at Barn Elms.) Ivanov drove Keeler back to London that night, the apparent victor; according to Keeler, this was when they began a passionate affair. Before long the Russian was sharing her affections with the British minister for war.

So the patterns recur. Wealthy dynasties hold court at the top of the hill. Human bodies enter water and find the direction of their lives changed. Women are fought over and endure the violence of men and in turn manipulate the men who pursue them. Clandestine links are formed in English country houses with representatives of hostile powers, sealed over dinner or the body of a shared mistress. A ritual sacrifice, in the shape of the delusional osteopath, is prepared to deflect the wrath of the gods and the attention of the public from those in charge of the country. Yet a shift has taken place; those subjects will never regain their deference and unquestioning respect for the aristocracy and their political rulers. It is those long regarded as among the least respected subjects of the nation – showgirls, models, B-movie actresses, mistresses – that prove capable of overturning male power structures unchallenged for generations. The words of Denis Healey at the Labour Party Conference in 1945 – 'the upper classes ... are selfish, depraved, dissolute and decadent' – suddenly sound less like the rabble-rousing of an ex-communist firebrand and more like an accurate sociological report from Cliveden.

At the same time as this shift in attitudes is taking place, the culture of the ruling class also begins to lose its ascendancy. The house where Frederick, Prince of Wales in the mid-18th century commissioned the first performance of 'Rule, Britannia!' to be performed in the open-air Rustic Theatre overlooking the Thames plays host in 1964 to the Beatles, filming scenes for their movie *Help!* Gates are breached and plate-glass windows smash. The two-way mirror from Diana Dors' London flat is sold by her first husband Dennis Hamilton to his friend Peter Rachman, who installs it in his bedroom, where it is broken by his mistress Mandy Rice-Davies. Rice-Davis, who will die aged 70 during the completion of this book, is determined the Profumo affair will not blight her life. She holds her head high and waves to the crowd as she walks into court, where she claims she has had a sexual relationship with Bill Astor. (When told by the prosecuting council that he has denied it, she replies 'He would, wouldn't he?' Or perhaps, 'Well, he would, wouldn't he?' Or even 'Well he would say that, wouldn't he?': the various versions of her famous remark chasing each other through the public domain like echoes in the Sounding Arch.) Something has changed, for ever. The process does not begin or end on the hill above Taplow station, yet on its wooded slopes, or beside the river where the mineral springs bubble, it is hard not to imagine we catch an echo of female laughter.

DIVERSION: COOKHAM

AWAITING RESURRECTION

'When I started up this ward on this long journey
I felt like some engine of a long train when
starting to glide out of Paddington ...'
Stanley Spencer, Notebook 1945–7[25]

The atmosphere on the platform at Maidenhead from which the train to Cookham departs is quite different to that of the main-line; apparently in no hurry, the train stands for several minutes, gradually gathering passengers. When it does leave, trundling slowly out of the station, the sensation of riding on a single-track line, curving in an arc away from the main route beneath a bridge into an ivy-lined cutting then emerging so that the trees in the back gardens of houses either side of the track loom equally close on either side, is immediately captivating. The line has been known affectionately as the Marlow Donkey by locals since the 19th century; whether this nickname derives from the pack animals that pulled barges along the river before its arrival, a particular locomotive or the donkey engines then used in the docks is unclear.

One man who knew this railway well was Cookham's most famous son, the artist Stanley Spencer; indeed, it played a central role in his life, forming a connecting route between his village and the outside world and providing a setting for some intense emotional experiences. The village gave him a sense of emotional security through its close community and acted as a portal to the unseen, spiritual dimension that nurtured his work. 'Cookham is a kind of newspaper to me,' he told an interviewer, 'through the pages of which I am anxiously glancing in the hope of finding something about myself ...' Unlike many of those who make a pilgrimage to this secluded spot, I am here to learn rather than visit an old friend. Up until this time I have not been strongly drawn to the figurative and narrative aspects of Spencer's art, with its religious imagery, sexual neurosis and determinedly English localism. But perhaps this lack of sympathy is just another symptom of the 'great malady' Baudelaire called 'the horror of home', a sickness I have determined to overcome by travelling in my own country.

The station at Cookham is some way from the village, in the neighbouring hamlet of Cookham Rise, which grew up along the track with the arrival of the railway. My visits are made towards the end of January, a month during which the village of Cookham itself, positioned as it is between the Thames and its tributaries, has been cut off from motor traffic by flooding. To walk from the station to Cookham is to retrace a route Stanley knew well: down Station Hill, past the Old Swan Uppers pub and out on to Cookham Moor, taking the raised pedestrian causeway created long ago for just such conditions. The village in the distance looks impossibly rural, given its proximity to Maidenhead and Slough, as if frozen in time. The waters have retreated somewhat but are still pooled on either side of the causeway. Where they have withdrawn a strong aroma of floodwater and crushed vegetation fills the air, rising from battered stands of bulrushes that appear lifted straight from a Spencer painting. (Already, it seems, I am entering the pages of Stanley's newspaper, my vision of the world infiltrated by his.) I'm reminded of the account in his notebook, dated 6 December 1947, of his return to Cookham after serving in Macedonia in the first world war with a farthing in his pocket, having crossed Europe by rail in a cattle truck.

> As we ran into Maidenhead station I saw the cutting that branches round to Cookham with its foreign & un-Cookham-like appearance, which it always had, looking even more so as if trying to kid me it did not go to Cookham. I felt assured when walking from the station I arrived at the west end of Cookham moor. There in the distant eastern end of the causeway were the cowls of the malt houses glistening in the evening sun. Only a few weeks before I was saying to myself 'I would have to go a 300 mile journey if I wanted to see them. Too far removed'. The cowls looked like huge white moths settled on some twig or wall with wings closed in the midst of trees of Cliveden woods & the houses & chimney smoke of the hamlet ...[26]

Spencer grew up, one of eight surviving children, in a house built by his grandfather on the high street. His father, William Spencer, was a piano teacher and Stanley and his siblings had to make sure they finished breakfast and cleared away in time for the first of his pupils to take their place in the queue that formed in the front room of the already crowded house. When, aged 17, Stanley gained a place at the Slade School of Fine Art in London he left each morning on the 8.50 train, wearing an Eton collar and a tweed jacket, returning on the 5.08 from Paddington, both too poor and too much a home bird to stay in the city overnight. The first day he met his fellow students was in a rest period in the 'Life Room', where he found them smoking and drinking tea out of old marmalade jars. The young artist C. W. R. Nevinson came over and pointed out some marks on the floor, telling Spencer they were the traces of previous students who had 'melted' under duress.

Spencer's humble background and lack of conventional education marked him out from most of his fellow students. His primary school was a tin shed beneath a tree at the end of the garden next door. The building had been erected as a business concern by Spencer's father, a village school in which he appointed himself head teacher. However, it soon became clear that giving music lessons was more remunerative than being a schoolmaster, so responsibility for the education of the children who attended passed to Stanley's sisters Florence and Annie. Much of the knowledge Spencer acquired as a child was gained within the home. His father was an autodidact who, as Stanley's artist brother Gilbert put it, 'went after education through the company he sought'.[27] He had a genius for cultivating patrons among high society, many of whom he met through his teaching, through concerts he staged for his son Will and his work as organist at Cookham, at St Nicholas church at Hedsor and at St Jude's in Whitechapel. He was intensely ambitious for his children; Will, a musical prodigy and composer, seems to have been driven to a breakdown by his father's relentless drive. Both Will and his brother Harold attended the Royal College of Music, paid for by the Duke of Westminster and a Mr Beaumont, while Stanley's fees at the Slade were paid for by Lady Hedsor. Until he attended Maidenhead Technical College as a teenager – where his father insisted that on no account must he be made to sit any kind of examination – Spencer's education had been largely confined to the house in which he grew up, a buzzing hive full of music, drawing and amateur dramatics, the shed in the next-door garden and the fields and lanes around Cookham. This was enough to mark him out among the more cosmopolitan of his peers at the Slade. The fact that he disappeared back to Berkshire by train at the end of each day added to his unworldliness. Unsurprisingly, he was given the nickname 'Cookham', which he accepted with pride.

Spencer's experience of the Great War was bookended by train journeys. On the day he left to take up his place in the Royal Army Medical Corps, to avoid emotional partings with family and friends, he walked to Maidenhead the back way, along Sutton Road, instead of making his way through the village and taking the train at Cookham station. Setting out beneath blue skies, he soon encountered a downpour, which caused his straw hat to disintegrate, forcing him to question why God should rain so emphatically on his attempts to do his patriotic duty. Arriving at his destination he recalled: 'The very thing happened I did not want to happen. I met my father on Maidenhead station with his cycle; he had cycled from Cookham to Maidenhead to say goodbye to me … I got into the train, along with several other recruits & just as the train starts, my father called through the carriage window to the man in charge of us, "Take care of him, he's valuable", which made me feel very awkward … I felt so horribly like the curly-headed little boy going out into the wide, wide world, & all by himself.'[28]

Every family must have its black sheep. Among the Spencer children there was one who eluded his parents' attempts to shape his career. Horace was the darling of his mother, but, as Gilbert wrote, he 'was totally different to the rest of us and in the quiet of our home life at Cookham he found little to his liking'. When he showed an interest in falconry, his parents bought him a sparrow hawk that moved into the crowded house, filling it with its insistent cries for raw meat. Once the unfortunate bird died, killed when the village butcher sold Horace salt beef by mistake, Horace progressed to an interest in entering the Church. This was overtaken by what was to become his consuming passion: conjuring. Gilbert's description of a family Christmas at Fernlea doesn't sound altogether quiet. 'Father played *The Harmonious Blacksmith* with the keyboard covered by a cloth,' he remembered. 'Percy sang. Horace produced cards out of Father's tailcoat pocket and other beautifully performed tricks.' The young magician soon progressed to performing locally. The *Maidenhead Advertiser* reported in 1912 that 'the audience was kept in continual good humour by Mr Spencer's extremely witty patter and humorous sallies. His amazing tricks with cats, rabbits, chickens etc. caused general astonishment, and at the end of the evening's show he received quite an ovation.'

Horace had some success, touring a magic show in the United Kingdom and abroad and performing on ocean liners, but financial security eluded him. In 1941 *The Magic Wand* magazine contained an article by Arthur Hambling, revealing the technique behind 'Horace Spencer's Levitation of Tumblers', a popular trick involving a handkerchief borrowed from an audience member, a book and two glasses. 'Horace Spencer presented the effect with much humour,' wrote Hambling, whose account was accompanied by a helpful diagram. 'He told a story relating to a waiter who was quite casual in the handling of trays and glasses. While pattering, the audience saw the book and tumblers assume apparently impossible angles.'

Unfortunately, Horace was a little too casual in the handling of glasses himself; in short, he became an alcoholic. He moved back to the Cookham area, living in lodgings he shared for a time with the young American actor John Forrest, to whom he passed on his love of magic. (After his best-known film appearances were behind him, Forrest concentrated on building a second career as an internationally touring magician. He told an interviewer in 1996 that 'everything I have done has been to do with illusion. Acting, painting and making things appear and disappear' – a list of activities that sounds remarkably like life in the Spencer household during Stanley's childhood.) As Horace's career declined, he took to cycling around local pubs in the evening, performing card tricks in return for drinks. Returning from one such expedition in March 1941 considerably the worse for wear, riding along the towpath at Boulter's Lock in Maidenhead, yards from the house where Diana Dors would later hold court, he fell off his bike and dropped five feet into the river. Two weeks passed before his body was found.

Cookham's combination of rural tranquillity, proximity to the motorway network and twice-daily direct service to Paddington means that in the 21st century it is one of the richest villages in England, numbering TV presenters, sports personalities and semi-retired rock stars among its inhabitants. Houses along the river shelter behind walls and Entryphones; the high street bristles with restaurants and gastro-pubs. These changes had already begun a century ago when Spencer wrote to his friends Gwen and Jacques Raverat, former fellow students at the Slade, in 1913: 'I hear that the London General Omnibus Company is going to run a service through Cookham. Cookham is taking "great strides" & is fast becoming a popular riverside resort ...' The village has always been a place of dreams, a characteristic of this stretch of the river. Its dreamers have ranged from aristocrats and the super-rich, building themselves palaces on the heights from which to look down on its waters, to those seeking a rural setting in which to raise their families while they toil in London; from poets, novelists and painters to day trippers come by train, escaping the clamour of urban life for a few hours by taking a boat out on the river.

Most visitors to Cookham pay a visit to the Stanley Spencer Gallery, situated at the corner of the high street, and I am no exception. It is housed in the former Methodist chapel where Stanley's uncle used to preach, and where the young Stanley was fascinated by the way the 'Entirely Sanctified' congregants would 'flop down' when overcome with the spirit. 'My eyes were well down

& I was trying to imagine what shape they were in', he recalled, 'on that sacred piece of ground that "counted" for "coming to the Lord", just that hard patch of linoleum floor … It seemed to be the "take-off" place for their Methodist heaven.'

Methodism had a strong hold among the tradespeople of the village and the non-conformism of his mother's side of the family connected him to an earthy, animated religion very different to that being expressed in the ancient Anglican church at Cookham; yet his father was an Anglican and was organist in such churches and Stanley loved their architecture and sense of history. The gallery was established after Spencer's death with the help of William Waldorf Astor, who was one of Spencer's patrons. The aristocrat and the artist were introduced by a mutual friend, the writer Maurice Collis, who recalled their first meeting:

> I led the way in my car to Spencer's house, that queer little wretched residence where he lives alone and paints in his bedroom. He came to open the door, his usual debonair talkative self, and we went up the squalid stairs to the bedroom. The bed was covered with cardboard, drawings and photo-graphs of paintings … He spoke of his grandfather, the grocer, his father, the organist, of his many brothers, of his patrons in the past. Astor was impressed with him and asked him to come to Cliveden and choose a subject in the park for a picture. 'I will send my car for you,' he said. 'Only the first time,' Spencer replied. 'I would rather be free and come by bus after that.'[29]

An unlikely friendship grew up between the two men and Spencer painted the Viscount's portrait; he was also a regular dinner guest at Cliveden, where his habit of wearing his pyjama trousers under his suit, a practice he adopted in winter months and for which he appeared to make no exceptions, caused some amusement. Waldorf enthusiastically promoted and supported Spencer's art and spoke at his funeral in Cookham, describing him as a genius. Had Spencer recovered, Astor had decided to support him financially to enable him to finish what he thought was going to be the artist's greatest painting, *Christ Preaching at Cookham Regatta*. Instead, he paid Spencer's hospital fees. That it is now possible to see the artist's work hanging in a space in which he and his family had prayed and then to wander out into the locations he depicted, many of them easily recognisable, is due at least in part to Astor's generosity.

On an impulse I walk down Odney Lane, past the Odney Club, a holiday centre owned and maintained for its employees by the John Lewis Partnership, and cross a bridge on to Odney Island. Two young mothers, deep in conversation, push buggies along a path by the riverbank, pausing for their babies to gaze at a group of swans that weave their necks in supplication. What is it about being separated from the land by water, even by a relatively short footbridge, which immediately shifts the ambiance of a place? Cookham is rich in exotically named islands and backwaters, adding to its magical atmosphere. This, after all, is the stretch of river that enchanted the young Kenneth Grahame, brought to live in his grandmother's house at Cookham Dean from Scotland after his mother's death and his father's descent into alcoholism. The two years he spent here seem to have been among the happiest in his life, the source of his enduring love of the river and the raw material he would later shape into *The Wind in the Willows*. He returned to Cookham Dean, bringing his family to live in Mayfield House, from where he sent a copy of the book to one of his most devoted readers, American president Theodore Roosevelt. 'The book hasn't come, but as I have never read anything of yours yet that I haven't enjoyed to the full,' Roosevelt wrote in a letter in October of 1908, 'I am safe in thanking you heartily in advance. Of course [referring to Grahame's own description of his book] it won't have "any problems, any sex, any second meaning" – that is why I shall like it.'

Even with the river swollen with floods it is easy to imagine Spencer and his friends bathing here on languid summer afternoons. 'Few things are pleasanter on a hot day than a plunge into one of the deep, quiet, shady pools in which the Thames abounds,' Charles Dickens wrote in *Dickens's Dictionary of the Thames, 1887: An Unconventional Handbook*. However, he goes on to warn of the ever-present dangers of submerged obstacles and clinging weeds, perils that have persuaded him against 'so great a responsibility' as recommending particular bathing spots.

The melancholy fate of Mr. Argles, who lost his life in August, 1879, in one of the best-known and most frequented bathing-places on the river – Odney Pool at Cookham – ought most strongly to point to this moral. Canon Argles, after his son's death, writing to the *Times* on the subject, said that a guide-book, which his son had in his possession at the time of the fatal accident, stated that there was 'splendid bathing in Odney Weir'. And splendid bathing at Odney Weir, under normal circumstances, there undoubtedly is, as the writer, from many years experience of its waters, can aver; but the season of 1879 was in all respects exceptional, and there can be no doubt that the suck of the stream, owing to the great rush of the water which it is impossible accurately to gauge from the appearance of the surface, developed some peculiar source of danger unknown at quieter times.

I follow the Thames path beyond the village, frustrated initially by being taken on a long detour in order to skirt the exclusive, gated properties located on Formosa Island. As I regain the river and catch the gilded tower of Cliveden flashing in the afternoon sun high up on the opposite bank, I shrug off my habitual response to the sight of red-eyed cameras, high fences and 'Private Property' signs. For all I know it is precisely the wealth of a proportion of its inhabitants that has enabled the preservation of the physical appearance of Spencer's kingdom. Half-close your eyes so that the award-winning Indian restaurants and gift shops blur into the background and it is not hard to imagine the artist pushing his pram – which is still preserved like a holy relic in the gallery – stuffed with oil paints and canvases along the high street into the churchyard. Here he had an early epiphany, again described to Jacques Raverat in a letter in 1911 with his characteristic mix of mysticism and irreverence. 'I rose from the dead last night. It happened like this. I was walking about in the churchyard when I suddenly flopped down among the grave mounds. I wedged myself tightly between these mounds – feet to the East and died. I rose from the dead soon afterwards because of the wet grass. But I did it in a very stately manner.'

It is impossible to visit the graveyard today, with its gap-toothed headstones jutting out of the ground at odd angles, some of them dating back to the 17th century and decorated with skulls and cherubim, without thinking of one of his best known works, *The Resurrection, Cookham* (1924–7). Spencer himself is in the painting, leaning nonchalant and naked against a gravestone, as the earth erupts around him with the awakened dead. Location, for Spencer, is both extremely specific and a thin veil; among those rising from the graves are people of African descent, unlikely to have been residents of the parish at the time. Cookham, for Spencer, is both unique and the whole world. I enter the ancient church to find myself confronted by a striking sculpted marble frieze erected in memory of a retired naval man, Sir Isaac Pocock, who, his tomb informs me, was 'suddenly called from this world to a better state' in 1810, after a heart attack suffered while punting on the river. Pocock is depicted swooning, supported in the arms of a woman who may be his wife or an angel, the Thames boatman he has hired to scull the boat transformed into Charon ferrying him across the Styx. In the background of Spencer's painting, resurrected souls are borne away on pleasure steamers: was the artist's vision of the Thames as a border between two worlds inspired by Pocock's tomb? Spencer himself now lies in the graveyard, planted with his first wife Hilda in the centre of his own painting, awaiting resurrection.

Spencer was irresistibly attracted to strong, dominant women. It is no surprise he was struck by Diana Dors, when he met her at a cocktail party at the house of the physicist, Sir Charles Ellis, in Cookham; he declared he wanted to paint her, as she had 'a simple beauty. Her pouting lips are particularly pretty'. She never sat for him. A study for *The Beatitudes of Love* that is on display when I visit the Stanley Spencer Gallery portrays a man and a woman touching their grotesquely extended tongues, the male figure, with its pudding bowl haircut and owlish glasses, unmistakably a self-portrait. Spencer's tongue is blunt, hers a sharp and pointed spike; his body small and limp next to her overpowering female presence. Although Slade pupil and fellow artist Hilda Carline was the mother of Spencer's daughters, he abandoned her for the voracious Patricia Preece, who seems to have had no qualms in exploiting the artist's submissive infatuation in order to part him from his money; she even left him behind on their honeymoon, replacing him with her lesbian lover. But it was to Hilda he remained constant, emotionally at least, until his death. It was to her that he wrote an extraordinary love letter composed, probably in 1949, on board the morning train from Cookham to Paddington.[30] It is a letter that records the unfolding process of its own redundancy, as when it is completed he will have arrived at her house in Hampstead and have no need of it; that encapsulates within it separation and anticipated union, the erosion of distance through travel and the physical experience of the railway itself, its seclusion and its crowds.

In Train, Cookham Station.

It was too raining to write on Stn. Platform. So far I have a carriage to myself. I'm off now ducky, off to see you. Just that, the joy of that, the boundless joy of it. I specially did not buy a paper, so as to be able to devote every shortening mile between us to the thought of you. I loved writing, my love, in the midst of the loud voices of ladies coming to town & real-thing business men. I love my errand. Nearly Maidenhead now, ducky. There will be lots of people getting in …

There is a poignant moment as he approaches Hanwell, with its view of its vast mental hospital from the window. His cousin, Amy Hatch, with whom he had explored the Berkshire countryside as a young man, ended her days there; Spencer helped care for her and used to visit her at the hospital.

I thought, I like it when we get between Hanwell and Southall. One can often see where I used to go and see Amy. I believe she rests in the big cemetery one sees from the train adjoining St Bernard's Hospital. I still have to collect her things from there … This is the place. The scenery I see from the train would be about ¼ of a mile from Hanwell at any time.

He measures his emotional distance from Hilda in railway miles and delights in the way it can be erased through means of the train:

The division between me & you is like the division between Hampstead & Cookham. I like it myself, it's like performing a miracle.

This mechanised miracle leaves its imprint on the letter through the very act of writing on paper – an aspect of rail travel less felt today by those of us tapping on electronic keyboards.

We are nearly at Paddington now.
   We are slowing up among a lot of stationary trains and have now stopped. This you can see from the writing, soon the writing will be jerky again. I was going to write a special love letter bit … But we are entering the station, drawing to a stop, stopped.

Even as he progresses across London by a series of buses – *I only have to love, the bus does the taking of it to you … And now I am in the 24 bus … It is our home, this 24 bus. It is like being with you. I feel sheltered and secured in a you-room now* – he is reminiscing about all his previous journeys through this territory, right back to when he first encountered the city as a student and an anxious commuter, in the grip of another love affair that would shape his life and cause him to feel the pangs of separation.

And now we turn into Hampstead Road … I used to come here for composition lessons with Ihlee & Lightfoot. [The artists, Rudolph Ihlee and Maxwell Gordon Lightfoot]
   I thought I would never get back to Cookham …

Of course, the opposite turned out to be true: he never left.

DIGRESSION
TRAIN VISION – MOTION AND EMOTION

'I also wondered why in our language [Turkish] the same
French loan word, *makinist*, designates both the person who
runs films and the person who runs railway engines.'
Orhan Pamuk, *The New Life* (1994)

The window in a train is an optical instrument that converts the view
from the carriage into a series of frames. We are used to this, but it
is worth remembering that train travel introduced human beings to
an entirely new way of seeing. Never before had we been able to slide
through the landscape, watching it endlessly, panoramically unfold.
Never before had we experienced 'optical flow' – the rushing and
blurring of objects near the track and the apparently slower, statelier
movement of scenery further away. Some early travellers by rail couldn't
cope with this confusion of images. After all, what we 'see' is simply
light bounced off objects and converted by receptors in our retinae into
electrical impulses that are unscrambled and decoded in our brains,
with reference to a stored databank of what we have seen before. What
passed in front of the carriage window lay outside previous human
experience; it shouldn't be surprising that some of the first people to
be exposed to it simply rejected this startling new version of the world.

The Victorian author, artist and critic John Ruskin had built his
aesthetic appreciation of landscape on leisurely sketching tours on foot
and by horse-drawn coach. Looking at his detailed botanical drawings,

for instance, it is easy to see why he detested the flickering, jolting view from the train, accompanied in those early days by cinders, sparks and the rattle of wheels. The 'iron road', he wrote in a letter in January 1871, was the 'loathsomest form of devilry now extant ... destructive of all wise social habit or possible natural beauty, carriages of damned souls on the ridges of their own graves'. All travelling, he maintained elsewhere, 'becomes dull in exact proportion to its rapidity'.

Yet this blurring, together with the sounds of the railway and the sensation of being hurled forward at a speed greater than that achieved by any living thing, is essentially modern. We are only enabled to see in this way by a machine – we cannot do so on our own. Might this newly available perceptual condition have other benefits?

Scientists have long proposed a connection between physical and mental states, a famous example being the link between smiling and a sense of wellbeing. When people are happy they often smile; conversely, if they are instructed by researchers to smile, it seems they feel a corresponding increase in positive feelings – this is known as the 'facial feedback hypothesis'. I have often wondered why I find train travel conducive to thinking and imagined perhaps I had discovered a feedback hypothesis of my own. When people daydream, listen attentively to a piece of music or eavesdrop on an overheard conversation, their eyes tend to slip out of focus. Might the reverse effect of this phenomenon mean that the blurring of vision caused by the velocity of a moving train creates its own feedback loop, readying the mind for concentration or dream?

Charles Darwin noted the connection between the focus of the eyes and mental absorption in his book *The Expression of the Emotions in Man and Animals,* published in 1872. 'The vacant expression of the eyes is peculiar,' he wrote, 'and at once shows when a man is completely lost in thought ... The eyes are not then fixed on any object ... the line of vision of the two eyes even often become slightly divergent … Professor Donders attributes this divergence to the almost complete relaxation of certain muscles of the eyes, which would be apt to follow from the mind being wholly absorbed.' Sadly, he did not examine the phenomenon of divergent eyes in those gazing dreamily from a train window; however, in chapter seven of his book, entitled 'Low Spirits, Grief, Anxiety, Despair', he did take advantage of the opportunity train travel provides to closely observe the facial expressions of one of his fellow passengers. This chapter in the book explores the link between what Darwin calls 'for the sake of brevity, the grief muscles', including those that crinkle the brow or lower the corners of the mouth, and the mechanism in the eye producing tears. 'I may here mention a trifling observation, as it will serve to sum up our present subject,' he wrote. 'An old lady with a comfortable but absorbed expression sat nearly opposite me in a railway carriage. Whilst I was looking at her I noticed that her *depressores anguli oris* [the muscles that lower the corners of the mouth] became very slightly, yet decidedly, contracted; but as her countenance remained as placid as ever, I reflected how meaningless was this contraction, and how easily one might be deceived. The thought had hardly occurred to me when I saw that her eyes suddenly became suffused with tears almost to overflowing, and her whole countenance fell. There could now be no doubt that some painful recollection, perhaps that of a long-lost child, was passing through her mind.'

Darwin is, at this point, shifting his ground between science and art; exchanging empirical observation for the novelist's conjecture. It is almost as though the setting of the railway carriage, electric with implied drama, compels him to do so. Almost exactly half a century later, in 1921, that arch-modernist Virginia Woolf published her story *An Unfinished Novel*, which opens with the narrator sitting in a railway carriage, alternately perusing a copy of *The Times* and the face of a woman opposite her.

'Such an expression of unhappiness was enough by itself to make one's eyes slide above the paper's edge to the poor woman's face – insignificant without that look, almost a symbol of human destiny with it. Life's what you see in people's eyes; life's what they learn, and having learnt it, never, though they seek to hide it, cease to be aware of …' Gradually the other four occupants of the carriage disembark and the narrator finds herself and the distressed woman the only remaining occupants. The narrator's copy of *The Times*, it seems, 'is no protection against a sorrow like hers' – a sorrow she has entirely discerned from the woman's expression and posture. They fall into conversation and the narrator finds herself mimicking her new acquaintance's body language and finding that through its operation on her own physiology she feels the woman's emotion herself. Had Woolf read Darwin's description of a woman on a train? It seems likely, particularly in view of her precise description of the woman's gestures: 'Then she shuddered, and then she made the awkward angular movement that I had seen before, as if after the spasm, some spot between the shoulders burnt and itched. Then again she looked the most unhappy woman in the world.' The woman nervously rubs at a spot on the window and the narrator finds herself compelled to imitate her. 'There, too, was a little speck on the glass. For all my rubbing, it remained. And then the spasm went through me. I crooked my arm and plucked at the middle of my back. My skin, too, felt like the damp chicken's skin in the poulterer's shop-window; one spot between my shoulders itched and irritated, felt clammy, felt raw. Could I reach it? Surreptitiously I tried. She saw me. A smile of infinite irony, infinite sorrow, flitted and faded from her face.' The woman had communicated her emotion, 'passed her poison'. Their conversation ceases.

I don't know whether Darwin found the train conducive to thought; it is well known he favoured walking as an aid to mental activity throughout his life, so much so that at Down House in Kent he had a special 'sandwalk' laid out, which he termed his 'thinking path'. Looking at the edge of the track as the train rushes forward, the embankment resolves into layers, strata, as though the lines of the railway reveal similar lines running through all matter; vegetation a little further back is flung this way and that by the speed of our passage. This could hardly be described as 'dull', whatever Ruskin may have thought. In fact, it might allow us, 'damned souls' though we may be, to slip out of the present into another mental state, our eyes losing focus as our muscles relax to become 'lost in thought'. We have changed in response to technology of the train in a way Ruskin could not. An entirely new type of human has evolved on the tracks. It is as though a final picture should be added to the famous diagram representing human evolution, in which mankind gradually progresses through the stages from walking with knuckles on the ground to standing upright; the last figure represented should be sitting in a carriage with an open laptop or scrolling through messages on a phone. Such people are imbued with a 'commuter consciousness' that enables them to think, work and relax while travelling at speed. It is as if the railways came to prepare us for the present, readying us for the torrent of images and information that rush towards us every day, the multiple screens we routinely negotiate like the windows of a swiftly moving train.

II

'Railroad travel; like Jules Verne's ships and
submarines, it combines dreams with technology.'
Michel de Certeau, *The Practice of Everyday Life* (1984)

Passengers in a train carriage or a bus, its sides punctuated by extensive areas of glass, are made acutely aware of the position of the sun. Sitting next to a window on a bright, sunny day they may find themselves dazzled, forced to retreat behind eyelids into a flickering half-world of alternate shadow and glare, as buildings, trees, embankments or hills intervene between them and the source of light. These seats are best avoided if you intend to work on a computer or read; for that reason, on summer days they are often the last to fill. This may also have been the case half a century ago, in December 1958, when the artist Brion Gysin found himself travelling through the South of France on a bus, on his way to an artists' colony in Marseille. (Although he lived for most of his life in Paris and Morocco, Gysin was born at Taplow, within walking distance of the GWR line, in the same hospital in which Stanley Spencer died.)

Gysin was tired; he settled in his seat, closed his eyes and rested his head against the window. What happened next, invisible to the passengers around him, was a defining moment in avant-garde culture in the 20th century. In his journal he described it as 'an overwhelming flood of intensely bright patterns in supernatural colours exposed behind my eyelids: a multi-dimensional kaleidoscope whirling out through space ... I was swept out of time'.[31] Years later he told an interviewer that he thought the visions 'were some kind of spiritual grace that had been allotted to me', but that he 'found out later that it was a purely physiological neurological effect ... activity within the alpha rhythm of the brain'.[32]

What he had discovered, through the rapid play of light and shadow on his eyelids, was the so-called 'flicker effect', described by neurologist W. Grey Walter in his book *The Living Brain*, first published in 1953. Walter began researching the response of subjects to rhythmic pulses of light in an effort to understand epilepsy and the function of the brain. He discovered that maximum effects were obtained by synchronising the rate of flicker – he used stroboscopic lights – with the brain rhythms of the subject. Such effects sometimes occurred naturally and had been noted as early as the 16th century. Catherine de' Medici reported that the astrologer Nostradamus, during consultations held on the roof of her palace, would look at the sun with his eyes closed while moving his fingers rapidly back and forth in front of his face, presumably to gain access to the altered state from which he brought back the prophecies that were his stock in trade.

On his return to Paris, Gysin wrote to the writer William Burroughs, his close friend and collaborator, about his visionary journey. Burroughs had read Walter's book, in which the scientist had noted the intricate hallucinations that were an aspect of the brain's response to flicker stimulation. For Walter, they were an interesting by-product of his research into the operation of the brain; for Burroughs, they were potentially revolutionary, an end in themselves. 'We must storm the citadels of enlightenment,' he wrote back to Gysin in typically dramatic fashion. 'The means are at hand.' Encouraged by Burroughs and together with Ian Sommerville, a young science graduate from Cambridge, Gysin developed and attempted to market a device he called the Dreamachine, which could replicate the effects on the brain noted by Grey using a 78rpm turntable and a perforated cylinder with a light inside. Although it never achieved mass-market success as Gysin hoped it would, persuading people to replace TV with the entertainment available in their own brains, the Dreamachine became a countercultural status symbol associated with the more experimental fringes of the art and music scenes.

The bus that unlocked the treasure chest in Gysin's head was not unique; mass-movement technologies routinely provide transport of a kind different to that intended. At the dawn of the railway age, medical experts were particularly concerned about the vibrations endured by train travellers and the effect they had on their physical and psychological state. It was the first time the human body had come into intimate and extended contact with mechanical forces, apart from on the factory floor, and there was no knowing what the result would be. Particularly worrying was the fact that the velocity of train travel caused shocks to occur at a rate that made them impossible to distinguish from one another. 'The traveller's mind takes little note of the thousands of successive jolts which he experiences,' wrote a doctor in the *Lancet* in 1862, 'but every one of them tells upon his body.'

What made this subject especially fascinating to the 19th-century mind was that vibrations, whether in the body, the nerves, the air or in space itself, were seen as the medium by which thoughts and emotions were broadcast. Human beings were compared, in both medical journals and Romantic poetry, to sensitive stringed instruments, ready to respond to the slightest stimulus. 'Every strong sensation, emotion or excitement – extreme pain, rage, terror, joy, or the passion of love – all have the tendency to cause the muscles to tremble,' Darwin pointed out, who cited as an example 'the thrill or slight shiver which runs down the backbone and limbs of many persons when they are powerfully affected by music'.[33] Doctors had also become aware of the link between vibration and sexual stimulation, particularly in women. As late as 1910, one of the founders of sexology, Havelock Ellis, could write: 'It is well known ... that both in men and women the vibratory motion of a railway-train frequently produces a certain degree of sexual excitement, especially when sitting forward.'[34] Such illicit stimulation, of course, increased the likelihood of moral as well as social barriers being breached when strangers were confined together in the close proximity of railway compartments. These dangers could only be increased by the well-recognised narcotic effects of vibration, also cited in alarming detail by the *Lancet*, which could lull the female passenger into a deep and drugged sleep, making her vulnerable to the advances of unscrupulous predators. The author Stefan Zweig, in his last novella *Journey into the Past*, sent to his publisher before he and his second wife took their own lives in Brazil in 1942, relates the story of two lovers who have been separated by the first world war and its aftermath for nine years. Since they last met one has been widowed and the other married. They board a train together but are unable to speak openly of their feelings because of the presence of three lawyers who enter their compartment just as they are about to leave the station. The combination of social reticence and the mechanical operation of their chosen form of transport acts, as it does every day in carriages around the world, to turn their minds inward.

> With a slight jolt, the train began to move. The rattling of the wheels drowned out the legal conversation, muting it to mere noise. But then, gradually, the jolting and rattling turned to a rhythmic swaying, like a steel cradle rocking the couple into dreams. And while the rattling wheels below them rolled onward, into a future that each of them imagined differently, the thoughts of both returned in reverie to the past.[35]

More recent researchers have taken a somewhat different view of the effects of rail travel. The academic David Bissell argues that it is a mistake to think of the passenger as a passive recipient of vibration caused by the train, as this is an erroneous separation of the body and technology.[36] In reality, the body both transmits and absorbs vibration, which is itself a kind of 'motion without trajectory or displacement'. While the passenger might appear to be sitting in a seat, 'at the nano-scale, the body is never actually in contact with the seat', as vibration means it is simultaneously touching and not touching its surface. Sitting in a train, then, in some sense we *become* the train; the rigid boundary between it and us is compromised by its shuddering, just as objects on the table jiggle and jump and the landscape closest to the window dissolves, blurred by speed.

Perhaps the train itself is a kind of Dreamachine. A swift look around the carriage reveals many different mental states, from the animated to the somnolent. Passengers are both present and not present, rocked in Zweig's 'steel cradle', conscious yet for extended periods lulled through rhythm and vibration into something approaching an hypnotic state. As I write I am hurtling forward through space, a bright October sun flashing through the window, rendering these words intermittently invisible as the screen of my computer is turned into a mirror, in which my reflected hands hang suspended above the keys, figments in a machine-driven dream.

III

'Of a Saturday afternoon, as you wait in your corner
of the compartment for the starting of the train, the
window makes a frame for a glowing picture.'
Henry James, 'London' (1888)

During the same decades the railways achieved their nationwide expansion, a number of exotically named inventions – including zoetropes, phenakitoscopes and zoopraxiscopes – came on to the market, all designed to create the illusion of moving imagery. (Their design in many cases bears a remarkable similarity to Brion Gysin's contraption, and their aim, to trick the brain, is the same.) Their effects were achieved, using perforated cylinders, glass discs and photographic or drawn figures, through a spinning motion that created the impression of movement for a stationary audience.

Trains work on the reverse principle of such devices, moving the audience rather than the background, transforming the landscape into a constantly changing ribbon of images. It should be no surprise that trains are bound up with the foundation myth of cinema itself. For decades, film histories have recycled the story, unsubstantiated by any contemporary account, that the audience for the Lumière brothers' 50-second film *L'Arrivée d'un train en gare de La Ciotat* [37] flinched, screamed or even ran from the cinema as the locomotive moved towards and threatened to crush them. The story survives, it seems, preserved and disseminated by those requiring proof of the unique power of film to transport audiences.

What is clear is that both trains and film cameras have changed the way we see; and that, by boarding a train, we are in effect taking our place in a cinema of a kind. But how many of us would choose to go and sit through the same feature again and again? Repetition acts on our mental faculties like a drug. If every passing experience took up our whole attention it would be impossible to undertake the simplest routine tasks. The human brain has evolved to filter out sights and sounds we have seen many times before, leaving us ready to respond to what changes in a landscape: the arrival of a predator, for instance, or the distant sight of prey. The rest, particularly what we have seen many times before, becomes part of what Walter Benjamin called 'the optical unconscious', that area of our life that is seen but not processed as information, through which we pass as if in a dream. Once we have been exposed to the same image repeatedly, neuroscientists suggest, a more efficient encoding is achieved in the neural network and the brain no longer requires the high 'metabolic costs' of intense sensory engagement. Many travellers, if questioned after arriving at their destination, having spent their journey time gazing out of the window at a landscape they have seen many hundreds of times before, would be unable to recall what they had seen. The process by which we reach this state of reduced awareness through overfamiliarity with our environment is known as habituation. While this adaptation was a benefit when we lived on the savannah, hunting antelope on foot, in danger of attack by lions, in the highly mechanised society we now inhabit it can mean that much of our time is spent in a state best described as perceptually half-asleep.

There is also a reverse process that can happen after a period of time spent making the same journey. All of a sudden, a particular detail can emerge from the blur of barely perceived visual information and seize the attention, taking on a hyper-real quality; we will visit one of these sites later on our journey. Once this has happened, it is impossible not to seek out these features as they pass the window. In my own case, I found I would know subconsciously when such landmarks were approaching and look up from whatever I was doing, as if to check they were still there. In this mental state, the particular object or feature in the landscape I sought, although familiar, would strike me with fresh power as though seen for the first time. This seemed to me a remarkable discovery; after all, the work of literature has been at least partly an attempt to retain the vividness of our first encounter with things and experiences, to render the familiar unfamiliar and to fight against the way 'time poisons perception', as Michael Clune has put it.[38] In his book *White Out: The Secret Life of Heroin*, Clune argues that what keeps an addict enslaved to a drug is not so much its physical effects but the memory of the user's first, intense and never recaptured experience, a memory that, counter to all our other experiences of life, does not fade, remaining endlessly alluring. Addiction is nothing if not routine, a regular commute between dealer and shooting gallery in search of the sublime. Perhaps those who travel by train each day become addicted, in the way addicts appear to become as wedded to the paraphernalia and schedules surrounding a drug as they do to the drug itself, rituals written into their brains through repetition. Is it these similarities that allow the time-defying moments I noted to break through into consciousness, without the necessity of chemical enhancement?

I decided to ask other passengers whether they had experienced similarly intense encounters with objects within the landscape of their route; to my surprise, the small and unrepresentative sample I interviewed seemed to understand straight away what I was talking about. For one, it was particular trees that marked his passage along the line that seemed burnt into his consciousness; for another, a farmhouse that stood near the track which she regarded with undimmed fascination every day. Volker Straub, a genetic scientist at Newcastle University who is a regular rail commuter himself along the Tyne valley, recognised the phenomenon from his own experience and suggested it may be an evolutionary hangover from our nomadic past. Indigenous Australians believe their spirit ancestors moved through and shaped the landscape during the 'timeless' period of creation known as the Dreamtime. Their descendants retrace these ancient paths when they travel along what have come to be known (to Europeans) as songlines, navigating through songs handed down from generation to generation. That certain natural features in the landscape are given sacred status and ascribed personhood might, Straub suggests, act as a way of fixing these places, and thus the route between them, in the memory. In the same way, when features seen from the train take on an intensified reality, perhaps it is the brain's way of noting and remembering landmarks that might prove useful to the traveller, an aid to their survival; places of safety, sources of food or simply pointers to guide us home.

DIVERSION: MARLOW
THE BEAUTIFUL SPOTTED BOY

Every branch line is a digression from the narrative arc provided by the main route. The next time I board a train at Maidenhead, it is on an afternoon in May that combines bright sunshine and an icy wind. The season is a matter of interpretation; half the people stepping into the carriage are wearing heavy coats, the others are in T-shirts. A man and a woman sit across from me, engaged in a business discussion. She is middle-aged, of South Asian origin, dressed in a floral print, and keeps up a brightly optimistic chatter. He is a little younger, dark-haired with an Italian accent and a round, preoccupied face, wearing expensive jeans and a linen jacket. He bites his nails continuously, removing his fingers from his mouth only to inspect the damage caused by his latest attack. The train rattles along past the backs of houses, past the usual higgledy-piggledy allotments, through the station at Cookham and on into open country. Across the fields, a stone's throw from the track, the Thames oozes lugubriously by. The far bank is studded at regular intervals with villas, each with its motorboat attached. Various domesticated animals walk nonchalantly about, as if aware they could become the subject of a watercolour painting at any moment.

'Look at that,' the woman breathes. But the Italian-sounding man has become aware of a smell coming through the window, possibly emanating from the animals, possibly from the river. 'It isn't here all the time,' the woman tells him. 'And look at those houses!' But the man wrinkles his nose and says decisively, 'I do *not* think that is very attractive.' He puts his cowboy boot up on the opposite seat so he can get more leverage on his nails and concentrates on them for the rest of the journey, answering her remarks only with grunts. At Bourne End, the driver must leave his cab and walk down the train to take up a position at the back, so we can reverse direction and take a loop along the river towards Marlow. It is hard to believe such manoeuvres are necessary in a place only 20 miles from London as the crow flies. For some reason it puts me in a holiday mood.

Approaching Marlow by train is completely different from doing so by road, via a nondescript motorway junction. It is impossible not to be aware that this is the end of the line, which alters its character somehow, making it seem to the train traveller a place of refuge, or escape. I have come in search of two people for whom this was true in different ways. The first lies in the churchyard of All Saints' church, adjacent to Marlow's handsome suspension bridge. To reach it I must walk past a pub called the Marlow Donkey, after the town's idiosyncratic rail connection, and turn down the high street. The door to the church is open, as I have been told it will be. A woman is pushing a vacuum around near the altar and doesn't hear me enter. The portrait I am seeking hangs high on the back wall, in an area set aside for children's activities. Its subject is George Alexander Gratton, better known during his own day as the 'Beautiful Spotted Boy', or the 'Spotted Negro of Renown'. I wait for the trajectory of my unwitting companion's droning circuit to place a pillar between us, and then stand on one of the children's benches to take a closer look.

George was born on the island of St Vincent in the Caribbean in 1808, the year following the abolition of the slave trade. It is a matter of dispute if just one or both his parents were slaves; according to J. S. Lingham, the author of *The Cabinet of Curiosities* (1851), the name Alexander was that of the slave owner and Gratton the name of the slave overseer on the plantation where they lived. George was born with a rare condition known as piebaldism, or vitiligo, which in people of African descent results in dramatically contrasting white patches on the skin. His career in showbusiness began disturbingly early; as a baby he was exhibited at the local market for a dollar, but someone obviously saw greater earning potential in him and by the time he was 15 months old he had been shipped to Bristol and then onwards to London. According to some accounts, it was at the Bartholomew Fair in Smithfield Market that he came to the attention of the travelling showman John Richardson, a native of Marlow, who specialised in exhibiting 'freaks of nature'; he is said to have paid a large amount of money for George which, although often cited as proof of his concern for the boy, must also give some indication of the profit he felt he could earn through his affliction. We can get a glimpse of the atmosphere of one of Richardson's shows from Charles Dickens, who, in *Sketches by Boz,* remembers attending one as a young man at Greenwich Fair. In it, 'a dwarf, a giantess, a living skeleton, a wild Indian, "a young lady of singular beauty, with perfectly white hair and pink eyes", and two or three other natural curiosities', Dickens tells us, were 'usually exhibited together for the small charge of a penny'. It is easy today to take a superior view of such spectacles; until, that is, we turn on our TV and catch an episode of Jerry Springer or any of the multitude of other programmes that serve up human misery as entertainment. Old-fashioned freak shows can appear tame in comparison.

George stares wistfully out at us from the painting, apparently commissioned by Richardson 'from the life' in 1811. He is carrying a bow, half-drawn, and seems to be posing as Cupid, a quiver slung over his back, in a tunic that leaves his arms and legs exposed, the better to show off his 'piebald' markings. We can only agree with

J. S. Lingham that 'in figure and countenance he can truly be called a beautiful child' with well-proportioned limbs and pleasing features, 'his eyes bright and intelligent and the whole expression of his face both bright and lively'. He has the triangular white mark on his forehead and white patch in the centre of his hair that are characteristic of his condition. Vitiligo sufferers of African heritage seem to have held a particular fascination for white audiences, both in North America and Europe, from the 18th century to the early 20th. They were often billed in sideshows as 'leopard people', half-human, half-beast; but the particular frisson they delivered may have had more to do with the fact that the patches on their skin were of a startling whiteness, equal to that of the skin of any slave-owning aristocrat. If all that determined whether someone was a full human being or a slave was skin colour, piebaldism appeared to challenge the status quo. It looked like a work in progress. The period saw many attempts to draw up taxonomies of human beings, similar to the classifications of the biological world created by Linnaeus in his *Systema Naturae* in 1735. If all black people were to turn white overnight, what would become of such reassuring boundaries? Such unfathomable questions convinced many that the Spotted Boy must be a fake. As late as 1910, Charles G. Harper, the forthright author of *Thames Valley Villages*, declared: 'We shall probably be not far wrong in suspecting Mr. William [sic] Richardson of a Barnum-like piece of showman humbug in putting this child forward as a "Negro Boy". The boy, we cannot help thinking, was sufficiently English, but was a freak, suffering from [a] dreadful skin disease.'

The story goes that Richardson adopted George and paid for his education; he certainly had him christened in a church in Surrey in 1810. Such concern for his wellbeing didn't stop him exhibiting the child for up to 12 hours a day, until George's premature death at the age of 'four years and three quarters' from a tumour to the jaw.

Richardson was said to be devastated and had the boy buried in the crypt he had reserved for himself at Marlow, holding an elaborate funeral and later having himself placed in the same grave, with his and the child's headstones side by side. I want to see the graves and decide to ask the woman in the church whether she knows where they are. She sees me approaching and gropes for a moment to find the switch to turn off the vacuum. She seems happy to accompany me into the graveyard, although I am not convinced she knows which grave belongs to the Spotted Boy. She is in her 70s and has lived in Marlow all her life, she tells me. We walk slowly, stopping at various points as she shows me restoration work that is going on in the churchyard. Eventually she identifies two gravestones that stand side by side. I bend down to have a look but the inscriptions are either worn away or obscured by bright yellow lichen. The woman tells me these are the graves she always understood to be those of the Beautiful Spotted Boy and Richardson.

'Marlow was well known for its gypsies and show people when I was young,' she says, leaning on one of the graves, 'so it's not surprising Richardson lived here. There were a lot of big gypsy families in the town, people who worked on the fairgrounds and that sort of thing. I suppose it was all the grazing there was for the horses along the river. Some of them have got houses now, of course. Some of them are quite rich. Marlow was an ordinary town in those days. A lot of people worked in the paper mills, or the furniture trade in High Wycombe. There were proper shops then, the high street wasn't all cafés like it is now.' Effortlessly, she jumps back a further century. 'Before the railway came, Marlow was on the main stagecoach route from London to Oxford. There were big coaching inns here. I remember the pub up in the part of town where I live – it had all the stables out the back that were for the horses to rest in. People used to take their produce up to London by horse and cart.'

Marlow may or may not have been an ordinary town but it has long attracted unusual visitors. Four years after George Gratton was buried here, in March 1817, the poet Percy Bysshe Shelley took up residence in West Street, in a cottage then called Albion House. It was an unconventional household. Shelley's wife Harriet, whom he had abandoned for Mary Godwin, had drowned herself in the Serpentine a few months before their arrival. It emerged after her body was dragged from the lake that she was pregnant and had been virtually destitute. The fact that she was still officially married to Shelley cast the poet in a bad light. He hurriedly married Mary, in order to head off further scandal and to gain custody of his children. Mary's stepsister Claire, with whom Shelley had an intense and ambiguous relationship, came to live with them, along with her illegitimate daughter Alba, the fruit of a liaison with Lord Byron. Marlow offered protection from public scrutiny to this unusual ménage and a place to work far from the smog and bustle of London. Shelley loved the water; as the poet Edward Thomas has written, 'From the time he went to school to his last residence in England, Shelley was never long away from some part of the River Thames.'[39] He spent hours floating in his boat, or seated beneath the canopy of Bisham woods, engaged in drafting *The Revolt of Islam*.

Meanwhile, in the house on West Street, Mary pored over the final drafts of *Frankenstein: or, The Modern Prometheus*. The idea for the novel had come to her two years previously in a villa on the shores of Lake Geneva, when she rose to the challenge issued by Lord Byron to the assembled house party to write a Gothic story. Mary had returned from Switzerland with the novel growing within her, along with Percy Shelley's child. She was 18 years old. Only the story came to full term; the baby was the first of three that she and Shelley would lose. Perhaps the notion of the creation of life through science had particular resonance for one from whom life had been stolen; but there may have been more local influences at play on the final draft that evolved in Marlow. It would have been inevitable in such a small town that the story of the Beautiful Spotted Boy came to the ears of the Shelley household. Several critics have linked the *daemon,* or monster, in Shelley's novel to contemporary accounts of escaped slaves that were popular at the time, with their portrayals of journeys towards both physical and mental emancipation. As Jean-Paul Sartre wrote in the preface to Frantz Fanon's *The Wretched of the Earth,* 'The European has only been able to become a man through creating slaves and monsters ... On the other side of the ocean there was a race of less-than-humans, who, thanks to us, might reach our status a thousand years hence.'[40]

As I stand talking with my guide, a tall, slim man comes loping through the graveyard at a great rate, heading for the church. I suspect he might be the vicar, although he is not wearing a dog collar. 'I was just saying,' the woman tells him, 'these are the graves of the Spotted Boy and Richardson, aren't they?'

The man pauses, smiling. 'They might be, I'm not sure. I've thought of looking for them myself. He needs Patricia, our local history expert, doesn't he? Patricia knows all these gravestones, she's researched them all.'

He touches a stone tentatively and suggests that the best way of deciphering its message might be to trace its inscription with my fingers – this is Patricia's technique, apparently – then continues on his way to the church, where he has a meeting to attend. The woman sets out in his wake more slowly, and I find myself alone beside the graves. I kneel down to take a closer look, but hard as I try I can't make out what is written on either of them. I try running my finger along the grooves in the stone with my eyes closed, as if it were written in Braille, but it remains illegible, the anonymity of those sleeping beneath it intact.

LOCATION: READING
OSCAR'S BALLAD

'I never saw a man who looked
With such a wistful eye
Upon that little tent of blue
Which prisoners call the sky'
Oscar Wilde, *The Ballad of Reading Gaol* (1898)

'I never travel without my diary,' Gwendolen Fairfax says in *The Importance of Being Earnest*. 'One should always have something sensational to read in the train.' However sensational the book I am holding, as the train leaves Reading bound for London, I often raise my head to glimpse one of the most poignant sites in British literary history: the red-brick turrets of Reading Gaol, which lie to the south of the line. Designed by the young George Gilbert Scott, the prison was described in the *Illustrated London News* in 1844 as 'the most conspicuous building' in Reading and 'by far the greatest ornament in the town'. It was here that Oscar Wilde served out all but five months of his two-year sentence to hard labour for 'gross indecency', emerging a profoundly changed man.

Wilde was familiar with fashionable society in Reading and its environs. As well as visiting Taplow Court, he had on two occasions hired houses by the river at Goring-on-Thames, where his behaviour scandalised local inhabitants, particularly the vicar who arrived on a pastoral visit to find Wilde in the garden wrapped in a towel. 'You have come just in time to enjoy a perfectly Greek scene,' Wilde told the startled cleric, pointing to Lord Alfred Douglas, who was lying naked on the grass. Wilde loved Goring, at least until the harmony imposed by the nearness of the river was broken by one of the inevitable rows he had with Bosie (his pet name for Douglas), or the arrival of his wife and children from London. 'I have done no work here,' he wrote to a friend. 'The river gods have lured me to devote myself to a Canadian canoe, in which I paddle about. It is curved like a flower.' When he arrived in Reading by train in 1895, bound for the gaol, he had left no such idyll. His previous address had been a squalid cell in Wandsworth prison, where the stink of the slop bucket was so strong it made him faint. At Wandsworth he had become ill and desperate, by his own account longing for death. The authorities

grew worried and decided he should be moved somewhere with a gentler regime. So it was that Wilde, 'a *flâneur*, a dandy, a man of fashion', as he described his former self, one of the greatest celebrities of his age, found himself travelling by railway in an arrowed prison suit with the hands that had written so many elegant lines manacled together before him. At Clapham Junction station at 2 p.m. he had to disembark to change trains, which required a wait of half an hour. He was recognised, and swiftly found himself surrounded by a circle of jeering and spitting onlookers. On that platform, the extent of the hatred a great many people felt for him, stoked by accounts of his trial in the press, was revealed to him in all its savagery, and the polished persona that had taken years to create was destroyed. The event had a profound effect, part of the regulated timetable of his decline and humiliation. 'For a year after that was done to me,' he wrote in *De Profundis*, 'I wept every day at the same hour and for the same space of time.'

As he grew stronger, Wilde was at first filled with rage, and then with the conviction that only through acceptance could he fashion a new life outside the prison walls. So began the painful construction of another Wilde, one he believed had been there all along but was only now revealed through the intensity of his suffering. 'There is only one thing for me now,' he wrote, 'absolute humility.'

On his release from Reading, Wilde was taken by train once more to London, to spend a final night in Wandsworth, a journey we will return to. Shortly afterwards, he left England for good, but he did not forget Reading. You can take a poet out of prison it seems, but you can't so easily take prison out of a poet. From Paris, under the nom de plume C.3.3., his old cell number, he published *The Ballad of Reading Gaol*, a burning indictment of the conditions in British prisons and of the death penalty. Gone is the refined language of Wilde's previous poetry; instead, he adopts the ballad form, a currency familiar to those who had suffered alongside him, 'the poor thieves and outcasts' he claims in *De Profundis* were in many respects more fortunate than himself. They had only to travel 'as a bird might fly between the twilight and the dawn' to find people who knew nothing of their crime. In contrast, the global celebrity has come 'not from obscurity into the momentary notoriety of crime, but from a sort of eternity of fame to a sort of eternity of infamy'. In this, as in other aspects of his fall from grace, Wilde's fate foreshadows the internet age.

In France, Wilde lived under the name Sebastian Melmoth, taken from a popular novel of the day by Charles Maturin called *Melmoth the Wanderer*. Maturin's starting point for the book was a passage in one of his own sermons. 'Is there one of us present, however we may have departed from the Lord, disobeyed his will and disregarded his word ... who would ... resign the hope of his salvation?' The eponymous hero of *Melmoth the Wanderer* was such a man, who imagined himself so strong and intelligent that none of the physical, spiritual and intellectual laws that governed others applied to him. Wilde was not exaggerating too much in implying that before his trial his indifference to the morals of the public he encountered on the platform at Clapham Junction could be compared to that of Melmoth. For Wilde and Bosie, sex with the rent boys they brought back to their adjoining rooms at the Savoy was almost a religion, a calling as strong as their devotion to literature; indeed, the two things were linked. 'What the paradox was to me in the sphere of thought, perversity became to me in the sphere of passion,' Wilde explained. Every man was duty bound 'to live his own life to the utmost', to be 'always seeking for new sensations' and to have the courage 'to commit what are called sins'. Drugged by fine food, wine and the thrill of the chase, Wilde had sown the seeds of his own destruction, leaving a trail of incriminating letters, inscribed silver cigarette cases, soiled hotel sheets and talkative chambermaids in his wake.

One anecdote survives from Wilde's journey by train, on his release from prison, to London; another platform epiphany, although of a different kind. Neither he nor the prison authorities wanted to make his reappearance in the world a sensational occasion. In an attempt to evade the reporters who were already gathering outside the gates, instead of taking Wilde to Reading station they placed him in a cab accompanied by the deputy governor of the prison and a warder in plain clothes and proceeded to the next stop down the Great Western line, at Twyford. There he noticed a bush growing by the platform that was just coming into bud; after his long confinement, his only glimpse of the outside world 'that little tent of blue' above the exercise yard, his visual sense was overloaded and he broke down. Holding out his arms towards the insignificant plant, he exclaimed, 'Oh beautiful world! Oh beautiful world!'

'Now, Mr Wilde, you mustn't give yourself away,' said the warder. 'You're the only man in England who would talk like that in a railway station.'

LOCATION: READING

A PLACE OF VANISHINGS

Oscar Wilde was not the only person to disappear from the world after touching down at Reading. Just six days before the station was due to open in March 1840, linking the town to the nation's capital by rail for the first time, Henry West, an unmarried young carpenter from Wilton in Wiltshire, was working on the roof when the area was hit by a freak tornado. The wind lifted him up and transported him some 200 feet, where his insensible body was discovered in a trench some time later. It was said, as is customary on such occasions, that he was killed instantly.

The swiftness of Henry's transition from life to death made a strong impression on his fellow workers, who erected a monument to his memory fashioned from a railway sleeper, inscribed with a verse admonishing all to be ready to face such a call themselves:

Sudden the change
I in a moment fell and had not time
to bid my friends farewell.
Yet hushed be all complaint,
'tis sweet, 'tis blest
to change Earth's stormy scenes
for Endless Rest.
Dear friends prepare,

take warning by my fall,
so you shall hear with joy
your Saviour's call.

Reading was, briefly, the terminus of the line and Brunel had grand plans for building a landmark station here, but he was thwarted by the budget-minded directors of the GWR. Instead, he constructed one of his early 'one-sided' stations, the up and down platforms of which lay alongside one another, served by the simplest amenities. Brunel claimed the single-sided design afforded greater convenience to passengers; but while it is true that those wishing to travel did not have to cross the line, trains, in order to reach them, did, with an obvious impact on the service. Henry, then, was not engaged in constructing a building of great distinction when he met his end. Brunel's original station lasted a mere 20 years, while the single-sided design persisted into the 1890s. I first became aware of Henry's story when a friend sent me a photograph she had taken on her phone of the brass plaque containing the verse and Henry's dates on the wall of the station itself. When I searched for it following the recent redevelopment of the station, disorientated by the change I found around me, at first I failed to find it. Had his memory been swept away by a wind of a different kind, I wondered, the wind of change finally delivering a station building to satisfy Brunel's ambition for this strategically important location?

II

Reading's power as a place of disappearance is not limited to people, but extends to physical objects. T. E. Lawrence disembarked to change trains here in the autumn of 1919. He was travelling accompanied by the first draft of *Seven Pillars of Wisdom*, composed, according to his own account, with the help of notes he had 'jotted daily on the march' while in the Middle East and written up during the Paris Peace Conference. He left a briefcase containing the 250,000-word manuscript, along with some of his original notes, on the train when he stepped down to the platform. It was never recovered. He claimed to have rewritten the book over the winter of 1919–20, 'with heavy repugnance ... from memory and my surviving notes. The record of events was not dulled in me and perhaps few actual mistakes crept in – except in details of dates or numbers – but the outlines and significance of things had lost edge in the haze of new interests'. Lawrence was, as Robert Graves tactfully put it in *Lawrence and the Arabs*, 'an exasperatingly complex personality', and the story may have been a strategy to protect himself against accusations of inaccuracies in his account. I prefer to believe it. Working on an earlier book of my own on the train, approaching my deadline and making final checks on the manuscript, I took five notebooks with me on my journey to work in the morning instead of one, as was my habit. Four remained behind when I changed trains, as Lawrence had done. I always put contact details in the front of my notebooks, a trick Lawrence should have observed; to my gratified amazement, I got a call from the lost property office at Reading, to say they had three of the four in their possession if I wished to come and collect them. One notebook remained lost, part of the editing process, kicked under a seat by a passenger perhaps or thrown in a plastic bag by a cleaner as they passed through the carriage, hurrying to clear away the flotsam and jetsam of a previous journey before the wheels started to turn once more.

Reading station was not Lawrence's only connection with the Thames valley. The success of *Seven Pillars of Wisdom* and public fascination with the figure of 'Lawrence of Arabia' made him uncomfortable, and he attempted to vanish by enlisting in the Royal

Air Force. His unease was shared by others. Harold Nicolson recorded in his diary for 8 April 1940 a journey 'on the early train' to London with a group of friends, discussing 'why I hate T. E. Lawrence so much'. The reason, he decides, is 'that he acquired a legend without deserving it, he was fundamentally fraudulent. Walter Elliot asks if I really think that the Arab campaign was fraudulent and I say No, but everything that came after. The Pillars of Wisdom and that inane translation of Homer.' Twenty years earlier, such voices had been in the minority. While Lawrence was stationed in Plymouth, riding his Brough motorcycle along a street in the city, a peahen voice screamed 'Aircraftman!' and he found himself flagged down by Nancy Astor. She wanted to learn to ride a motorbike. Lawrence visited her at Taplow and she took to racing on two wheels from Maidenhead to London, to the consternation of local police. 'May I ask if we are ever to see you again,' she wrote rather plaintively to Lawrence, when he once again disappeared off the social map. 'My grammar is bad but my affection grand, enduring and well worth your keeping ...'

Reading can also lay claim to another inveterate traveller, as ill at ease in the place of his birth as Lawrence, a compulsive voyager who eventually found his way to his own desert solitude. The first time he ran away from his home in the Ardennes, Arthur Rimbaud was 15 years old. He didn't have enough money for the train fare to Paris so he travelled without a ticket. The city was seething with socialist intrigue and insurrection leading up to the Commune of 1871, and Rimbaud, despite his youth, had already cultivated a suspicious air. On arrival at the Gare du Nord he was arrested, thrown in a police van and locked up in the notorious Mazas prison. In 1874, a mere four years after this dramatic first arrival in the capital of the country of his birth, Rimbaud was in Reading. Many people take four years to write a book; in Rimbaud's case, if we discount his correspondence, four years was the length of his literary career. It included at least one poem written on a train, when he was 16 years old.

Winter Dream

When winter comes we will board a small pink railway carriage
Upholstered in blue.
We will be comfortable. In each soft corner
A nest of mad kisses lies waiting.
You will close your eyes, in order not to see, through the window,
The evening shadows leering.
Those snarling monsters, a tribe
Of black devils, black wolves.
Then you will feel a scratch on your cheek –
A little kiss will run around your neck
Like a crazy spider.
And you'll order me 'find it!' bowing your head,
And we'll take all the time we need searching for that creature
as it continues to scuttle.

In a railway carriage, October 7, '70

During those four years of intense creativity, Rimbaud conducted a drunken and destructive affair with the older, married poet Paul Verlaine, a tortured entanglement which ended in a shooting incident in Brussels; Rimbaud, wounded in the wrist, denounced Verlaine to the police, effectively condemning him to imprisonment and social disgrace. (Like Wilde 20 years later, Verlaine was undone by a younger poet; like Wilde, despite repentance and a religious conversion, Verlaine sought out the agent of his downfall on his release and attempted a reconciliation.) Rimbaud returned to London, where he had lived with Verlaine. In June 1874 he became ill and was hospitalised. His mother and his ever loyal sister Vitalie came to his aid. Some sort of reconciliation took place, and Rimbaud appears to have been gripped by a determination to begin a different life. On 7, 8 and 9 November 1874, an advertisement ran in *The Times*.

A PARISIAN (20) of high literary and linguistic attainments, excellent conversation, will be glad to ACCOMPAGNY [sic] a GENTLEMAN (artists preferred), or a family wishing to travel in southern or eastern countries. Good references. – A. R., no 165, King's Road, Reading.

The references, if requested, would presumably have been a work of poetic fiction. Nothing came of the advertisement, but it at least serves to locate the elusive poet. Rimbaud did get a job: perhaps in Scotland, perhaps in Scarborough, perhaps in Reading. Pilgrims seeking to retrace his footsteps in Britain, from the flat he shared with Verlaine in Camden Town to the rooms he hired for his mother and sister in King's Cross, lose his trail here, in this unremarkable Berkshire town, its position on the rail network meaning he could take off at a moment's notice to any part of the country. Over the next four years, Rimbaud never settled anywhere for long. He gave up poetry, so he disappears from the page as well as the map. He travelled widely, twice crossing the Alps into Italy on foot, a doctor remarking at the time of one of his collapses that his ribs had worn through the wall of his abdomen due to his excessive walking. Eventually his trajectory from Reading took him beyond Europe, to Aden, Yemen and finally across a burning Ethiopian desert to his last home, the sacred city of Harar.

LOCATION: READING
A STATION REBORN

Despite the relentless progress of globalisation, Reading and Harar remain reassuringly different. One an ancient city in the Ethiopian highlands, said to be the fourth most sacred in the Islamic world, its walls patrolled by spotted hyenas; the other a county town in a fertile English river valley, subject to some of the worst rush-hour overcrowding in the country. More passengers are funnelled into and through Reading every year; to cross from one platform to another at busy times is to enter a whirlpool created by the competing pull of different destinations. This is the third busiest rail interchange outside the capital; 15.5 million passengers enter and leave it annually, while nearly four million use it to change between lines. From here, routes radiate out towards Southampton, Cornwall, Wales, the Midlands, the north and Scotland. Reading's strategic importance has only been increased by becoming the western terminus of Crossrail. It would seem reasonable to expect a state-of-the-art transport hub at such a key fulcrum in the network, yet for many years the reverse was true; according to a government white paper, Reading acted as a 'strategic pinch-point' in the Great Western route, with only four lines running through the station and trains regularly stacked up outside, waiting for platform space.

Over the four-year period from 2010 to 2014 travellers on the line watched a transformation take place. The station stayed open, but around, above and alongside it another structure took shape, emerging from the early morning mists like a ghost city, first a sketch and then a skeleton swarming with orange-jacketed workers. I became fascinated with observing the seemingly impossible task under way: constructing a new station without disrupting the tidal flow of passengers through the existing one. New canopies, silver on the outside and lined with panels in a deep blue metallic finish, followed the trajectory of the escalators on to and along the platforms, swooping down in lines pleasantly evocative of dynamism, modernity and motion – all the qualities missing from the station's previous incarnation. The best conjuring trick of all was the slotting into place of the huge new bridge, or transfer deck, which was built offsite and then manoeuvred into position over the tracks. Once open, it seemed to me that Reading had the fluidity of some of the most striking railway architecture of mainland Europe: Calatrava's Eurostar station at Liège, say, or Rem Koolhaas and OMA's station at Lille, albeit on a scale suited to the surrounding town. Those responsible, Grimshaw Architects, have been involved with some of the most radical buildings of the past 30 years. Were they aware, I wondered, of the historic significance of the space in which they were building? Did the little man with the tall hat cast a shadow across their drawing boards?

At Grimshaw's London offices I meet the two architects who have overseen the project: Mark Middleton, the managing partner who negotiated and won the contract, and Declan McCafferty, who brought it to completion. The practice has long specialised in railway architecture, having worked on stations at Ashford International, Waterloo, London Bridge and Southern Cross in Australia, as well as on phase one of the redevelopment of Paddington. They are obviously excited by the renaissance of rail in Britain and around the world, and remarkably open about the challenges and frustrations of working on such large collaborative projects. While Declan runs through some slides documenting the evolution of the project, I ask Mark if he had been conscious at Reading of working in an iconic architectural space.

'The practice has a long association with the Great Western main line,' he says.

'Paddington, more than any of the other stations I have worked on, has loud echoes of its Victorian past ... It still has something of the Sherlock Holmes about it. Brunel had a singular vision of how things should be, right or wrong. He was doing the work of an engineer, an architect and an industrial designer rolled into one, and I've got to say we feel a lot of kinship with him because of that. I'm not saying our work is on the same level as Brunel's – but I am saying there is some sort of esoteric connection there, because he loved engineering and the beauty of what he did came from the engineering. The best Victorian engineering always has character. If you look at the work we did at Paddington, with all those stainless steel castings in plain view, that's because we wanted it to have character.

'You can do all the analysis you like,' he continues, 'but you've got to understand the space as a user first. You've got to be there in the winter. You've got to be there in the summer. It's a different place at holidays and at peak times. I'm one of these people who never learnt to drive so I rely on public transport. When I was a student I worked for BR architects department and I've always been an avid watcher and user of stations. I've been using Reading for years.'

The bridge, with its panoramic overviews in both directions up and down the track, is one of my favourite features of the new station. Mark and Declan obviously agree.

'It looks vast now,' Declan says, 'but it's designed to have capacity for growth until 2033, by when we expect a 50 per cent increase in passengers.'

'You get fantastic views of the sunset and the early morning sunrise from up there, facing east and west,' Mark adds. 'We had to fight very hard to keep those glazed sides on the bridge because engine drivers object to any kind of distraction, like seeing people walking about, for obvious reasons. They would prefer it all to be closed off.'

'Look at this,' says Declan, putting up a slide. 'This was a couple of days after we opened.' The photograph shows the back view of a woman standing on the bridge. It is evening, and she is in front of one of the windows, face to face with a vast purple sky, taking a photograph. The image reminds me that at Reading the line runs directly east to west, so the commuter's direction of travel, especially during the shorter days of winter, is always oriented towards sunrise or sunset. I like the fact that the design of Grimshaw's transfer deck has taken this simple fact into consideration. By doing so, they join an architectural tradition that reaches back to the Stone Age.

How does it feel as an architect, I wonder, to deliver a beautiful building and then see it compromised by the addition of retail outlets, signage or security cameras? Mark has no patience with such sensitivities. 'A lot of architects swish around with their felt hats and say, "Darling, you've messed up my space", and I think that's wrong. I can think of a good example of this. Everyone thought Stansted was a beautiful airport when it opened because it was all on one level and you could see the planes taking off, but you could only do that because [Sir Norman] Foster designed it without any retail. As soon as the retail went in, it completely buggered up the concept. Therefore I would argue the concept itself was slightly flawed – to make it work he had to take one of the major components out of it. We all know airports are basically shopping centres with planes attached. In many ways a railway station is like a high street and should be embedded within a town and a community, rather than being separate. I think stations have got a real part to play; they have divested the responsibility they have to the community. There are a lot more things they could provide to the local neighbourhood, rather than being that dark spot where you think at 8 p.m., "Ooh, I don't want to go by there because it's where all the hoodies hang out." We should embrace retail instead of treating it as if it's grubby; make the station a nice place to visit, so people enjoy going there.'

It's easy to get swept along by the arguments made by architects to justify their buildings. This, after all, is what they do: pitch ideas, create castles in the air held aloft by words, drawings, 3-D printed models that would crumble to dust between the fingers in seconds. Before anything is constructed in the real world it must be constructed in the minds of their clients, and this can only be done through the power of the architect's self-belief. Brunel, of course, was the supreme battler, often winning the right to pursue his own, occasionally disastrous course through an elemental force of will. His decision to build a single-sided station at a point where lines converge from Wales, the north and the south-west was certainly not one of his best decisions. In addition to the new station, an elevated section of railway known as the west Reading viaduct has recently been completed to allow high-speed trains to cross the freight lines when entering the station. 'It is thought this is the first time this has been achieved since Brunel built the first layout in the 1840s,' a publication from train operator First Great Western says pointedly.[41] Sitting in a carriage waiting to depart, looking across the broad platforms to where the clock tower of the Victorian station is just visible above the curved lines of the canopies, the space Grimshaw have created still feels so new that to stand within it is like inhabiting an artist's impression. The sky is impossibly blue. A train slides into position on the other side of the platform, its silver-headed guard leaning out of a window. He, the orange-jacketed dispatch crew who are chatting with each other on the platform and the Amazonian young American woman pulling a heavy suitcase who approaches them to ask for directions, all appear to be actors in a play, put on for my benefit. Most of the people getting on to my train have their eyes glued to their phones, of course, and are seemingly unaware of their surroundings. We have become used to such transformations of the built environment that surrounds us and it is increasingly difficult to imagine the impact railway architecture must have had on those seeing it for the first time.

DIGRESSION
A DIFFERENT CLASS

'I particularly approve of and welcome the
arrest of the millionaire saboteurs in the
first- and second-class railway carriage.'
Vladimir Lenin, telegram to V. A. Antonov-Ovseyenko
(December 1917)

'Whatever improvement in communication will enable the poor man … to carry his labour, perhaps the only valuable property he possesses, to the best market, and where it is most wanted, must be a decided advantage, not only to him but the community at large.' The words are those of the Conservative politician and prime minister Robert Peel, made in a speech at his constituency, Tamworth, in 1835, in support of the opening of a line between Derby and Birmingham. In the new, industrial age, factory workers should be able to circulate in the same way as the commodities they produced, and the swiftly expanding railway network would be the means of making this happen. The great stations the Victorians built shared their architectural vocabulary of glass roofs and iron columns with market halls. Instead of delivering fish, meat or vegetables to the metropolis they delivered that other resource vital to its existence: human workers – a function they continue to fulfil to this day.

Not everybody shared Peel's enthusiasm. The Duke of Wellington warned that allowing the working classes to move around the country at will was a recipe for revolution. William Wordsworth and John Ruskin were both convinced the expansion of the railways would lead to the destruction of the countryside they cherished by provoking an invasion by the urban masses. Even the first railway entrepreneurs were not keen on their custom. The Great Western Railway began operation with a two-tiered business model: firstly, they aimed to move freight faster and more efficiently than the canal system. Secondly, they would provide transport for the moneyed middle classes and the aristocracy. Paddington station had a separate waiting room for the royal family to use when they were on their way to Windsor, while special wagons were laid on to accommodate the horses of those going hunting and the carriages of those who wished to take along their own transport between the station and their country seat.

Provision for less prosperous travellers was not quite so generous. In the first years of rail, so-called 'goods passengers', reduced by this designation to the status of things rather than people, rode in open freight wagons, with no protection from either the elements or the impact of collisions.

Third-class services travelled much slower than normal trains and at deliberately inconvenient times, leaving Paddington at 4.30 a.m. and Bristol at 9.30 p.m. It was just such a pre-dawn departure from Paddington that was involved in the accident in the Sonning Cutting, near Reading, on Christmas Eve 1841. The train was pulling two open, third-class carriages, peopled with travellers *The Times* described as 'chiefly of the poorer class', as well as 17 heavily laden goods wagons. It emerged at the inquest that these unfortunate passengers were mostly stonemasons working in London, returning to their families for Christmas. A landslip in the cutting, which is nearly two miles long and 60 feet deep, had covered the tracks with soil and debris. The report written the following day for the privy council by the inspector-general of railways, Lieutenant Colonel Sir Frederick Smith, creates a vivid picture.

> When the train reached [Sonning Cutting], the engine came in contact with an obstruction, which threw it off the rails, and its velocity being in consequence suddenly checked while the wagons retained their impetus, they ran forward on the passenger carriages, smashing one and considerably injuring the other, and I lament to say, killing 8 and wounding 17 passengers.
>
> At the time this dreadful accident occurred it was quite dark ... It was found that the concussion had thrown the whole of the passengers out of the carriages.

Smith was clear that the number of deaths and injuries suffered was due in no small part to the design of the accommodation provided. The effects of the derailment could have been lessened if the carriages had been fitted with spring buffers, he concluded. Moreover, 'the third-class carriages used on the occasion of this accident were not of such a construction as the public have a right to expect'. While they were equipped with seats 18 inches high, the sides of the carriage were only two feet off the floor, 'so that a person standing up is ... in great danger of being thrown out of the carriage, and those sitting near the sides are also in danger of falling; besides which the exposure to the cutting winds of the winter must be very injurious to the traveller who, proceeding from London to Bristol, often remains exposed for ten or twelve hours, a great part of which is in the night time'. Such accidents, coupled with the generally contemptuous treatment meted out to third-class passengers, provoked so much public anger that in 1844 an act was passed requiring companies to run at least one 'workman's train' per day, with covered carriages, at a rate of no more than a penny a mile.

As the second decade of the 21st century began, the division between first- and standard-class travel returned to the centre of political debate in Britain, and it has remained there ever since. The railways were born in an intensely class-conscious society. It is therefore no surprise that early entrepreneurs built the divisions they felt their customers – particularly their wealthier patrons – would expect into the miniature versions of that society sent trundling down the line. What *is* perhaps surprising is the way in which any discussion about first- and standard-class tickets in the present day can still short-circuit, amid smoke and sparks, revealing with X-ray precision the deep-seated attitudes of those speaking and exposing divisions that stretch far beyond the tracks. Those commuting in standard class at peak times, who have spent thousands of pounds a year on their season tickets, are often forced to stand in crowded carriages. On the London to Bristol route, many first-class carriages have recently been 'remodelled' to provide more standard-class accommodation. Primarily this has been undertaken to ease overcrowding, but is it also a pre-emptive move against a rumbling insurrection? The sight, glimpsed through the window from the platform, of first-class passengers lolling in capacious seats in half-empty compartments can stir revolutionary feeling in the most sedate passenger's heart.

For this reason you would imagine a first-class carriage would be about as desirable a place to be observed for an image-conscious politician as a lap-dancing bar or a backstreet bookie's. Nevertheless, at least three members of the political class in recent years have boldly blundered into controversy linked to rail travel, to the despair of their PR teams and the horrified delight of the public. The amusing thing about such incidents is the way they reveal how little some career politicians understand the lives of those they supposedly represent. The first two actors in this comedy of manners mixed themselves a toxic cocktail that combined rail travel, the media and the MPs expenses scandal. Eric Pickles, then the shadow secretary of state for communities and local government for the Conservatives, made what was to become something of a cult appearance on BBC1's *Question Time* in March 2009. Live on air, Pickles tried to justify the fact that he claimed for a second home on the outskirts of the city when he owned a central London flat. To jeers of derision he admitted he had only a 37-mile journey, but maintained the rigours of travel made it essential he kept up his flat in London. He had tried commuting for a short period, he explained, during a family illness. 'It was an extremely difficult experience and I will explain why. Because the House of Commons works on clockwork. If you are on a committee you have to be there precisely. Particularly someone like me ...' He appeared to be unaware that other professionals, such as doctors, nurses and teachers, also travelled long distances, worked long hours and were expected to turn up on time.

The second player to take the stage was the long-serving Conservative MP for Macclesfield, Nicholas Winterton, who in a radio interview on BBC Radio 5 Live in February 2010 declared himself furious that MPs were no longer allowed to claim for first-class rail travel. As someone with responsibilities who worked on the train, he could not be expected to mix with the 'totally different type of people' with a 'different outlook on life' who travelled in standard class, often accompanied by their noisy children.

When told that they very well might be undertaking work themselves, he replied: 'They may be reading a book but I very much doubt that they are undertaking serious work and study, reading reports, amending reports [like] members of parliament do when they travel.' This was the sound of someone committing political *hara-kiri* on air, a slow-motion suicide to which he had been delivered by rail. Shortly after the broadcast he was publicly disowned by his party and retired at the next election.

The third of our trio of politicians to find themselves caught in the first-class elephant trap was the architect of Britain's austerity plan, as well as the champion of the HS2 and HS3 rail projects, George Osborne. A reporter for ITV news, Rachel Townsend, travelling south towards London from Wilmslow on the same train as the politician on 19 October 2012, overheard a conversation between a ticket inspector and Osborne's aide. Osborne was travelling on a standard-class ticket but refused to move from the first-class compartment in which he was sitting, appearing to feel that his status as an important public figure entitled him to the seclusion it offered. The ensuing David and Goliath contest between powerful politician and railway employee was tweeted live as it happened by Townsend; eventually, the ticket inspector triumphed and Osborne's party paid for an upgrade.

Unfortunately for Osborne, Twitter moves faster than a train. In less than an hour, before he had arrived in the capital in person, the story of the chancellor's journey had broken on television channels. Rather like the Slough murderer John Tawell, he was preceded by news of himself, captured through an electronic technology and disseminated while he was still captive in a speeding carriage. The man who famously assured the country 'we are all in this together' as he began making deep cuts in public funding had demonstrated that, when it came to railway travel, well, no we were not. By the time his train pulled into Euston station a disparate but excited reception committee had gathered, formed of reporters, photographers, representatives of the National Union of Students and others who had followed the story on Twitter, forcing him to make an undignified exit through a security gate to a waiting governmental car.

• There is a direct correlation between the distance travelled to work and the seniority of position of the person commuting. According to the Office for National Statistics, 36 per cent of people in high-skilled jobs in London commute from outside the city. This is similar to North America, where so-called 'mega-commuters', with a journey of more than 90 minutes each way, tend to be male, older, married, make a higher salary, and have a spouse who does not work. Where does this leave Peel's poor man, hoping to carry his labour to market?

The truth is that today rail travel is so expensive, even middle- and upper-middle-class households struggle to find the money for season tickets. In 1893, a songwriter named John Parnell published a broadside ballad, sold for one penny, called 'The Railway'. Its sentiments still resonate, after the passage of 120 years.

> *And so the years roll onward*
> *While the workers utter the cry,*
> *Which rings in the ears of manhood,*
> *And rises aloft to die.*
> *Till the hour cometh of change,*
> *Like the steady tide of the sea,*
> *When the people shall travel for nothing,*
> *And the Railways shall be free.*
> *When the State shall know the value,*
> *Of which there is no doubt,*
> *Of the right of a free-born people*
> *To freely move about.*
> *For a land which is locked by money*
> *Is a land of death and decay,*
> *Where the weak man gets still weaker,*
> *And the strong man fades away.*

Today's commuters still sift themselves before their train arrives, first-class passengers dawdling near the entrance to the platform, standard class walking briskly away from the barriers in the hope of finding a seat. It is always amusing when an announcement is made, just as the carriages come to a halt: 'The train arriving at Platform 1 is in reverse formation.' Suddenly, it is first-class passengers who must hurry along the platform, jostling and pushing their way through the returning standard-class passengers, who, on this day at least, will arrive at their destination before those who have spent more for their tickets. So the last shall be first and the first last, as the King James version of the Bible has it. How long, someone of a radical disposition might wonder, before such a reversal happens in the society that lies beyond the railway platform?

LOCATION:
THAMES VALLEY
OF SWORDS, SWIFTS AND SHIELDS

Riding the line along this river valley we are following the contours of the land, joining a network of tracks, pathways and roads that have existed for centuries. Objects unearthed here from the Roman period reveal that people were already travelling to work two thousand years ago – itinerant traders moving along the valley, bringing goods from places far distant in the empire; plough teams passing between farmsteads; locals making their way to markets, to shrines for festivals and to the larger centres to register for the census.

As well as providing a means of transport to the Romans, the river may have acted as a border in the eras that preceded and followed them, although such things are hard to prove. What archaeology can tell us is that the Thames had special significance to prehistoric peoples: swords, axes, helmets and shields were placed in its waters in the Bronze Age, not for storage, but precisely because they were difficult to retrieve. (Perhaps a folk memory of this practice gave rise to the Arthurian legend of Excalibur rising from the surface of a lake.) Were they the weapons of defeated enemies or of warriors retiring after years of battle? Did they mark a border or signify a votive offering to a watery god? Contradictory theories abound.

What is certain is that the landscape through which the train passes was a place of sacrifice. These people were making a bargain with forces larger than themselves; so are today's train travellers. Their offering was of some of the most powerful and precious objects they possessed. Centuries later, ours is of time spent on the train, time itself now being one of the highest-value currencies of our age.

As the river curves and meanders its way towards London and the sea, the railway at one minute loses sight of it then runs close alongside and leaps across it again, so these two pathways are as interwoven as we are with our past. The Thames holds those hours, days and weeks that I, along with millions of others, have spent travelling; they lie there in its depths, alongside spearheads and ancient skulls, a deposit laid down to ensure the prosperity of the tribe.

II

One of the sustaining myths we live by is that human beings are completely different from other animals. This, of course, is far from the case. We are closer in our genetic make-up to a chimpanzee, for instance, than a chimpanzee is to a gorilla. Nevertheless, we need to maintain the myth in order to justify our exploitation of the earth's resources, quite apart from any religious meta-narrative we may adhere to. In many ways we are unique; but in our bodies and the make-up of our brains we carry the traces of the staging posts we have tarried at on our evolutionary journey, and our behaviour and motivations are often not so different from those of our non-human cousins.

Take, for instance, commuting. It is tempting to see the vast mechanical networks we have created in the last century or so to transport people back and forth each day as further evidence of the gulf that separates us from the animal kingdom – but this is to concentrate solely on the external trappings of our activities.

A commuter is someone who lives in one place and earns his or her sustenance in another, and is therefore compelled to make a journey at more or less the same time every day. The same could be said of a seagull that travels inland from the coast each morning to follow the farmer's plough, or an urban fox that times its visits to a street to coincide with the hour the garbage is put out. Human travellers have long marvelled at the ability of animals and birds to migrate huge distances without the aid of map or radar. Certain species, it seems, have a small crystal of magnetite buried in their skulls, an in-built sat nav aligning them with the earth's magnetic fields. Among them are human beings; we carry our crystal, our miniature lodestar, in the ethmoid bone between our eyes. Repeated journeying along the same axis, day after day, must code our route on to this internal GPS. No wonder long-term commuters, when they lay aside their season ticket, at first feel a sense of euphoric release but then sometimes experience a lack of purpose or direction, as if they had been cut loose from the elemental forces that govern life on our planet.

Some years ago I lived in the King's Cross area of London, a few minutes' walk from the Gothic towers of what is now the international station at St Pancras. I heard somewhere that the swifts roosting among its red-brick cliffs for the mid-summer months travelled every day to the fens of Cambridge and East Anglia to hunt their insect prey, a round trip of as much as 150 miles – a fairly serious commute, by any standard. Of course, to a bird that leaves its home in Malawi or the Democratic Republic of Congo to breed in northern Europe, such distances mean little. Tied as I was to the surface of the earth, I was cheered by distant glimpses of these phenomenal travellers scything the upper air, their screeching calls to each other rendered inaudible at ground level by the roar of traffic and the squeal of brakes.

From the beginning of May to the end of August swifts are a common sight from the train, hunting the flatlands, river valleys and water meadows on the approach to the city. The rigours of their journey put ours in perspective; they have crossed forests, oceans and the ever-expanding Sahara to share this space with you. They have no need of railways or other aids to locomotion – commuting to their feeding grounds they routinely fly at 60 miles an hour, even faster when they stoop and dive in pursuit of their prey. Much of their life – including their ability to mate and even sleep on the wing, high in the air at night – remains as mysterious to us as ours must remain to them.

Two hyper-mobile species, we pass each other at high speed, each wrapped up in the pursuit of the insubstantial and elusive things that sustain us – microscopic insects, drifting airborne spiders, money, prospects, hope.

DIGRESSION
MAGIC, EDUCATION AND THE
HALF-SOVEREIGN ACCIDENT

'Cervantes, who wasn't dyslexic but was left crippled
by the exercise of arms, knew perfectly well what he
was saying. Literature is a dangerous occupation.'

Roberto Bolaño, the Caracas speech accepting
the Rómulo Gallegos Prize (1999)

Like literature, the art of magic can also be hazardous, as Stanley
Spencer's brother Horace discovered when he fell from his bicycle
into the dark waters of the Thames. (Was he too some sort of
offering; a sacrifice offered to the river gods by the Magic Circle
perhaps?) The association in the public's mind of Brunel, the
architect of the impossible bridge at Maidenhead, with the art
of illusion was further compounded by an event in 1843, one of
several near-death experiences that punctuated his career. The
story has everything. A hero, blessed with apparently limitless
energy and scientific expertise, is undone through the most trivial
circumstances. What is it that finds the chink in this invincible
warrior's armour, that seeks out his Achilles' heel? Love – more
precisely, parental love. For those brought up on a diet of Bible
stories and classical myth, the combination in one figure of
strength and weakness, of semi-divine powers and intensely human
vulnerability, is a potent one.

Brunel's work often kept him away from his family – as he said prophetically in his private journal when thinking about marriage, 'my profession is after all my only fit wife'[42] – but when he was at home he enjoyed playing with his children. On 3 April 1843 he bounded up the stairs from his ground-floor office at 12 Duke Street to the nursery and began entertaining them with magic tricks. One of his favourites was the classic illusion in which a conjurer appears to put a coin in his mouth and then produce it from his ear, as if it has passed through skin, bone and the teeming brain. Stage magic was an abiding interest with Brunel, perhaps because it depended on principles diametrically opposed to the empirical laws governing the life of an engineer. Like many interested in theatrical magic, he enjoyed pitting his wits against those who attempted to defy science with the spiritual hocus-pocus that became increasingly fashionable as the century progressed. 'His power of observation was singularly accurate,' his friend William Hawes wrote to Brunel's son, when the latter was engaged in writing his biography. 'He was not satisfied with a hasty or superficial examination, nor with the mere assertion of a fact; his mind required evidence of its correctness before he could receive and adopt it. I may illustrate this with reference to the experiments he made with French mesmerists, and the pains he took to expose the farce of table-turning and its accompanying follies.'[43]

On that fateful day in April 1843, as if in retribution for his questioning of the supernatural powers of others, Brunel's sleight of hand failed him and physical reality painfully asserted itself. While attempting the trick, he swallowed the coin by mistake and it lodged in his windpipe, threatening to end his dual careers of engineer and amateur magician at the same moment, before the horrified gaze of his children. For the next two weeks he suffered from what was referred to as 'a troublesome cough', according to an account published in a letter to *The Times* by his brother-in-law

Seth Thompson. On 18 April the eminent physician Sir Benjamin Brodie was consulted. He confirmed that the coin was lodged in the windpipe, probably at the bottom of the right bronchus, and was movable. Indeed, when Brunel bent over a chair, 'he distinctly felt the coin drop towards the glottis'; when he stood up it sank back into its position, triggering a severe fit of coughing that incapacitated him. Rather than despair, Brunel turned to his powers of invention for remedy. Together with the doctor, he devised an apparatus that would allow him to be turned upside down, in order that gravity might combine with his cough to expel the coin.[44] This procedure was put to the test on the 25th, but Brunel's cough became so violent that his life was judged to be in danger and it was discontinued. Two days later, Brodie tried a different approach, performing a tracheotomy through which he hoped to remove the coin with the help of forceps. However, the insertion of the forceps caused such an adverse reaction that the attempt was abandoned, although the wound was kept open with a tube in the hope that the coin might be persuaded to exit by that route once Brunel was strong enough to endure another attempt.

Public interest in Brunel's condition was intense. In the words of the *Illustrated London News*, the details of Brunel's private life with his children afforded 'a glimpse ... equivalent of a revelation [of] the natural man disconnected from the engineer'. His fate was the subject of conversation everywhere, and 'for a while kept all the world in suspense from the value of the life in jeopardy [and] the singular nature of the accident'.[45] On 13 May, Brunel was judged to be recovered sufficiently to be placed on the apparatus and turned upside down once again, a figure more akin to the reverse hanged man in the Tarot pack than an eminent engineer. After he was struck gently on the back he coughed two or three times; able to breathe through the wound in his throat, he didn't choke as the coin moved upward, striking his upper front teeth with a sound he later said was the best he heard in his life, before dropping to the floor. When Thomas Babington Macaulay, who would achieve fame as the author of *The History of England*, ran along the street towards The Athenaeum, shouting, 'It's out! It's out!', everyone was said to have understood him immediately.

What is significant about this story, beyond any incidental interest it may have, is the way it has come to us. Throughout his career Brunel made every effort to manage the way he, and the works he was engaged in, were reported in newspapers and magazines, the social media of his day. In current parlance, he was a master of spin who wished to 'control the conversation'. It should come as no surprise that the account *The Times* carried of the accident, in the form of the letter from Seth Thompson, was published at his own request. The trivial, albeit uncomfortable, event that came to be known as 'the half-sovereign accident' is put to use to polish and refine Brunel's image. Rather than being portrayed as a fool come to grief through his own carelessness, Brunel is praised for his sang-froid, his presence of mind under pressure. Potential investors in an apparently risky business proposition – a huge, transatlantic steamship, for instance, larger than any the world had yet seen – would surely be more likely to trust their money to the hands of a man who had demonstrated he could remain calm, even while choking. His very public career had made him expert at managing what author Ben Marsden has called 'the narrative of failure'.[46] To be able to turn stories of mistakes into ones of eventual success, of late delivery into heroic perseverance, was vital in an age when so much engineering was experimental, made up as it went along.

Brunel had been well schooled in public relations by his father Marc, who countered the negative criticism that surrounded the numerous accidents and delays in the construction of the Thames

Tunnel with a small industry producing souvenirs, pamphlets, guides and even its own broadsheet, illustrated by his son. Thus, a disastrous incursion of water into the tunnel became the story of the young Brunel's heroism in rescuing a drowning man; another flood, which the young engineer survived but which resulted in the death of six workmen, is now chiefly remembered as further proof of his courage and apparent indestructibility. As well as providing evidence of Brunel's coolness to add to his already documented courage, the half-sovereign episode granted the public a 'revelation' – a picture of Brunel as a devoted family man. Being shown in such a light was always thought good for business, as the painter William Powell Frith was to demonstrate by including his own family on the concourse at Paddington in *The Railway Station*.

The reality, of course, was that Brunel worked astonishingly long hours and for considerable periods was scarcely at home. His children, like his employees, were expected to match his industry. The promise he held out to his sons, once they were too old for conjuring tricks, was a helping hand into business, the same his father had offered to him. His eldest son and namesake Isambard Junior was born in 1837 with a birth defect that resulted in an odd, shuffling walk. This could have been corrected with a fairly simple operation but his mother, who seems to have countered both Brunel's firmness and his frequent absence with a maternal solicitude, would not allow it. At the age of seven the boy was sent away to boarding school. 'You are wrong in supposing that I cannot feel your parting from dear Isambard,' Brunel wrote to his wife Mary in 1844. 'I hope the poor little fellow is not very unhappy but it is what all must go through and he has infinitely less cause for pain than most boys in beginnings. I made my beginnings in ten times worse circumstances and now he will soon get over it. Give my love to the dear boy and tell him I have smoked his cigar case twice over.'

Denied an operation, Isambard Jr is expected to overcome his physical abnormality through his own efforts. The small amount of direct correspondence to him as a child from his father that survives encourages him to walk properly and listen to his drilling master, as well as to study hard. Brunel wrote to him in 1852, the year he went to Harrow, on the subject of mathematics.

How for arithmetic? I think I must take you in hand at Christmas for I fear very much that the quality of your arithmetical knowledge is very queer, whatever the quantity and that is probably small. Half a pint of poor small beer is not nourishing and cannot be called a malt liquor diet, neither can I imagine Harrow arithmetic to be much better. It is very distressing but one must put up with it as one would if brought up in a country where it was the practice to put out one eye.

For Brunel, not to educate the young in science was to deliberately handicap their ability to participate in the technological age evolving around them, as ludicrous a decision as putting out an eye. His own father had introduced him to mathematics and geometry at a young age, with a particular emphasis on the importance of direct observation through drawing. To these had been added Latin, Greek and classical history, the education of a gentleman. His schooling in French, perfected during the time he spent being trained and educated in that country, gave him access to French scientific literature not available to British rivals, while his membership of clubs and institutions provided access to private libraries and the latest journals and magazines. His office at Duke Street contained a large collection of books on architecture and he enjoyed the works of Shakespeare enough to want to amass a collection of paintings based on the plots and characters they contained. He was even a published author himself – his 'Treatise on Draught' was published to accompany William Youatt's *The Horse* in 1831 – but was disparaging of his own literary ability while expert at marshalling others to his cause. Throughout his career he experienced stinging criticisms in the press of his various schemes, countering them in campaigns he was to refer to, with regard to the media interest in his *Great Eastern* steamship, as 'a wordy war with all comers', often deploying a blizzard of scientific evidence and mathematical calculations.

Brunel, then, was a very literary engineer, at a time when such entrepreneurial figures were keen to establish their intellectual credentials. It is not surprising, therefore, that he quickly grasped the potential of the train carriage as a place for reading and writing. The public he imagined would utilise his line was an elite, educated one. Gentlemen engaged in business could doubly benefit from the time saved between their destinations and the ability to work while they travelled, something they would have found impossible to do when subjected to the lurching motion of a stagecoach. Other readers, male and female, young and old, would be able to pass the time with newspapers, novels and magazines. It was at least partly to achieve the necessary combination of speed and smoothness to enable this imagined clientele to read that he rethought the technology of both locomotive and track in designing his broad-gauge railway. The nature of his ambition is clearly stated in his diary entry for 5 December 1831, in which he reports on his first ever experience of travelling by rail.

I record the specimen of the shaking on the Manchester Railway. The time is not far off when we shall be able to take our coffee and write whilst going noiselessly and smoothly at 45 mph – let me try.

Brunel's early training in architectural drawing had made him adept at reproducing perfect circles and his pocket notebooks contain many examples of pencilled circles and target-like figures, recorded as tests of the vibration of the track. In 1838 he travelled on the Manchester line again, drawn by a Lion engine. As well as making his usual visual tests of the track's smoothness, he complained in writing to his notebook that his hands were very cold and drew a humorous self-portrait. It shows the famous engineer, top hat in place, 'going at 28 miles an hour', seated on a carriage bench with his hands thrust deep in his pockets.[47] Once more Brunel is constructing his self-image, although this time it is only for his own amusement.

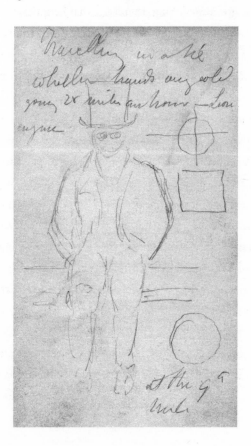

The effect of the railways on the availability of literature has been well documented. It began in the 1840s when goods on offer at stations largely consisted of pirated reprints of American bestsellers and racy French novels, via the 'cleansing' of the trade by W. H. Smith when they bought out all the station bookstalls, to Allen Lane's cathartic moment on the platform at Exeter station in 1934 when, faced with the paucity of reading material on display, he decided to launch the affordable paperback imprint that became Penguin Books. The 'fine flare' of one of Mr W. H. Smith's bookstalls, Henry James wrote in his essay 'London', 'is a feature not to be omitted in any enumeration of the charms of Paddington and Euston. It is a focus of warmth and light in the vast, smoky cavern; it gives the idea that literature is a thing of splendor, of a dazzling essence, of infinite, gas-lit red and gold. A glamour hangs over the booth, and a tantalizing air of clever new things. How brilliant must the books all be, how veracious and courteous the fresh, pure journals!'

James writes, of course, of a time when such publications remained physical objects with texture and heft, fashioned from the same carbon we are ourselves, which could be arranged to best advantage beneath the gas illumination of a station bookstall. Today, words also leap through space towards us on hand-held devices and those without access to the internet live as if, in Brunel's words, 'in a country where it [is] the practice to put out one eye'. Isambard Jr did not become an engineer, although his younger brother Henry Marc did. Instead, he wrote a biography of his father, who died when his oldest son was only 22 years old; too young, perhaps, to have proved that he was equipped with 20:20 vision, or that his education had proved adequate to negotiate the modern world.

LOCATION: DIDCOT
FARM BOYS AND NAVIGATORS

Before the railway brought trains to this valley, it brought the men who dug the cuttings and laid the rails. The arrival of the navigators, or navvies as they became known, was dreaded by local residents, as their reputation for hard drinking, fighting and stealing preceded them down the line. The technological advances of the Industrial Revolution had thrown many out of work in artisanal trades, swelling the ranks of cheap labour. Rail contractors based their calculations on the ability of a navvy to dig and throw on to a truck 20 tons of earth a day. In addition to railway building, the docks, the canals, mining and brickworks all remained un-mechanised and dependent on labour. Not all those who supplied it came from mainland Britain. Around a third were Irish Catholics, admired by gangmasters for their strength and endurance, prepared to work for less than anyone else; reason enough for outbreaks of violence between them and their Presbyterian Scottish and Protestant English co-workers. Paid intermittently, sometimes in kind, uninsured against injury, the navvies were forced to fend for themselves, erecting huts and tents in makeshift camps, often accompanied by their wives and children, more like a unit of mercenaries than the railway workers of today. Without any amusement in the few hours they had of leisure apart from that provided by local inns, made wild by drink they often turned to mischief or sport. In a time when there was no regular police force to maintain the peace they posed a serious challenge to the communities in which they settled.

Somehow, through a combination of threats, promises and strong-arm tactics, contractors managed to keep the navvies in harness and the railway crept westward from London to meet workers forging east from Bristol. In 1839, 300 navigators made their camp near Didcot. If these hard-bitten men imagined the countryside would yield up its riches without a struggle, or that its inhabitants would be easily intimidated, they were mistaken. The farm boys of Berkshire and Oxfordshire, muscles hardened in the fields and at the plough, were not likely to yield ground easily to the farm boys of Donegal. This valley, after all, had seen invading armies before: Celts, Romans and Danes had all come and gone.

Tame Farm, long held by the Tame family, bordered the line and it amused the navigators to let the farmer's cows into the corn, wrecking the crop and making the animals sick. One of the sons of the farm, Edmund Tame, was exceptionally strong, known locally as 'a perfect Samson'. Six feet two in his stockinged feet, already in his early 40s, he could bend half crowns between his fingers, lift enormous weights and tear up packs of cards. The navvies had their own champion, a man named Thompson; an inch taller than Tame, his strength, built by shifting tons of earth and rock with picks and shovels, and his fighting ability, honed in workers' camps along the line, were legendary. These giants, then, one rooted to the earth, one ploughing resolutely through it, had moved inexorably towards each other, their progress as stately as the passage of two planets through the skies, until they reached a point of collision. It is probable that the navvies, with their sporting instincts ever alert to the possibility of a contest on which they could place a bet, had provoked the Tame family deliberately. If this was indeed their intention, they got their wish.

One evening, not far from the river Thames, the two warriors met. Navvies gathered on one side of the makeshift ring and locals on the other. It is likely that money changed hands. This was bare knuckle fighting, to the finish, the kind of match the Marquess of Queensberry hoped to regulate with his famous rules some 30 years later. The smack of fist on flesh, the sprays of blood and the casually spat, irreplaceable teeth aroused those watching to a frenzy. More was at stake than mere money. The pride of men who had little else to call their own was pitched against that of men rooted in and shaped by the landscape. For the farmers and farm workers, the world around them was formed by their own labour; it was this world the railway carved through, its disruption as much social as physical, its hard-edged geometry connecting them to a disturbing, exterior universe they had never before encountered. They had more than a title to defend.

At the end of each round the champions staggered back to their corners, knuckles and noses bleeding, carthorse chests heaving, to be doused in water and pushed back in the ring. In the fourth round, Tame landed such a blow to Thompson's head that he collapsed and remained insensible for a full six hours, unable to move. To their credit, the navigators cheered Tame from the ring (or had they bet against their own man?). In any case, no further trespasses were reported; the argument had been won.

Today, for the first time in over a century, we are seeing proposals for a dramatic expansion of the railway network in Britain. Once more, plans have been laid to drive high-speed trains through English farmland, this time from London towards Birmingham and on to Scotland and from east to west to join the great cities of the north; once more they are being met by opposition. These new trains, as new trains always do, come weighted with symbolic freight: on one side, the destruction of the rural landscape, including areas of particular environmental sensitivity; on the other, nothing less than the regeneration of the nation's economy. The fight is being conducted through media campaigns, petitions, public meetings and the lobbying of members of parliament. Our governors, looking to public investment in infrastructure to lift the economy out of recession, deplore the morass of consultations and legal challenges such projects face.

Perhaps they could take a lesson from the last great age of railway construction in settling the dispute; the savings in time and legal costs could be considerable. Might a champion as fearsome as Farmer Tame emerge from the downlands of the Chilterns? And might not the company formed to push through construction of the line put up a rival to stand against him as formidable as Navigator Thompson? As onlookers, clustered round the ring, where would you place your bets?

LOCATION: DIDCOT
THE CATHEDRAL OF THE VALE

I had not been travelling long before I fell under the spell of the coal and oil-fired power station at Didcot known as Didcot A.

First, there was the simple geometry of its shapes – a scattering of modernist building blocks placed incongruously in a rural setting: six cooling towers, a vast rectangular turbine hall, a 270-foot chimney studded with red lights to warn off low-flying aircraft. Second, and more importantly, there was the array of atmospheric effects the station produced. On clear, winter days Didcot announced its presence shortly after the train left Oxford, some 10 miles away, with a plume of white water vapour rising into the sky. At other times the graceful silhouettes of the towers were barely visible through the mist of the river valley as we drew parallel to them on the approach to Didcot station. Every day was different. At sunset the clouds that arose from the mouth of the towers could be tinted pink or purple; if you were lucky enough to pass at exactly the right moment, the entire side of the glass-clad turbine hall would ignite, gilded in orange solar fire. On cold, frosty mornings when it was generating at full capacity, the power station almost disappeared behind its self-generated veil of steam. The adjacent opencast landfill site, with its swarm of wheeling birds and fluttering flags of plastic caught in bushes and fences, merely added to the post-apocalyptic splendour of the scene.

I have already written of how such objects, seen a thousand times, can suddenly be transformed through a mysterious mental process, reappearing transfigured, never to be forgotten. Once this has happened they function in the landscape like the 'punctum' in a photograph that Roland Barthes speaks of in *Camera Lucida* – the detail that somehow connects with and 'wounds' the viewer, giving emotional resonance to the whole composition. The cooling towers would surface from the dreamlike state in which much of my journey was subsumed, like breaching whales; soon I was photographing them, standing in the corridor with my head out of the window, or shooting through the glass from my seat. I had no interest in obtaining a sharp image; the blur and judder produced by the train became part of the composition, a futurist rendering of an icon on the point of disappearance. Gradually, I built up a library of images; their infinite repetitions, rearranging the same shapes in a landscape again and again, somehow reminded me of the still lives of the Italian painter Giorgio Morandi, endlessly shuffling his collection of bottles and vases on a shelf. Still lives, snatched at speed; looking at them one after another on my laptop, each a record of a few seconds culled from hundreds of days, produces in me a vertiginous feeling, as if I was replaying a single moment of my life over and over again.

It is perhaps not widely known that Didcot A is the work of a leading modernist architect, Sir Frederick Gibberd. Once voted the worst eyesore in Britain, it has come to be held in affection by many of those who live closest to it (as well as by those, like me, whose lives have somehow been shaped by passing it every day). Gibberd was more than an architect; he was also an evangelist for the centrality of architecture to culture and for the importance of the modernist movement of which he was a part. As early as 1938 he wrote a book called *The Architecture of England from Norman Times to the Present Day* that was an attempt to popularise his ideas for a general audience. Long out of print, it is written in pithy, staccato sentences that vibrate with optimism for the future, employing extensive integrated illustration rather in the manner of Le Corbusier's *Towards a New Architecture*. 'Like most authors who do not write primarily for a living,' he admits, 'I have an axe to grind. It has two edges. The first is this. If you understand the evolution of English architecture you will do all in your power to encourage its further growth in the Modern movement ... The second edge to the axe is that the more you appreciate English architecture the less it will be destroyed.' Like all modernists of his generation, Gibberd particularly appreciated buildings in which form followed function. He writes well in *The Architecture of England* about the construction of railway stations in the 19th century, and the way in which the use of iron and glass created 'a thin skin that keeps out the weather and keeps in the light'. For the creators of such buildings he coins a new term. 'When an engineer is gifted with a sense of form he is an architect. During the 19th century a few great engineers possess this aesthetic sense, and to distinguish them from those not so gifted and from the architects who employed themselves in reviving past styles, I have called them "architect engineers" ... They design with keenly analytical minds unencumbered with nostalgia for the past.' This quality, one we are left in little doubt by his book he aspired to himself, he attributes to Brunel; Paddington station is one of three examples singled out in his list of 'Buildings to See' at the foot of the page.

Among Gibberd's other projects were Liverpool Metropolitan Cathedral, colloquially known as Paddy's Wigwam; Harlow New Town; the InterContinental hotel at Hyde Park Corner in London; the original terminal at Heathrow airport; and the Central London Mosque in Regent's Park in London. For Gibberd, the mosque was another opportunity to explore the balance between a building and its environment, its relation to the park, the Nash terraces that bordered it and the view of its dome through the trees. The building had special significance for me at another time in my life. I lived on the edge of Regent's Park as a student and often used to cut across it when returning to my lodgings in the early hours, having mastered the art of scaling the railings that surrounded it. At such times I would be entranced by the mournful howling of wolves from London Zoo and, as dawn approached and the shape of the mosque emerged from the mist, by the muezzin's call, drifting over the already rumbling streets. Strange that two buildings by a single architect, whose identity was unknown to me for years, should have been part of my daily rituals in such different settings. The power station swiftly acquired the nickname the 'Cathedral of the Vale', giving it quasi-religious status. The architect of one cathedral by design had become that of another by popular decision. It is tempting to think the sinuous lines of Didcot's cooling towers fed into both the curved roof of Paddy's Wigwam and the dome of the mosque in Regent's Park, buildings powered by different energies that are nonetheless as central to current geopolitics as power generation itself.

It is no coincidence that the power station is visible from the train. Didcot A was sited here, at a junction at the centre of the national rail network, so that coal could be shipped to it from mines in the east Midlands. On arrival, it was shipped by conveyor belt to the pulverising mill, where it was crushed to dust by steel balls, each a ton in weight. When British coal was deemed to contain too much sulphur it was replaced by coal from Bolivia, shipped across the Atlantic to Bristol, at what overall benefit to the environment it is hard to say, once again completing its journey by train to Didcot. A branch line to the station brought in the coal in hoppers that discharged their load automatically. The conveyor belt from the loading bunkers to the furnace was two and a half miles long.

In 2008, the European Union set new limits for power stations on the emission of sulphur dioxide, nitrogen oxides and dust particulates, in legislation called the Large Combustion Plant Directive. To meet these targets a station designed in the 1960s would need either to be retro-fitted with costly technologies to control its emissions or to switch to burning non-polluting fuels. The only other course open under the legislation was to opt out; stations that did so were given a final 20,000 hours' operating time before closure. On Friday 22 March 2013 the station ceased operation for the last time and the clean-up of the site began, a prelude to all the buildings being demolished. (Didcot B, the natural gas-powered station on an adjacent site, will continue operation.) For the time being, the towers remained: breathless, silent, somehow robbed of their aura along with their function, marking a fulcrum in the route where the track from Bristol swings east to London.

Of course, I feel no nostalgia for the burning of fossil fuels per se; the problems associated with coal-fired generation are well documented. However, the knowledge that something is destructive does not prevent us from appreciating its beauty. Part of this appreciation comes from its sheer scale: the distance between the two sets of cooling towers at Didcot was a mile. The thrill of the sublime, that mixture of awe and terror that poets and painters of previous generations experienced in rocky mountain gorges or in the face of an immense ocean, we now feel in concrete chasms of our own making, faced with monsters that have slipped beyond our control and turned to bite the hand that gave them life.

A week before the station closes I join what is to be the last public tour of the site. I cycle from the station at Didcot and report to the gatehouse that sits in the shadow of the three north towers. 'How will you feel when they come down?' I ask the middle-aged woman who signs me in, pointing through the window.

'I class them as my three kings,' she says. 'I feel safe, knowing they are there. You'll probably think I'm crazy, but I even try to get

Christmas cards with them on. When you go away from Didcot – say you go on a foreign holiday – when you see the smoke in the sky you know you are nearly home. What other landmark has the town got?'

We are a small group. The artists Barbaresi and Round are coming to the end of a residency at Didcot, during which they have uncovered many interesting documents in the station's archives. One is a series of black-and-white photographs of the site of the power station before it was built, taken by Gibberd from various viewpoints in the surrounding countryside, on to which he had drawn the shape of the as yet unbuilt cooling towers in black ink. This was how architects worked, before the advent of computer-aided design software – by putting themselves in the landscape, rather than allowing a machine to imagine it for them. A local filmmaker, photographer and writer, Martyn Bull, has traced all but one of the locations in the photographs and rephotographed them, including the built power station. Gibberd clearly thought long and hard about the visual impact of the station and considered its layout carefully. However, there is a further, probably apocryphal story that attributes another hand a role in its appearance. Apparently a model of the station before it was built was on display at the Royal Fine Art Commission, on which Gibberd served. The legend has it that the sculptor Henry Moore, also a member, happening to walk by, paused a moment to rearrange the layout of the towers. It is a lovely thought; the artist, so used to working from maquette to monumental scale and to considering the impact of sculptural form on the landscape, makes a readjustment; the architect, himself a collector of contemporary art and sculpture and owner of works by Moore, accepts his intervention gracefully and turns it into reality. If the story is true, Didcot A was Henry Moore's largest sculpture.

It is Rachel Barbaresi, of Barbaresi and Round, who has invited me to join the visit, along with Martyn, who is keen to capture some final sound recordings and images. We don hard hats and protective goggles and set off in a minibus. Our guide is a woman who has been taking tours around the site for the past 20 years; the fact that this may well be the last one she leads adds to the poignancy for her and triggers reminiscences. The first place we stop off is at the foot of one of the southern cooling towers. Each tower stands on stilts. Inside them a continual waterfall cascades downwards into a deep pool. Didcot A had a licence to take up to 45 million gallons a day from the Thames to reduce the ferociously high temperatures at the plant. River water was directed along concrete channels that fed a network of pipes cooling the high-pressure turbine, before completing its journey by falling through the cavernous interiors of the towers. Cooling towers rely on something called the Venturi effect: air is sucked up through the tower structure, by a combination of their curved shape and the fact that moist air naturally rises. As it does so it cools the falling water. The pools attract heron that come searching for the fish inhabiting the eerie space beneath the cascade. How the fish get there is something of a mystery; they clearly haven't swum up the channels, negotiating the various filters built into the system. The most likely explanation is that fish eggs attached themselves to the herons' legs while they stalked the shallows of nearby ponds and rivers in search of prey and were released when the herons made speculative visits to the power station; a perilous form of public transport, on a par with human infants hitching a ride with a mass murderer. Once the falling water cooled sufficiently it was fed back into a relic of an earlier technological age, a ninth-century channel that runs through the site known as Moor Ditch. Along this ancient waterway it returned to the river – excepting, of course, that part of itself, as much as 13 million gallons a day, that emerged from the tops of the towers as cloud, a ghost river drifting on a course of its own.

Inside the coal unloading house built over the railway track, the control panel for the extractor fans in the roof is coated in a thick layer of black dust. We climb the steps of the tower where a man is still employed to keep an eye on the huge coal yard. A million tons of coal was stored here at any one time; in these last days of the station's operation, it is being ordered in a single trainload at a time, making a tiny black pile in acres of ebony, crisscrossed by the tracks of yellow and red caterpillar vehicles that now stand parked and silent in a row. From his eyrie the man points to a line of hills in the distance that have been hidden from view by stockpiles of coal the entire time he has worked at the station. We wander the walkways of the vast turbine hall, a cathedral awaiting its Reformation, looking down on a forest of pipes here and there emitting a plume of steam, and the vast generator, boiler and turbines that mysteriously convert the dark matter of pulverised coal into power and light. In the main control room a handful of men in boilersuits sit in front of arrays of dials, switches, buttons, warning lights and levers that look impossibly antiquated, lifted from a Bond villain's lair. Others gaze from high-backed swivel chairs lit by the blue glow of large illuminated screens, their job simply to watch, hour after hour, keeping a visual check on the plant's operation. One man introduces himself; he has worked at the plant for the past 35 years. 'They put the computers in during the 1980s,' he tells us, with a dismissive wave at the screens. 'I preferred it when it was all manual.' He walks to the desk and puts his hand on a toggle lever. 'You could feel what you were doing then. A little movement like this' – he twitches the lever to the right for a second – 'you knew that was 30 tons of coal.'

II

The first visible stage of the demolition of the power station will be the destruction of the three northern cooling towers closest to the town.

Unsurprisingly, there is a high degree of interest in the timing of the 'blowdown' and many people are determined to watch the towers fall. It soon becomes apparent that RWE npower, the operators of the plant, have no interest in making the erasure of Didcot's best-known landmark a public event; the deadline they finally announce is between three and five in the morning on 27 July 2014. The news that the demolition has been scheduled to take place during the night causes a great deal of comment and protest in the area. The distinctive profiles of the towers have loomed over the town for the past four and a half decades and are bound up with its sense of itself, not least because so many of Didcot's inhabitants have depended on the livelihood the station provided to support their families. Former employees have spoken of the sense of solidarity and community they found within the perimeter fence of the station. At the same time, what they produced – energy – was invisible. The countless thousands of tons of coal that have arrived by rail to be pulverised into dust and burnt have been transformed into – what? Workers at the car factory a few miles down the line in Cowley could see the results of their labour on the roads around their neighbourhood, but those at Didcot had nothing so tangible to show for the hours they put in at the power station. The towers, therefore, along with the huge columns and cloud formations of water vapour they emitted, visible for miles around, gave a physical expression to the activity of their lives. Those with a working knowledge of the station would know how to read their aerial calligraphy, be able to deduce from them how much energy was being produced. Even though they stood on a private and closely protected site, the towers were very public, the signals they sent up part of the visual landscape for many thousands of people, from local residents to those walking the hills, speeding past on trains, in cars or in planes flying overhead. Surely the moment of their disappearance should be public also?

An online petition started by a Didcot resident asking for the demolition to be moved to 6 a.m. swiftly gathers 3,000 signatures and the support of the local member of parliament, but the company responsible for the demolition are adamant that safety factors must make this impossible. 'We entirely recognise that many people would want to see the cooling tower blowdown,' a spokesman states, 'but it isn't advisable given the nature of explosive demolition and the unknown weather conditions on the day, which could affect the direction of the resultant dust cloud. Clearly, the more people that turn up to see an activity such as this, the more difficult it is to ensure the safety of those attending.' The developers of a partially completed housing estate called Great Western Park, which is located on a raised site in the town overlooking the power station, initially offer a space as a viewing point for the community; then, apparently under pressure from the demolition contractors, they withdraw the offer. However, on the grapevine we learn that residents of the estate are being provided with letters to allow them access to the estate after it is closed off. As only one, standard letter is being sent to each house, photocopies are soon in circulation, and it proves fairly easy to obtain the documentation we hope will provide us free passage to a good viewing position on the night in question.

On the Friday preceding the demolition, Martyn and I take a walk around Didcot in burning sunshine, checking out viewing spots. The central role the railway played in shaping the town is still apparent in its layout. Effectively, the station divided the settlement into two: the original Old Didcot, with its hybrid Romanesque-Norman church, handful of substantial houses and farm workers' cottages to the west and the new town, developed after the arrival of the railway, to the east. Such was Didcot's insignificance as a rural village at the time the railway was built that the spelling of its name had not even been formalised. In contemporary correspondence and newspaper articles it is variously referred to as Dudcot, Didcot and Dudcote; it was the opening of Didcot Junction station (as it was first known) that permanently fixed the town's name, just as the station clock set the watch of anyone in the neighbourhood prosperous enough to own one. Didcot's primary function in Brunel's plan was as an important interchange between lines – not many farm workers would be making excursions to London – but his eye was also on profitable freight. To increase paid traffic he constructed Station Hill, connecting the station to the nearby turnpike road. Ever the complete planner, he was aware that those employed by the railway would need somewhere to live. As early as 1846 he drew elevations of '4 Room Cottages to be built in pairs' for railway staff, which were eventually constructed 40 years later, red-brick terraces which, along with houses by local speculators, remain a distinctive feature of the town. Landlords were able to charge more for these new houses than for accommodation in the old village that surrounded the church, meaning only railway workers could rent them. The two communities became increasingly divided.

This small town, then, bears the imprint of two 'architect engineers': Brunel and Gibberd. I can't help being struck by similarities between them. They both had a distinctive, somewhat flamboyant appearance: Brunel with his tall hat, cigar and curls spilling over his collar; the well-tailored Gibberd, the son a gentleman's outfitter in Coventry, with longish hair and a luxurious handlebar moustache. They both had to overcome physical frailty: Gibberd, as he told an interviewer, 'made a hobby of going into hospital' after contracting rheumatic fever as a child and was no stranger to pain as an adult; while Brunel was injured numerous times during the course of his career, submitting himself to a schedule while working on the Great Western that, although it 'laid the foundations, or rather built the fabric, of his reputation', as his son put it, 'also undermined his constitution, and eventually shortened his life'.

Both men were artistically as well as technically gifted. Brunel's brother-in-law, the artist and Royal Academician J. C. Horsley, described him as having 'a remarkably accurate eye for proportion, as well as a taste for form. This is evinced in every line to be found in his sketchbooks, and in all the various features of his architectural works.' Gibberd believed in the magical process that happened on the page. 'I think most brilliant engineering is not done on a computer,' he told Roy Plomley on *Desert Island Discs* in August 1983. 'You start with a blank piece of paper and you haven't a clue what is going to happen. It's a marvellous adventure. Suddenly you get a brainwave and you almost fancy you feel divinity within you breeding wings, to quote Milton ... That is the distinction between art and technology.' As well as being gifted draughtsmen, both were passionate about collecting the art of their contemporaries. Brunel's house in Duke Street, London, which was subsequently demolished, was filled with rare furniture, china, bronzes, elaborately carved fireplaces and doorways, silk hangings and Venetian mirrors. In the late 1840s he commissioned a series of paintings on Shakespearean themes for his dining room at Duke Street, the engine room of his active social life. Those he invited to contribute included some of the leading painters of the modern British school: Edwin Landseer, Augustus Leopold Egg, C. W. Cope, Clarkson Stanfield and Charles Robert Leslie. Typically, his ambition for his scheme went far beyond domestic decoration. In the first place, the acquisition of art was an outward sign of success, confirmation of his status as a gentleman at a time when the profession of engineer was still establishing its place in the social order. Secondly, he intended to create a collection of national interest, connecting England's great cultural past with its current generation of artistic innovators. Several artists declined Brunel's invitation, perhaps wary of the engineer's reputation for micromanaging all he commissioned; among them was William

Powell Frith, who a little over a decade later was to create his own tribute to Brunel's world in *The Railway Station*.

Frederick Gibberd also collected art. Less wealthy than Brunel, he concentrated on works he could afford, buying watercolours by living British artists. Over time he built up a remarkable collection of works on paper by leading figures including John Piper, Edward Bawden, Paul Nash, Elizabeth Blackadder and Victoria Crowe.

From the station we climb the hill towards the church and the few remaining buildings of Old Didcot. At Great Western Park, metal fencing is already being assembled in preparation for the following night. We walk through the eerily quiet estate to where a brand-new children's playground overlooks the cooling towers. The playground is full of the latest equipment: a wooden climbing frame with a rope net, swings and seesaws, a roundabout, all standing on some kind of bright yellow artificial shock-absorbing material traversed by a path outlined in a swirl of blue, like a river running through a desert. The composition is completed by the inclusion of picnic tables and a scattering of large rocks, reference perhaps to the prehistoric sites characteristic of the area. Standing in front of the industrial landscape of the power station, the playground looks like another, smaller energy factory, chock-full of the machinery of leisure. This is clearly where we want to be when the charges ignite.

In the bright afternoon sunlight the estate looks startlingly new, yet its architecture is firmly based on the past. Some houses even have Georgian-style porches, bolted on to their facades. Brunel, as we have seen, was involved in the creation of new housing for railway employees; at Swindon, his sketches fed into Digby Wyatt's designs of cottages, amenities and the layout of an entire workers' village. The development at Swindon also alluded to the past in the 'nostalgic' Victorian manner so despised by a modernist like Frederick Gibberd, whose most significant contribution to the British landscape was the design of a new town at Harlow in Essex. Both Brunel and Gibberd intended in their later years to live in houses where there was space to explore their interest in landscape on a larger scale. Brunel purchased an estate at Watcombe in Devon, amid countryside he had fallen in love with while prospecting the GWR line and where he planned to commission a house and lay out its grounds. His sketchbooks suggest he was also going to install his collection of paintings in a specially designed room in the house, but pressures of work dogged him relentlessly and the engineer's early death closed the door on the Shakespeare Room for ever. Frederick Gibberd was more fortunate. He demonstrated his commitment to his own architectural ideas by moving to Harlow, the town for which he had created the master plan, living in a house with a seven-acre garden that, together with his wife Patricia, he spent his remaining years designing and filling with sculpture.

It is 2 a.m. on Sunday morning. The inhabitants of Didcot do not seem to have obeyed instructions to either stay within their homes or view the explosion from a safe distance. Many are holding 'blowdown barbecues' in their gardens, making the most of the warm weather. A sizable crowd has already assembled at the bridge over the railway at Foxhall Road. I had considered the bridge as a possible location for historical reasons. Firstly, this was where the inhabitants of Didcot assembled in 1840 to watch the first train thunder through the station at a terrifying 30 miles an hour, a messenger from the future. Secondly, it will not offer itself as a vantage point for much longer: it is scheduled to be swept away in the coming electrification of the line, as it is too low to accommodate the new, larger trains that will arrive once the process is completed.

We leave our car in a side street to walk to Great Western Park, trying to look as though we are casually returning from a late-night drink despite being weighed down with tripods and camera bags.

Security men in high-visibility vests guard a gateway in the security fencing. Martyn asks one of them politely to let us through. 'Residents?' I assure him we are and fumble in my pocket, bringing out the folded photocopy of the letter. 'Oh, in that case we can't keep you out,' he says, grinning and waving us past the barrier without bothering to look at it. Was that a conspiratorial wink he gave me? We hadn't thought it would be so easy. We walk through the estate down to the vantage point next to the playground, where a crowd is gathering. The towers are floodlit and show grey-blue and ghostly against the night sky. In the playground a group of young men have swung themselves to the top of the climbing frame, their hooded silhouettes picked out against the towers. Others are sitting on swings or spinning slowly on a roundabout. Some people have brought deckchairs and blankets. A group of young men sit around a table stacked with beer, while half a dozen Filipino women sit on the ground. One holds up a parasol, blooming like a pale flower in the dim light, presumably as protection against the predicted rain of dust. We find a position for our tripods among the swiftly expanding plantation of cameras in front of the playground and settle down to wait.

It is 3 a.m.; a man draws our attention to the international space station blinking across the sky above our heads. (The power station it is passing over was completed a year before the first men walked on the moon.) 'It will be visible for three minutes,' the man tells us, consulting an app on his phone. We might glimpse it again in 90 minutes' time on its next circumnavigation, if it is not too light by then. Martyn, whose trade demands he is informed on such matters, tells me that nautical dawn will be at 3.41 today and that dawn itself is scheduled for 4.38. The later the demolition happens, the more he will capture on film.

The crowd in the park is steadily growing; clearly not all those present can be residents of the estate any more than we are. An ex-army man stops to talk to a group sitting behind us. He's worked on big demolitions in his time, handled detonators. 'They're always grumpy, the guys that do it,' he tells his friends. 'Drilling holes in concrete all day. The explosives give them a headache.' He's had a text from a friend in the police force, telling him the demolition will be at 4 a.m. There will be a warning siren 15 minutes before the blast. Someone else knows someone working in demolition in the Midlands who knows someone on the Didcot job, who confirms the blowdown will be at four 'on the dot'. Quarter to four comes and goes with no siren. One of the young men who have been drinking keeps falling asleep and then waking up and asking if his mates have seen the explosion. 'They're still there,' they tell him. 'God, it's like watching paint dry,' he complains, putting his head back on the table. The sky is brightening, streaked with herringbone cloud, and the towers are becoming more and more solid. At 4.45 the siren finally goes off. A drone enters the sky from the east, flashing purple and red like a Technicolor butterfly, positioning itself for the best shot. It is soon joined by two others that ascend from Great Western Park. Shortly before 5 a.m. there is a warning shot, intended to clear the chimneys of wildlife. A few seconds later there is a flash at the foot of the towers, followed instantly by a loud crack and a roar. I'm fumbling with my phone, trying to take pictures and see what is happening at the same time like everyone else, the contemporary condition. The central tower falls first, emitting a kind of smoke ring as it descends, a ghost image of itself that hangs for a second or two in the air, closely followed by those on either side, the clean lines of their geometry suddenly twisted and fluid, the mouths that for so long have pointed at the sky for a moment turned towards us in astonishment before all three crash to the ground in a spreading plume of dust that drifts towards the watchers on the bridge.

Demolition. Progress. Doubtless both Brunel and Gibberd would have enjoyed the moment, recognised the need to clear away these relics of an outdated technology, even if what will replace them is not yet clear.

ENCOUNTER

YOU ONLY HAVE TO GET LUCKY ONCE

In the buffet car a well-built man with an Australian accent is talking to a colleague who is travelling to the station where he will pick up his train. He must be off duty as he is wearing his own clothes. He ignores the swaying of the carriage, even as it negotiates the points where the line divides at Didcot, resting easily with his back against the wall and his feet firmly on the floor, well into the corridor. He is tall enough to have to stoop slightly beneath the curvature of the roof of the carriage. On the wall at his elbow is a poster that details the kind of treatment routinely meted out to railway personnel by the public. 'We will not tolerate verbal abuse, threatening behaviour or physical assaults on our staff,' it reads. By coincidence, such incidents are exactly what he is discussing with his colleague.

He doesn't appear surprised when I introduce myself and explain my project, and is happy to tell me about his work. He is a Revenue Protection Inspector; RPIs, as they are called, are employed in addition to regular staff and make unscheduled appearances to check on the validity of people's tickets. Their role can make them unpopular with the regular fare-paying public, let alone with those wishing to evade payment altogether. Customer bulletin boards are full of stories of overzealous inspectors enforcing heavy fines on confused and vulnerable pensioners; how many of these are apocryphal it is hard to tell. This man works a stretch of line running through the Vale of Evesham, the West Country's market garden, towards Worcester. 'People think it must be a peaceful place where only farmers and retirees live,' he says, 'where there hasn't been any trouble for hundreds of years. But it isn't quite like that.'

It seems there is a category of passengers, mainly male, aged between the ages of 14 and 25, who have no intention of paying for a ticket and respond to any challenge with the threat of violence. 'They square up to you,' he tells me. 'They say, "We're not paying and if you come near us we'll hit you." I usually tell them, "If you're going to do something, go ahead and do it. I'll get a few weeks off to recover, a bit of extra holiday, and you'll get the law on your tail." Given the size of me, that shuts most of them up. It's all bravado with most of them. I had one the other day, who shoved his face right in mine when I asked for a ticket and said, "I'm not paying – what are you going to do about it?" I said, "You can either buy a ticket from my colleague here or we can take it further: I'll take down your details and we can prosecute you for fare evasion." Of course, they never give you their right names or addresses. He said, "I'll be waiting for you outside the station." I told him, "Fine, I'm going to be getting a wash and changing my clothes, then in about half an hour I'll be coming out to get a taxi. If you want to hit me you can do it then. But remember, there's cameras all over the place; it's up to you." He wasn't there when I came out. But if you show people like that fear they are going to run with it.'

Is the abuse you get alcohol-related? I ask. Does it mostly happen after the pubs close?

'No. We get a lot of trouble in the middle of the day, not so much in the mornings or the evenings when it's busy. Last week I had three lads who were travelling from Pershore to Evesham during the day. When I asked to see their tickets they said I was just picking on them because of the colour of their skin. I said, "Look, mate, the only colour I'm interested in is the orange of your ticket. If you haven't got one you'll have to buy one." They said, "Come near us and we'll hit you." So I said, "Go ahead and hit me then." I'm quite sizable, so that helps. Some of my colleagues who are a bit smaller or skinnier get shoved around. We need to keep reporting these incidents to show where the trouble spots are ... The worst is being the only RPI on a train at night. Sometimes the police just stick their trouble on a train and I'm like, look mate, there's only one of me, how am I supposed to sort it out?'

I guess this kind of thing goes with the territory in your job, I say. Does it prey on your mind when you leave work? Does it stay with you?

'No, not really. Maybe I stay steamed up for an hour or two, then I just let it go. We're lucky, there's not much knife crime in our area, not like the places some of my colleagues work. It's like they tell you in training: you've only got to get lucky once to catch them – they've got to be lucky all the time. If someone gives you a hard time once and gets away with it, the next time you see them you can stop them getting on the train. That's a win. If you can't take their money, at least you can inconvenience them.'

We shake hands as he and his colleague get off at Reading and he smiles, the frown that had stayed on his face when he was talking about the challenges of his job disappearing. He is well qualified to take on railway bandits, I decide. His rugby player's physique and humorous, characteristically Australian response to male aggression must be a uniquely baffling combination for the small-town bullies he encounters in the English countryside. Once again the railway carriage fulfils its function as a microcosm of society, this time revealing things about us that perhaps we would rather not know.

DIVERSION: OXFORD
PLOTTING ROUTES AND SENSING SOULS

'Can anything be more eternally immutable than Oxford Station?'
asked Kenneth Grahame, in his essay 'Oxford Through a Boy's Eyes'.[48]

Berlin, Vienna, have built, and re-built, and built again, their
monumental stations. Hundreds of feet below the surface of
London, stations have sporadically spread after the manner of
mushroom spawn. I have even lived to see Waterloo Station
reconstructed and re-built. But Oxford Station never varies and
today is exactly as it flashed upon my eager vision in [18] '68.
That it has been re-painted since then I know, for I was once
staying in Oxford when this happened, and used to go specially
to gaze at the man told off for the job, and admire his deliberate
brushwork and the lingering care with which he would add a
touch and then step back to admire it. But even then, when he
had at last done, the station looked exactly as before.

What a tribute this is to the station itself and its designer!
Had there been anything needed to achieve perfection, this, of
course, would have been added long ago. But nothing has ever
been added, so nothing can have been needed, and Oxford
Station, in its static perfection, will be there to greet him as
now, when the proverbial stranger comes to gaze on ruins of
Christ Church from a broken arch of Folly Bridge.

If Grahame had returned to Oxford station at the beginning of 1999 in order to check up on the painting job, he would have found its 'static perfection' had not lasted quite as long as he imagined it would. The GWR station had been replaced with an undistinguished structure built in the 1970s and 'improved' in 1990, with the addition of a bridge. The adjoining station for the 'Varsity Line' to Cambridge, situated on Rewley Road, despite having received Grade II listing in recognition of its architectural importance, was under threat. Since the line to Cambridge had been closed in 1967, the building had been put to commercial use. In a surprise ruling in 1998, the environment secretary John Prescott ruled that despite its listing it could be demolished and removed from the site entirely to make way for a new business school, along with the plane trees that graced its forecourt, without recourse to a public inquiry. Grahame's wandering shade would have encountered protesters handing out leaflets to those arriving to board trains. Others, like characters from the Wild Wood in *The Wind in the Willows* perhaps, had occupied the old station building and built shelters in the trees, from which vantage points they monitored the movements of their enemies.

The protesters at the station were not just tree-huggers (the derogatory term used at the time to describe those calling for a radical green alternative) or railway preservationists; there was widespread concern in the city that the business school due to be built on the site, part of the University of Oxford, was being funded by the billionaire Saudi-Syrian businessman, Wafic Saïd. Saïd had brokered the controversial al-Yamamah arms procurement deal between the Thatcher government and Saudi Arabia, an agreement that encapsulated a persistent theme in British foreign policy towards the Middle East; allegations of corruption surrounding the deal were sidelined, allowing jet fighters, missiles and other weaponry to be traded directly in return for barrels of crude oil. In the face of such synergies of global interests, local concerns about the erasure of history were swiftly brushed aside.

Transport infrastructure, of course, needs to constantly adapt and mutate to accommodate the changing needs of travellers. Passenger numbers at Oxford are set to continue increasing, particularly with a new connection to London Marylebone opening soon and the proposed reopening of part of the Varsity Line. Did the Victorian station at Rewley Road merit preservation? It was constructed with a single, double-faced platform partially covered with a roof designed by Sir Charles Fox of Messrs Fox & Henderson, who worked on both the vast exhibition hall erected in Hyde Park for the Great Exhibition and Brunel's station at Paddington. As historian Richard Morris has written, Oxford was 'a kind of remote vestibule to the Crystal Palace, employing the same innovatory techniques of system building, ornament and glazing'.[49] Although low in height, its use of prefabricated cast-iron pillars and its glazed atrium spoke of its connection to the cutting-edge architecture of the mid-19th century. Perhaps Mr Prescott felt the developer's promise to reconstruct the original station buildings in a railway museum in rural Buckinghamshire was sufficient to satisfy local concern. Such Disneyesque solutions carry little weight with archaeologists or serious historians. To quote Richard Morris again: 'The uprooting of a unique building from the neighbourhood it helped to create will impoverish that neighbourhood. Exiled to rural surroundings in another county, it will be a pitiable object. But left where it stands, Rewley Road station could [have] again become what it was: a gateway in time and place, wherein the innovatory technology of one great age could be confederated with that of our own.'

On this occasion, the university had no compunction about discarding a visible symbol of the city's – and arguably the nation's – past. Of course, university authorities had also opposed the coming of the railway to Oxford in the first place, worried that it might 'imperil the morals of their students', and had held the nearest station at bay 10 miles outside the city at Steventon until 1844. So determined were they to protect the aforementioned morals that special clauses were added to the bill for the Oxford Railway Company of 1843, for the preservation of university discipline. The vice-chancellor, 'Proctors or Proprotors, Heads of Colleges and Halls or their deputies and the Marshal of the University' were granted access to stations at train times in order to check 'whether any members of the University were travelling or attempting to do so'; in addition, it was proposed the company be forbidden to convey any member of the university 'below the degrees of Master of Arts or Bachelor of Civil Law', even if they had paid their fare, introducing a degree of complexity to ticket inspection unseen before or since.

Anyone present at the station just before dawn on 9 September 1999 would have seen the joint machinery of academe and state move into action to end the standoff. By the time I arrived to catch a train a few hours later, 'law and order' had been restored; policemen were chatting with the university's own security guards, a private army deployed to protect the site of the proposed business school. They stood among the wreckage of what appeared to have been a minor hurricane. The trees had not so much been felled as snapped off, presumably with the help of heavy machinery, their split and jagged trunks still a man's height above the ground. These stumps, as well as a few shell-shocked protesters, kept their vigil for a few more days, before all sign they had ever been there disappeared.

· Oxford is a city with an international profile and an ancient university, but a relatively small (if rapidly growing) population of 150,000 or so. Compare this with the number of visitors who come to the city each year. *Nine and a half million.* Over a million more people than live in New York City or Greater London travel to Oxford annually to gawp at its architecture, traipse through its colleges, board its tourist buses, eat its indifferent sandwiches, marvel at the quaintness of its alleys and cobbled backstreets and try their hand at its ancient forms of self-propelled river transport. As an anonymous and satirical author wrote in 1894, 'it is gratifying to observe that, whether or not the University succeeds in its educational mission, it leaves nothing to be desired as a place of amusement for the jaded pleasure-seeker'.[50] A sizable proportion of the visitors attracted to the city arrive through the portal of the station on Botley Road. In addition to this traffic, nearly a third of Oxford's inhabitants commute elsewhere for their jobs, many of them to London. For these travellers the station at Oxford is a kind of second home, its staff paid-up members of an extended family shepherding us to and from our destination each day.

Providing information to commuters, who at least know where they are going if not always how they are going to get there, is one thing; providing help to those unfamiliar with the English language or the workings of the British transport system quite another. John is in his 60s, Oxford born and bred, and has been working on the information desk at the station as long as I have been travelling through it. In effect, he and his colleagues are the face Oxford presents to the world that arrives at its door. Like many of those who work on the railway today, John has family connections with the industry going back two generations. As he spoke I felt his memories establishing a visceral connection with a time when the railway was still young.

'My grandfather was a steam-train driver, my dad was a fireman, that's the guy who stokes the trains; I had two uncles who were signalmen as well, so I've come full circle by working on the railway. My granddad lived in a two-up, two-down in Jericho [now a desirable area of north Oxford with small terraced cottages, originally built to house workers in the iron and printing industries]. It was a slum in those days.

'He had 18 kids, my granddad. Food was scarce. He always had a shotgun with him, so did my uncles. So if he saw a hare or a rabbit when he was driving the train he'd shoot it, stop the train, go back and pick it up and then carry on. That was a marvellous nutritional meal!'

'He had racing pigeons, too. A working-class sport, pigeon racing. When a pigeon got to a certain age and he was doing shunting on his engine he'd take it three miles from home and then let it go. When it got a bit older he'd take it further. Perfect training. By the time it came to the race he had the best pigeons going!'

It is hard now to imagine a time when an engine driver could take a shotgun, or a crate of pigeons, into his cab, or reverse his train in order to pick up a dead hare. Despite the strength of his family connections, John didn't follow tradition by going straight into working for the railway when he left school. For six years he worked for the council, building roads. Then he spent time in the car factory at Cowley, on the production line, before getting a job in a paper mill on the Thames at Wolvercote, 'the oldest paper mill in the world. It closed, which was sad. It had been going about 700 years!' This seemed to provoke a change in direction, into jobs dealing with people: the homeless, the mentally ill, foreign students – all ideal places to learn skills necessary to deal with the flow of customer enquiries at a busy station.

Our conversation is conducted in fits and starts as a stream of visitors approaches the information desk. Signalling problems on this particular day are causing congestion on the line and a number of cancellations are beginning to show on the information board above our heads. Confused and harassed passengers, many from overseas, are trying to work out how they will get to their destinations on time. 'What do you mean, cancelled?' an irate man asks, placing his ticket on the desk in front of John. 'How will I get to Bognor Regis?' John taps at his keyboard, searching out alternative connections. 'Bognor Regis,' he says ruminatively. 'That's what I call it when a man goes to the toilet. When a woman goes, I call it Lyme Regis.' The man snorts with laughter; John's surreal patter seems to have defused his anger. A businesswoman has just realised her secretary has included her seat reservation rather than her ticket in the material she was handed on leaving the office – can she use it to travel? Unfortunately not. She withdraws to make an urgent phone call and after some time reappears with the correct ticket, only to find her train has just pulled out. Yes, she will have to buy another ticket, as her seat was booked on a particular train and at a particular time. She is going to miss her meeting in London. She maintains an icy calm but I don't envy her secretary's chances of promotion.

During a brief interlude between enquiries, I ask John whether he remembers any particularly dramatic incidents at the station.

'About 10 years ago,' he says, 'it was a foggy night, really foggy. A train had just left Platform 2 going north and it had some sort of mechanical problem, so they told him to pull in the sidings and they'd call an engineer. In the sidings there's a place where the drivers and the cleaners can get a cup of tea and he probably thought he'd go and join them. He was only about 26 years old, this driver. It was so foggy and dank he got disorientated and he ended up falling in the canal. They had to come out with a police helicopter with a heat-seeking device to find him. Although he'd only been in the water a short time he got hypothermia and they had to rush him to the John Radcliffe hospital.'

Before I can ruminate on how many stories I have discovered on my journey that have involved people falling, cycling, diving into, being baptised or nearly drowning in water, a woman approaches the desk who is trying to get to Shrewsbury, despite the cancellations that continue to appear on the departures board. 'Shrewsbury – that's a nice part of the world,' John mutters as he looks at his screen.

Do you find yourself imagining the destinations these people are going to? I ask him when she has gone.

'When I joined the railways you had to go on a route-learning course,' he explains. 'It was a good way to go around and see the area. I do it through books as well. When I read a Thomas Hardy book I think of Dorset. With Dylan Thomas it's New Quay, Laugharne and Swansea. I've been to Edinburgh for the Inspector Rebus novels. I love Edinburgh, it's my second-favourite city after Oxford. With Nottingham and Derby it would be Alan Sillitoe and *Saturday Night and Sunday Morning*. I find characters – even fictional characters – make you appreciate a place more. When you walk down the street you can sense the souls as I call it, the history.'

'Sensing the souls' seems a good description of what I am trying to do on my travels, and I am grateful to John for it. There are two souls in particular who haunt my thoughts.

Kenneth Grahame attended St Edward's school in Oxford, where he was head boy and distinguished himself both on the sports field and in his academic work. It is clear he could have gone on to a place at Oxford University, something he set his heart on, but his guardian was not prepared to finance his studies. Instead, Grahame went to work in the Bank of England, beginning as a 'gentleman clerk' and becoming its youngest ever secretary at the age of 39. Grahame 'lost' Oxford, just as he lost the youth he spent 'messing around in boats' on the banks of the Thames. One vanished world he attempted to recapture through his literary creations, including *Pagan Papers* and *The Wind in the Willows*. The other he hoped to experience vicariously through his son, Alastair, who he was determined would study at Oxford University. Alastair's life was not easy. Born premature, blind in one eye and with a severe squint in the other, he seems to have had a number of both physical and emotional problems. His parents gave him the nickname 'Mouse'. His behaviour at school and with other children was disruptive, loud, sometimes violent. At the same time he had a voracious appetite for being read stories, as well as powerful creative urges of his own – he had dictated a three-act play before he could read or write himself and was described by one who knew the family as 'a baby who had swallowed a dictionary'. He loved dressing up and longed to run away with the circus, a fantasy shared by his father, trapped in his routine job at the Bank. Aged seven, Mouse rejected his zoomorphic nickname and announced he had changed his name to Robinson; his father began addressing the letters he sent him accordingly. Rather than confronting his behaviour, the boy's parents shared a fantasy their son was an eccentric genius.

The Wind in the Willows began as tales told to Alastair, continued in the form of letters when he was sent away to the seaside with his governess. The epistolary versions of the stories have a more overtly moralistic streak than the final book.[51] Toad, to some extent at least, is Alastair: boastful, prone to acting on impulse, carried off by fantasy. Mole shares his short sight. Even the wicked weasels, perhaps, running wild in Toad Hall, echo some of his worst behaviour. (At least the anthropomorphised animal characters don't include a mouse.) Grahame's own life had been curtailed when he was forced to drop his studies and enter the Bank. His son would therefore live the life he wished he had lived himself. Alastair was given the finest hot-house education: sent first to public school at Rugby, he was removed after a few weeks and sent to Eton, where the pressure to achieve and fit in with the other boys drove him to a nervous breakdown. By pulling strings, the well-connected author secured a place for his troubled son at Christ Church, Oxford. Now Alastair could do what circumstances had prevented Grahame from doing and study at Britain's oldest university.

Neither father nor son has left a record explaining what happened to end Alastair's Oxford career, so perhaps it is legitimate to imagine what was going on in his mind. The young undergraduate would have been conscious of at least three versions of himself, none of which he could outrun. There was the one that existed in the ambitions of his father and the sentimental dreams of his mother – the talented but misunderstood genius-child whom they had nevertheless kept at arm's length for much of his childhood, particularly when he became difficult, with their separate holidays and his mother's hypochondria so often confining her to her bedroom, beyond his reach. There was the character he could now discern ruthlessly anatomised in his father's book, on display for all the world to see. And there was Alastair himself, squinting, physically clumsy, socially awkward, who found his academic work impossibly difficult yet couldn't tell his father he wanted to leave.

On an evening in May 1920 a fellow student noticed that Alastair took a glass of port with his evening meal in Hall, something he hadn't seen him do before. He then left college and walked to Port Meadow, the floodplain northwest of the city bordering the Thames, where commoners have for centuries grazed their livestock, a strange hinterland frequently underwater in winter months, attracting migratory birds and skating parties. A place of blurred boundaries, where perhaps he could struggle free of the constrictions that encircled him ever tighter within the walls of the university. He may have sat for a while beside the water, his mind half on the book in his pocket he was meant to revise for an exam the following day, which he had no hope of passing. Perhaps he was remembering the stories his father had told him about the river's inhabitants, half-human creatures that knew his joys and sorrows better than his fellow students would ever do. Perhaps, somewhere in the back of his mind, he heard an echo of Toad's conceited, delusional song, composed when he escaped from prison and evaded recapture by jumping from the footplate of a locomotive:

The clever men at Oxford
Know all that there is to be knowed.
But they none of them knew one half as much
As intelligent Mr. Toad!

It was two days before Alastair's 20th birthday. For him there was to be no escape. Leaving whatever hopes he had for the future behind him he went to the railway track, lay face down and waited for a train.

LOCATION: UFFINGTON

TUNING IN TO AN IRON-AGE BROADCAST

For a brief time between Swindon and Didcot the spine of the Berkshire Downs rises south of and parallel to the railway line. Formed from chalk laid down beneath the sea 150 million years ago from the powdered shells of molluscs and other small marine animals, their smooth, whale-like curves still speak of their oceanic origin. The Ridgeway, as the path that runs along their crest is known, once extended 400 miles from the Dorset coast to the Norfolk Wash, providing an elevated highway above the woods and marshes of the valleys. The thoroughfares of two civilisations face each other, across the plain. And then, at a certain point, the ancient flashes a signal to the modern, through time and distance: a system of communication that uses the material of the landscape itself, still functioning after millennia have rolled away, even to those travelling at a speed unimaginable to the people who carved their enigmatic totem on the hill.

On a good day, when the air and light are right, the White Horse of Uffington is clearly visible from the train, below the brow of the down – 374 feet long, its disjointed limbs take a moment or two to unfurl. On other days it is hard to see at all – a momentary splash of white against the turf, a brushstroke, a calligraphic sign. Either way, it is calling out, seeking attention – passengers in the train raising their heads for a few seconds from more recent forms of communication find themselves in conversation with a long-vanished people. This is a triumph of Bronze Age technology, still doing precisely what it was intended to do – a prehistoric broadcast, announcing 'We are here: you are entering our territory, the People of the Horse' – or, perhaps, 'Worship me – the Horse God'. Somehow, using techniques long lost to us, its creators were able to plot its shape so it is readable at a distance of miles. (Recent archaeological research has shown that gradually over the millennia, as it has been made and remade, the horse has 'climbed' the hill towards the flatter expanse at its summit, meaning it is less visible from a distance than it once was.) Close up, if you ascend to stand beside it, its visual logic disassembles, becoming as elusive as its meaning. Nevertheless, generations of locals have understood it well enough to find its eye, stand upon it, shut both their own and turn around three times before making a wish.

Near or far, the wonder is we can see it at all. 'His Head, Neck, Body and Tail consist of one white line, as does each of his Four legs,' wrote the Reverend Francis Wise in 1783, in his 'Letter to Dr Mead Concerning some Antiquities in Berkshire'. 'This is done by cutting a trench into the chalk about two or three feet deep and ten feet broad.' The trenches were filled with crushed chalk, but not sealed or buttressed against the elements. The horse only remains on the hillside, visible from the train, because for three thousand years (at the latest estimate) human beings have maintained and cared for it, repairing the results of erosion and the encroachment of grass and other vegetation. In the 18th and 19th centuries, the 'scouring' of the horse took place every seven years, on 17 and 18 September, and was preceded by a fair, or 'Pastime'. Booths and tents were erected on the hill and competitions held, the winners rewarded with prizes. Carthorse and donkey races, wrestling matches and sword fights were joined by more esoteric practices: gurning through a horse collar, chasing a cheese down a hill, and, in 1808, a women's smoking marathon, the prize of half a guinea or a gallon of gin offered to the woman able to smoke the most tobacco in an hour.

Uffington was king among the white horses of the West Country, but other, more recent carvings inspired equal loyalty among local inhabitants. Brunel's son Isambard Jr describes his father's reaction to one such monument as an illustration of 'his light and joyous disposition'. A Wiltshire village on the old Bath Road opposed the railway because they thought it would deprive them of profitable coach traffic. A hillside outside the village was the site of a horse that was the pride of the district (most likely the horse at Cherhill). Frustrated by their obstructive behaviour, one of Brunel's team of engineers suggested he should turn the troublesome villagers' horse into a steam locomotive. 'Brunel was much amused at the idea, and at once sketched off the horse from memory, roughly calculated its area, and arranged a plan for converting it into an engine,' Isambard Jr records. 'Ten picked men were to go down in two chaises, and by moonlight to peg and line out the new figure, and then cut away the turf, and with it cover up as much of the horse as may be left. From the tube was to issue a towering column of steam, and below was to be inserted in bold characters the offensive letters GWR.' Fortunately for the villagers, and possibly for Brunel's reputation, the joke was never carried through.

It probably shouldn't be a surprise that John Betjeman, most English of poets, made his home in Uffington from 1934 to 1945. It certainly feels a long way from Slough. It was to this village, with its thatched cottages, its ancient village shop and the church bells he learnt to ring, that he would return after working on the *Shell County Guides* at the Shell-Mex building in London on the South Bank of the Thames. Today the village is buried beneath the downs, accessible only by country roads. In Betjeman's day it had its own station on the main GWR line between Bristol and London, with another nearby at Challow Road, halts that have disappeared as completely as the people who carved the White Horse. So, as the cuts made to the railways in Britain in the 1960s following Dr Beeching's infamous reports demonstrate,[52] the promise of connectivity and its accompanying prosperity can be withdrawn as easily as it is granted, at the stroke of a pen.

The years Betjeman spent in Uffington were a time when England felt increasingly isolated by the rise of fascism in Europe and in need of nationalistic foundation myths of its own, around which its people could unite. The historian Arthur Bryant worked in a London school as a young man and was convinced the urban poor had been deprived of their birthright by not having experienced the English countryside. As long as they remained among 'the dark satanic mills' of the industrial city, he wrote in 1929, they could not be weaned from the dark forces of socialism. Only through reconnecting with the countryside's 'educative effect ... in the service of the state' would they find a place 'upon which the conservative heart of Everyman can cast anchor.'[53] Interest grew in the first half of the 20th century in Arthurian legends and other constructed mythologies. 'Never before have so many people been searching for England,' wrote H. V. Morton in 1927, a time when domestic tourism, thanks to the availability of affordable motorcars, was booming. Looking out from a hilltop across the mountains of Palestine, Morton experienced a nostalgic vision of 'a village street at dusk with a smell of wood smoke lying in the still air and, here and there, little red blinds shining in the dusk under the thatch'. (Give or take the colour of the blinds, he could have been describing Uffington.) This was, he remarks, 'the only religious moment I experienced in Jerusalem'.[54] Like all such revelations it encapsulates much. The move from 'abroad' to 'home'; from a politically volatile city to the stability of the countryside; from modernity to an apparently unchanging rural past. He admits, the England of his vision is not one he knows first-hand; he is a 'townsman'. But 'a little London factory hand' he has met has told him that the England he imagined he was fighting for in the first world war was not his street, or even his neighbourhood, but the green vastness of Epping Forest, a place he had visited on bank holidays; and so, Morton thinks, 'we all did'. Indeed, the verdant English countryside recalled from the perspective of the barren moonscape of the trenches is a recurrent motif in the poetry of the Great War.

For every Arthur Bryant who believed the working classes should be encouraged to visit the countryside, there were a dozen others who resented the intrusion of hikers, ramblers, trippers, trespassers, hostellers and other representatives of the lower orders, many of whom might be expected to arrive by train; they were, in the view of landowners, people who did not 'understand' the countryside – who were likely to drop litter, leave gates open and otherwise offend against its sacred rites. Their incursions, and the sense they were merely a vanguard of a greater invasion yet to come, gave added poignancy to literary depictions of a vanishing England.

The White Horse was a particular magnet for such mythologising. For many years it was thought to have been created on the orders of King Alfred of Wessex, to mark his victory over the Danes at the Battle of Ashdown in 871, allowing it to be co-opted into the story of nationhood. Of course, its origins lie much further back in time, as G. K. Chesterton acknowledged in the opening stanzas of *The Ballad of the White Horse*, written in 1911:

> *Before the gods that made the gods*
> *Had seen their sunrise pass,*
> *The White Horse of the White Horse Vale*
> *Was cut out of the grass.*

Before the gods that made the gods
Had drunk at dawn their fill
The White Horse of the White Horse Vale
Was hoary on the hill.

The very obscurity of the horse's origin suited literary mythologisers well. 'The chief value of legend is to mix up the centuries while preserving the sentiment; to see all ages in a sort of splendid foreshortening,' Chesterton explained in the introduction to his book-length poem. 'That is the use of tradition: it telescopes history.' By the mid-1930s one did not need a large telescope to see the old world was shifting. At such times a nation's writers turn inward, in search of sustaining myth. It is probably no coincidence that since the economic crash of 2008, writing that explores the rural British landscape has once again returned to the top of the bestseller lists. Some of its most notable examples are surprisingly devoid of political analysis, never questioning who owns the countryside; what agri-business is shaping it; or who has the right to walk in it, any more than the war poets who eulogised it from the perspective of the trenches had done. In this, of course, they are merely continuing a tradition established by 18th and 19th century landscape painters who cloaked the British countryside in a patina of classical grace, devoid of cow shit, mud and sweat. The reality of life for the rural poor in the railway age was somewhat different. An article in *The Saturday Review* of 16 January 1864 examines the proposition that the condition of the British poor is no better than that of the 'negro' slave in the Southern states of America. 'The slaves are separated from the whites by more glaring and ineffaceable marks of distinction', the article argues, but:

> ... distinctions and separations, like those of the English
> classes, which always endure, which last from the cradle to

the grave ... offer a very fair parallel to the separation of the slave from the whites. It is true that religion teaches the English gentleman not to despise the poor, and we recoil from that cruelty, as it seems to us, which prevents coloured people from riding with the white in American cars; but we must remember that we are not tried by any of the inconvenience which close contact with the poor would involve. If five farm labourers took five seats in a railway carriage, an English gentleman filling the sixth would find it hard to stand their smell, however benevolent and pious he might be; and it might have occurred to many attendants on the service of the English church that if the poor really came in the 'thronging numbers' which are invited, the building would reek with a stifling vapour.

Betjeman lived the dream promised by the GWR guidebooks of the 1920s, combining life in his rural idyll at Uffington with work in London. He also travelled widely on the railway, researching his guidebooks and visiting sites of architectural interest. His correspondence is full of rail journeys and complicated arrangements regarding the timing of meetings and return journeys. 'I shall be coming from Oxford by train reaching Wolverhampton Great Western Station at five-forty-five on Friday ... Alas I shall have to return by the ten twenty on Saturday morning.' Devoted as he was to all things Victorian, he loved railways, and was a strong advocate of the supremacy of rail as a form of transport over road. In 1963 he made a documentary for the BBC about a surviving steam branch-line railway that ran from Evercreech Junction to Burnham-on-Sea in Somerset.[55] 'Go away, you brute,' he says archly to a small truck that is holding up the train at a level crossing, 'you enemy of railways and comfortable travel.' Then, in the intimate tone he reserved for speaking to the British public, he uttered these prophetic words, three years before the descent of the Beeching Axe: 'You know, I am not just being nostalgic and sentimental and unpractical about railways. Railways are bound to be used again. They are not a thing of the past and it's heartbreaking to see them left to rot, to see the fine men who served them all their lives made uncertain about their futures and their jobs. What's more, it's wrong in every way, when we all of us know that road traffic is increasingly hellish on this overcrowded island and that 10 years from now there will be three times as much traffic on English roads as there is now.' The irony of such sentiments being uttered by a man who had done so much to promote touring by car through his work on the Shell Guides cannot have escaped all his viewers.

His routine during his first Uffington years hardly sounds arduous to a 21st-century commuter. His working hours at the Shell-Mex building were from 11 a.m. till 4.30 p.m. from Monday to Wednesday and, as he wrote to his former schoolmaster T. S. Eliot in 1936, he was 'free for luncheon on those days'. (Imagine working a five-and-a-half-hour day, three days a week, and being 'free for luncheon' – a meal that, by all accounts, the poet took seriously.) The farmhouse at Uffington gave Betjeman a place to which he could invite guests and entertain; visitors included Evelyn Waugh, Cyril Connolly, Gertrude Stein and Alice B. Toklas. He swiftly built friendships with other literary and artistic exiles in the surrounding countryside, including the aristocratic artist and composer Gerald Berners, at whose house in Faringdon he met Aldous Huxley and H. G. Wells. People began to talk of the 'Uffington set'. One of the more unusual visitors to the village was Lord Alfred Douglas, Oscar Wilde's former lover. When he was still a schoolboy, Betjeman had been fascinated equally by Bosie's poetry and the story of his love affair with Wilde and had begun a correspondence with him, to the horror of his parents. Now the ancient and somewhat decrepit roué came to stay, trailing the aura of a time when versifying and wit were accompanied by something altogether more dangerous.

Betjeman's workload increased along with his renown, expanding to include film reviewing and broadcasting, as well as a relentless number of talks and personal appearances. When the family moved to Farnborough, near Wantage, he would drive to Didcot and take the train from there. He was not a natural early riser; his family lived in dread of his terrible temper in the morning, when he was liable to accuse people of getting at him and hiding his clothes, until his wife Penelope suggested he see a psychiatrist to rid himself of his 'persecution mania'. On one occasion, a local girl who worked in the house remembers him losing his newspaper, which he wanted to take on the train, and saying evil spirits in the house had hidden it from him. Naturally, it was found on his chair, pushed under the table, after he left. Rather than persecution mania, perhaps he was just displaying behaviour typical of an exhausted commuter.

Despite the rigours associated with this style of life, trains provided Betjeman with space to write, think and maintain his correspondence. 'Cold from the G(reat) W(estern) R(ailway),' he wrote to the novelist Nancy Mitford in 1945, 'in which I have just been finishing the *Pursuit of Love*. I write to tell you on this lovely writing paper how v. greatly I enjoyed it.' Penelope claimed most of Betjeman's poetry was written on trains, as well as in waiting rooms, scribbled on flattened cigarette packets and on the back of restaurant menus. In his branch-line film, as the train rattles past Sedgemoor, he recites a poem by Thomas Hardy that he identifies as having 'a kind of railway metre'. Perhaps it is the mechanical tempos of trains we hear in his own poetry, their regular pulse inducing a kind of motion sickness in those accustomed to more adventurous rhythms. Some of his railway fragments were lost on his endless journeys. Others were reassembled in Uffington, with its chalk-white walls and thatched roofs that steamed after the rain as blue skies came 'racing over White Horse Hill', as he described in the poem 'Village Wedding'.

As an insignia, the horse seems to have retained its power. Time after time it has been snatched from the hill to reappear on T-shirts, book jackets, or as the trademark for a car dealership or a brewery. Many of these representations are based on aerial photographs, a vantage point seemingly anticipated by its prehistoric designers. This enduring legibility led to the horse being deliberately concealed for the only time in its history. In times of crisis, as another poet, Edward Thompson, described in 'England, June 1940', 'the chalk-limned Horses, the ancient Man ... turn traitors to our peace'. During the second world war the Ministry of Defence turfed the Uffington horse over, in order to prevent it being used as a waymark by German bombers en route to Swindon or Bristol. It survived that war, as it has every other conflict played out upon this plain, re-emerging to reclaim its place upon the hill. Without pointing Chesterton's telescope forward, into the future, who can say for how many centuries longer it will remain?

DIGRESSION

WHEN LONDON ENDED – FROM DAWLISH TO THE LAKE

This water is not still, the aftermath of an event, but active. Bubbling out of a hole beside the track, green, in places brown, moving fast enough to produce a thick white foam where branches trail across its surface, directing itself this way and that in brooks and streams as it takes over new territory. It all gives the impression of going somewhere – of being not so much an overflow as a relocated river. Beyond the raised embankment fields are sunk deep enough for only the tops of hedges to be visible. Just outside the station the train slows to a crawl and we sit, numbed, watching the swirling current beside the track. A young woman is pulling a refreshment trolley along inside the carriage at approximately the same speed as we have moved along the rails before coming to a halt. 'Would anyone like a complimentary tea, coffee, water?' she calls. The train operator is giving away drinks and snacks today in recognition of the inconvenience passengers are suffering, although the most jaundiced customer could hardly blame them for the weather. Judging by the view out of the window, more free water is probably not what we need, but I take a bottle anyhow, prompted by the deep urge we all have to accept anything offered without charge. The purchase of water in plastic, carbon-producing bottles in a country where drinkable water comes out of the tap is of course absurd, suggestive of a state of shortage – a situation the view from the window contradicts. Given the choice, I select 'sparkling', on the basis it least resembles what I can see running in the ditch beside the tracks.

It is very British, of course, to counter disaster with the dispensing of warm liquids, traditionally tea and coffee. This morning these drinks, accompanied by packets of sugary biscuits, feel more like offerings laid at the feet of the angry water gods than refreshments. The storms and floods of the last few days seem to have propelled us into the irrational. Even the weatherman on TV appears to be attempting his own kind of magic, stirring whirlpools of storms with his arm.

Railways seek out valleys and floodplains, avoiding contours that involve too much strain or friction or the cost of extensive tunnelling. For precisely this reason they are always at risk from encroaching water. Where the landscape forces them to run along the coast they also face attacks by the increasingly frequent and violent storms that have characterised our weather over the past few years. The line built by Brunel and opened in 1847, which runs south from Exeter along the Devon coast to Dawlish, is one of the most spectacular in the country. In calm weather, the uninterrupted view of the sea from the carriage has people crowding the corridor, cameras pointed to the horizon. I, too, have joined them, on a sunny afternoon in May, capturing an image of the azure bay, with a single orange-jacketed maintenance worker leaning back against the parapet beside the track as the train passed.

Even on less tranquil days, the spray generated by larger waves on carriage windows is exhilarating, in moderation, a traditional feature of the line that adds excitement to the journey. In the late 19th and early 20th century, most seaside resorts sold postcards of rough seas breaking on their foreshores. Visitors, well insulated against the weather and standing at a safe distance from the beach, could have an encounter with the raw power of nature and then catch a train back to their cosy inland home, taking a postcard with them as a reminder of their bravery. The artist Susan Hiller, who trained as an anthropologist, has collected hundreds of these postcards, combining them in a work called *Dedicated to the Unknown Artists*, an allusion to those who photographed the scenes and those, usually women, who were employed to tint them by hand, turning the angry sea into a commodity for the tourist market. Later, Hiller created her own digital prints based on these images, her manipulation shifting even further the colours of the waves that crashed on to the beach during long-forgotten storms.

The sea is all very well when it stays where it is meant to be. In February 2014 it revealed its destructive potential when it leapt out of one of those postcards, smashing through the seawall that supports the line at Dawlish, leaving the rails themselves hanging over a void, as ochre-coloured waves continued to explode upward into the new space they had created. A railway always floats above the earth on its bed of ballast, a bridge from here to there – a connection that in moments can be swept away. In Dawlish houses near the line shook as supporting walls collapsed and residents had to be hurriedly evacuated. It was, as one of them told TV reporters, as though a bomb had hit the town.

It is not the first time the sea has breached the wall on this stretch of line – a bridge was destroyed at Holcombe a mere seven years after it opened and repairs have had to be made on an ongoing basis ever since – and in a matter of weeks the line was open again. The regularity of the 'extreme weather events' we are now experiencing due to global warming has called into question our national reliance on this as the single route connecting Cornwall to the rest of the country by rail, and reopened discussion of restoring a long-disused inland route. One writer raised within earshot of the London to Bristol line and who dared to imagine a time when rising water levels would erase such technologies completely was Richard Jefferies. Best remembered today as a nature writer, Jefferies grew up on a farm outside Swindon, in the village of Coate. In an autobiographical essay, published posthumously, he spoke of the experience of walking across the fields as a boy to watch trains passing.

> Of one other path I have a faded memory, like a silk marker in an old book ... So full was the mind of romance in those days, that I used to get there specially in time to see the express go up, the magnificent engine of the broad gauge that swept along with such ease and power to London. I wish I could feel like that now. The feeling is not quite gone even now, and I have often since seen these great broad-gauge creatures moving alive to and fro like Ezekiel's wheel dream beside the platforms of Babylon with much of the same old delight.[56]

Jefferies spent much of his childhood rambling through the countryside around Swindon and the Vale of White Horse, hunting, fishing and boating on Coate Water, the reservoir bordering the family farm. Perhaps it was the apparent vastness of the reservoir to his childish eyes that sowed the seed for his only work of science fiction, *After London: or, Wild England*, published in 1885. The book is a post-apocalyptic account, in the tradition of Cormac McCarthy's *The Road* or Russell Hoban's *Riddley Walker*. In the aftermath of some never-explained event, London as well as vast areas of England have disappeared under water. Civil society, as it was known to Jefferies' 19th-century readers, has collapsed. 'The old men say their fathers told them that soon after the fields were left to themselves a change began to be visible,' the book begins. 'It became green everywhere in the first spring after London ended, so that all the country looked alike.'[57] With the precise eye of a farmer's boy he chronicles what happens when humans cease to steward the landscape: the collapse of dykes and dams, the silting of rivers, the swift reversion of farming land to impenetrable forest, scrub or marshes emitting poisonous vapour. Central England is submerged under a vast body of water known simply as the Lake, connected to the sea in the west by the Severn and the east by the Thames, divided into two unequal parts by the straits of the White Horse, a reference to Jefferies' childhood wanderings. Slaves outnumber the free 10 to one, towns are regularly raided by Irish and Welsh pirates and literacy is deliberately restricted to the noble classes. The technology of the 'great broad-gauge creatures' he spoke of in his memoir, along with the civilisation that gave birth to them, has disappeared for good.

> Beneath the surface of the Lake there must be concealed very many ancient towns and cities, of which the names are lost. Sometimes the anchors bring up even now fragments of rusty iron and old metal, or black beams of timber. It is said, and with probability, that when the remnant of the ancients found the water gradually encroaching (for it rose very slowly), as they were driven back year by year, they considered that they would all be swept away and drowned.

A little more than a century after its first publication, with rising water levels an increasing problem for coastal communities from Manhattan Island to Bangladesh, the book now seems eerily prophetic. Jefferies tried to create a world on the page as different to his own as he could, catalogued in forensic detail by his oddly dispassionate narrator, yet despite his best efforts to write a fiction, reality has moved to match his imagination.

LOCATION: SWINDON
A RAILWAY TOWN, PURE AND SIMPLE

'Swindon', explains *Through the Window: Paddington to Killarney*, 'is a railway town pure and simple – far more completely a railway town than any other place in Britain apart from Crewe. It can show nothing of history or art but plenty of engineering of the highest technical standard in all branches.'

The author is writing at a time when the Swindon Railway Works employed around 14,000 men and the thump of its drop hammers rattled the crockery in houses in neighbouring streets. As well as being a railway town, Swindon was a company town. The Great Western Railway company was involved in every aspect of civic life, from the moment Daniel Gooch selected it as a site for his engineering works. As well as providing housing for their workers by building the Railway Village, the Great Western Railway supplied them with pubs, social clubs, a church, recreation grounds and educational amenities. Very few aspects of life took place in spaces that were not in some way owned or influenced by the company. For many, a job in the works meant a job for life. When that life ended, funerals were likely to be paid for out of funds they had contributed to from their wages. Living alongside the tracks, building the locomotives and carriages and even the rails that carried passengers to London in one direction or Bristol in the other, employees in the railway's works rarely had the leisure or the funds to travel by train. Even in this, they depended on the largesse of their employers, earning free travel vouchers as a privilege for length of service. During the summer holiday period, chartered trains were laid on to take workers to the seaside or up to London for special occasions. Entire work teams exchanged the factory floor, with its soot, smoke and red-hot poured metal, for the beach. Those short of money packed their suitcases with food so they could cook up a meal in the rooms of their lodging houses.

Jack Hayward, now in his early 80s, was employed at the works in the 1950s and 1960s. Jack lost a leg when he was 14 years old as a result of osteomyelitis and couldn't work on the factory floor, but he managed to secure a clerical job in the office next to the blacksmith's shop.

'It was quite a shock when I started,' he tells me. 'What I found was a Dickensian scene. The books we wrote in were dog-eared and grimy. The shop floor was ash, so ash blew in every time the door opened. We used indelible pencils that you had to lick to moisten – when you licked them they turned purple. My boss always had the stub of a pencil on him and he'd be constantly licking it to write, so that his lips, mouth and tongue were purple.'

On his first day Jack wore his best suit, to look smart, with a white shirt and a tie. The time came for a walk around the shop floor and he followed his purple-tongued overseer through the door from the office. The scenes he encountered are still fresh in his memory.

'We stepped out into the smoke-filled, fume-filled shop. There was black snow falling, staining the whitewashed walls. It was unnerving, to be honest. There were two fires and two gangs of blacksmiths to each steam-hammer. The smaller hammers, making buffers and drawbars, were bad enough, banging and clattering, the sound bouncing off the walls – you couldn't hear to talk over it. Then there were the bigger, half-ton steam-hammers, making stampings of rods and beams. The big drop hammers were solid blocks of steel, weighing 50 tons, that were lifted up by hydraulic pressure and then dropped – they would shake the building when they came down. I could hear those at night where I lived, three miles away.'

The first thing Jack saw when he came through the door of the blacksmith's shop was an enormous electric saw.

'It was whizzing around without a guard on it. Just as I came up to it a blacksmith came across carrying a red-hot billet of steel in a pair of tongs, with a mate on either side, supporting it on a crowbar. He pushed the billet into the saw and a jet of sparks shot up into the roof and came down on me like a fiery rain, landing on my new suit. I brushed them off as best I could – luckily they didn't leave a mark! People today couldn't even imagine, let alone tolerate the conditions.'

It is hard, as I listen to Jack, to believe he is describing life in the mid-20th century – the age of The Beatles, Sputnik and mass-audience TV. He agrees.

'I've always felt I caught the tail end of the Industrial Revolution,' he tells me. 'The men's clothes hadn't changed – they wore heavy black twill trousers, black waistcoats with a shiny back, white collarless shirts and boots with studs in.'

The railway retains this ability to be at once futuristic and redolent of the past, in a way other forms of transport cannot. As the age of fossil fuels appears increasingly anachronistic, the high-speed train, powered by electricity or perhaps other scarcely explored technologies, looks more and more as if it may be the preferred option in the fast-developing economies of the east. Yet whatever the trappings of these new transport systems, they will feel instantly familiar, such is the strength of the connection forged between humanity and the train.

What was life like for those who worked inside the workshops and shunting yards that lined the tracks at Swindon, rather than viewing them, guidebook in hand, from the carriage window? An answer lies in the book *Life in a Railway Factory*, by Alfred Williams, published in 1915. A local man, Williams educated himself by going to nightclasses and specialised in descriptions of the Wiltshire countryside. His poems were reviewed in the national press; the novelty of a factory worker writing verse caught the public imagination, earning him the nickname 'The Hammer-man Poet'.

It was at a reception in London that a journalist first suggested he write about his job. The idea appealed to him immediately; the longer he worked at the factory, the angrier he grew about the conditions he saw around him. If he was to tell the real story, he realised, he would have to leave; the management had made it very clear they weren't going to allow him to write publicly about factory life while he was drawing a wage. Their threats did not intimidate him.

'I am not anxious to quarrel with any man,' he wrote. 'At the same time I am not disposed to be fettered, smothered, gagged or silenced, to cower and tremble, or to shrink from uttering what I believe to be the truth in deference to the most formidable despot living.'

Once a free agent, Williams did not hold back; in his portrayal, the factory is a microcosm of capitalism itself.

'The worker is everywhere exploited,' he wrote. 'The speeding up of late years has been general and insistent ... The actual exertions of the workman have been doubled or trebled, yet he receives scarcely anything more in wages. In some cases he does not receive as much.'

At certain moments Williams shifts from the general to the particular, as in this graphic description of an incident on the shop floor:

Some of the carrying is done with a kind of wheelbarrow that requires a special balance. The least obstruction will upset it ... Not long ago, as a youth was drawing a large, white-hot pile from the furnace to the steam-hammer, he slipped on the iron floor and fell at full length on his back on the ground. As he fell the bogie inclined forward and the huge pile slid down and lodged on his stomach, inflicting frightful injuries. He was quickly rescued from his tortuous position, but there was no hope of recovery from such an accident, and he died a day or two afterwards.

Witnessing such an event must have burnt a psychological scar in Williams almost as deep as the one seared into flesh by white-hot metal. The accident he describes took place over a century ago, before the outbreak of the first world war. Surely workers were protected from such danger by the mid-20th century?

Jack Hayward worked in various clerical positions at the factory; after a few years he was assigned the duty of overseeing the payroll, so that he grew to know everybody's wages. Surprisingly, he discovered the best paid among the non-management staff were two men in the carpentry division. To get such good salaries they must have had special skills.

'What do you think their job was?' Jack asks me.

I have no idea, I tell him.

He smiles, wryly. 'Making wooden artificial limbs.'

LOCATION: CHIPPENHAM

SOMETHIN' ELSE

In 1945 one war ended but another very different one was about to begin. A generation of young men had been consigned to graves far from home; those who survived were prematurely aged, as if weighed down by the responsibilities they had shouldered. From ground fertilised by their blood a new generation arose, no less determined to conquer the world. The enemy these war babies had in their sights was not some fascist ogre but simply the drudgery and drabness of everyday postwar life; their armoury included cars, guitars, dance moves and firm-hold hair treatments. In terms of lasting impact, the campaign they waged runs the second world war a close second.

No conflict is without its casualties. One of the most significant met his end at Chippenham in Wiltshire on 17 April 1960, at the age of 21. Eddie Cochran fulfilled every requirement of the rock'n'roll icon; impossibly good-looking, a vernacular poet who wrote and performed songs that expressed exactly what was on every young person's mind – 'She's sure fine-lookin', man, she's somethin' else' – while playing a fat orange Gretsch guitar and dipping his shoulders suggestively. (He never did quite master the Elvis hip-wiggle, although he attempted it on the first night of his British tour, in Ipswich, where he announced, 'It's great to be here in Hipswitch', and thrust his pelvis a couple of times, which made the girls scream.)

How did this young man, born in Minnesota but raised in California, meet his end in the middle of the night on the outskirts of a rural English town? To help me imagine the circumstances, I take the train to Chippenham and walk from the station, under the viaduct and back up Rowden Hill, to the spot where his car left the road. Cochran had just completed a British tour, co-headlining with Gene Vincent and supported by a number of British acts including Billy Fury and Johnny Gentle, concluding with a week of shows at the Bristol Hippodrome. He was riding high, earning £1,000 a week and on course to become the most popular American rock'n'roll star yet to hit the UK. However, he was also exhausted, cripplingly homesick and perpetually cold. Cochran hadn't been keen on touring overseas. He had a morbid fear of flying, but he was persuaded that once he was in the United Kingdom he could travel by train. The young British drummer booked for the tour, Brian Bennett, who later played in the Shadows, remembers: 'We travelled on British Rail for most of the tour, third class. During that time we formed the BRSM [British Rail School of Music]. As we were not driving in the dreaded Dormobile we had time to study music, practice …' A black-and-white photograph exists of Bennett, short-haired and wearing a fetching Nordic-style cardigan, lugging his drum kit along the platform of Bexhill station.

Sure enough, after their last show in Bristol, Vincent and Cochran were handed a bunch of train tickets to London for the following morning. Vincent was heading for Paris and more shows, but for Cochran there was also a plane ticket to the States, leaving Heathrow at 1 p.m. He was looking forward to spending time with his family and soaking up some sunshine, as well as fulfilling a recording contract, before resuming his British tour. Who persuaded whom that instead of taking the train to London in the morning they should hire a private taxi to drive them back to London that night? Johnny Gentle, who was also driving back to London, remembers Cochran asking if there was room in Johnny's car for him and his fiancée, Sharon Sheeley, who had flown over from California to join the tour. He had to turn them down as all the seats were taken.

The taxi that showed up had been used for a wedding that afternoon; Sheeley remembers it still had confetti on the floor. Its young driver, George Martin, must have been excited at having such glamorous passengers on board and would have been eager to impress them with his driving and the pace of his Ford Consul. The car entered Chippenham via the A4 Bath Road shortly before midnight, a route now lined with the drive-in stores from which people construct their lives: The Tile Gallery, The Kitchen Bedroom Bathroom Centre, Bathwick Tyres. By all accounts, it was travelling too fast; Sharon remembers Cochran repeatedly asking Martin to slow down. Unusually for one so young, he was keenly aware of his own mortality. Two of his friends, Buddy Holly and Ritchie Valens, had been aboard a plane that crashed near the town of Clear Lake, Iowa the year before, killing them along with their co-passenger J. P. Richardson, better known as The Big Bopper. Eddie had recorded a song in their memory just two days after their deaths.

Martin intended to take a short cut through Chippenham but lost his way, deciding instead to retrace his steps and pick up the A4 on the edge of town. Cochran and Sheeley were singing 'California, Here We Come' on the back seat. On a sharp bend on Rowden Hill, then an accident black spot, the car burst a tyre and skidded across the road, reversing direction and slamming into a lamppost with a noise that convinced some locals they had heard a plane crash. Those hurrying out of their houses to offer help saw Vincent, Cochran and Sheeley lying where they had been thrown on to the grass verge, alongside a large orange guitar, while photographs and sheet music fluttered in the breeze. Only two of them survived. At the precise moment the ambulance took Eddie away, onlookers recall, the streetlights went out, leaving the road in darkness.

I walk the short distance from the roundabout, flanked today by a garage and the Rowden Arms public house, to the spot where a plaque commemorates Cochran's life. Pebbledashed bungalows gradually give way to 1970s maisonettes and then to 1930s villas and, higher on the hill, one or two fine 18th-century houses. A blossom tree in the garden of number 36B is just coming into flower, its branches reaching across the low wall towards the verge where the plaque is situated. The faithfully rendered Gretsch guitar on the plaque is emitting white musical notes, which, I can't help noticing, have almost completely faded. It seems a strangely inconsequential spot for such a momentous event, and yet lines of connection reach out from it through time and space.

Trains are part of the DNA of popular music, stretching back to the early years of the 20th century and the birth of recording; from blues classics like Robert Johnson's 'Love in Vain' and Howlin' Wolf's 'Smokestack Lightning' to traditional numbers like 'This Train', a huge hit for guitar-toting gospel singer Sister Rosetta Tharpe. This shouldn't be a surprise; the neck of a guitar, after all, resembles a railway, with frets for sleepers and steel strings for rails. Popular songs both include train sounds within their structure – the rhythm of wheels on tracks, the lonesome whistle – and use them as a metaphor in their lyrics. Trains in songs bear listeners to heaven or hell, carry loved ones beyond reach, or symbolise the fact that life, like a railroad, heads in one direction and there's no way of turning it around, however soulfully Al Green might plead with the engine driver on 'Back Up Train'. Above all, trains represent escape to those chained by circumstance. The prisoner in Johnny Cash's

'Folsom Prison Blues' hears the train coming and imagines the rich folk it carries drinking coffee and smoking fat cigars in the dining car. He has accepted his fate, until the train whistle reminds him of the contrast between his situation and theirs: they are free to keep moving, he realises, 'and that's what tortures me ...'

While working on this project I listened to a lot of train songs and wrote about some of them on a blog. What happened next is a demonstration of the way the subject matter of a book can take over its author: I found new songs popping into my head at unexpected moments, asking to be recorded. That's how the album *Orphan Train* was born, which functions as a kind of soundtrack to this book, without alluding directly to the geography it covers. You can hear some of it by following the link given on the back flap of the book jacket.

Cochran was from California, not Chicago; unsurprisingly, therefore, it is the car rather than the train that features in his songs as a symbol of both freedom and of a young person's continuing and frustrating dependency on the adults in his life. In 'Summertime Blues' the teenage protagonist's parents tell him he will have to earn some money if he wants to borrow the car 'to go ridin' next Sunday'. When he skips work, pretending to be sick, his boss tells him (in a pantomime Italian accent) he can't use the car because he 'didn't work-a late'. While trains deliver you to a fixed destination, cars allow you to wander, cruising and listening to the radio, as Chuck Berry describes in 'No Particular Place to Go'. Rock'n'roll songwriters reflected the shift in American culture from public transport to the private automobile. Some people can still be found who deny this preference has been a disaster for the planet. None can question it killed Eddie Cochran.

It is hard today to imagine the cultural impact the visit by the two American stars had on a generation of musicians. A young Marc

Bolan carried Cochran's guitar from the stage door of a theatre to his car and later had his own guitar resprayed the same distinctive colour, in homage. (Seventeen years later, he too was to die in a car crash.) A 16-year-old Georgie Fame played in Cochran's backing band and heard his first Ray Charles tunes when the musicians jammed offstage. George Harrison followed the tour from venue to venue, soaking up Cochran's technique. Pete Townshend and Jimi Hendrix were similarly both in awe of and influenced by his playing. John Lennon may have got his early love for black leathers from Gene Vincent, but he let Paul McCartney join his group because he knew Cochran's 'Twenty Flight Rock'. A month after Cochran's death, 'The Silver Beatles' were themselves on tour in Scotland as Johnny Gentle's backing band, performing a cover version of 'Summertime Blues'.

The first policeman on the scene of the crash was PC Dave Harman, who impounded Cochran's guitar. He later changed his name to Dave Dee and formed a beat combo of his own, called Dave Dee, Dozy, Beaky, Mick & Tich, who went on to have a string of hits. According to some, he taught himself to play on Cochran's Gretsch, down at the station. Perhaps the strangest twist in the story was that later that night Gentle's party took the same route through Chippenham. Low on petrol and seeing a wrecked car by the side of the road about to be towed away, he asked the tow-truck driver whether he could siphon some fuel from its tank, common practice in postwar austerity Britain. It was only a couple of days later that he realised he and his companions had got back to London on Cochran's gas.

LOCATION: BOX
INTO THE TUNNEL

Box Tunnel took six years to construct and opened for traffic on 30 June 1841. It was one of the engineering wonders of the world. It is hard today to imagine the controversy and sheer terror the idea of running trains through such a long and deep excavation caused when it was first proposed. People worried about asphyxiation from smoke, about the steepness of the incline, about rock falls, about immoral acts that might occur in the compartments of carriages; perhaps most of all they were simply frightened of being propelled forward into darkness. It is worth remembering that trains themselves were not lit in these early days, so travelling nearly two miles in pitch blackness at a third of the speed of a modern train would have been a challenging experience. As one opponent of the Great Western Railway bill of 1835 put it, 'No person would desire to be shut out from daylight with a consciousness that he had [above him] a super incumbent weight of earth sufficient to crush him in case of accident.'

The tunnel took its toll on human life. Over a ton of dynamite a week was required to blast a route through the hill; shifts of as many as 4,000 men worked by candlelight around the clock, in constant danger of rock falls and floods, the debris of their excavations hauled to the surface by ropes wound by wretched horses that walked unending circles on the surface. On finishing their shifts, exhausted navvies fell into beds warmed by the bodies of the co-workers who had just left to take their place. Thus modernity was delivered using the most primitive means.

To best appreciate Brunel's aesthetic vision, a trip to the small village of Box is necessary, where a good view of the western entrance to the tunnel can be had from a nearby road bridge. I make my pilgrimage on an unseasonably warm February day. Above the tunnel's gaping mouth half a moon hangs in a sky a small, old-fashioned biplane is traversing, its propeller a white blur against the blue.

An oak tree festooned in ivy grows to the right of the tunnel, a detail from a Victorian sketchbook. Birdsong echoes in the cutting and a rabbit runs along the curve of the tunnel's retaining wall, disappearing behind its balustrade. For some reason, I find it moving to stand here. Why? Perhaps because I have seen Brunel's watercolour sketch for the tunnel entrance; although the actual tunnel has weathered, its appearance and colours remain remarkably close to

the way he conjured them on paper. To one side of the tunnel mouth a creeper grows upward, not large enough to suggest dereliction but just enough to add a Romantic detail of precisely the kind he employed on this stretch of the line. ('Tunnel No. 2', near Bristol, is fashioned to resemble a Gothic ruin. The ground to one side of the track slipped and rather than bank it up he decided to leave it 'unfinished' and plant it with ivy, intending it, according to his son and biographer, 'to present the appearance of a ruined gateway'.) The stretch between Bath and Bristol, during which contours were unavoidable and human sensitivities at their keenest, was the ultimate test of his skills. He was forced to dig seven tunnels and two deep cuttings between the nearby cities; and, as if determined to silence his critics in Bristol, always carping at his extravagance, he made a virtue of the difficulties he faced, going to extravagant lengths to decorate his tunnels with Norman and medieval architectural details. Brunel's line from London to Bristol is a conceptual work of art, one completed by its audience. In terms of his tunnel entrances, his viewers were largely limited to railway officials, engine drivers seated at the front of the train, those in the early days who rode in open carriages and glanced behind them through the smoke as they trundled out into the light and 21st-century pilgrims come to look at a page from the engineer's sketchbook made manifest.

At the east end of Box Tunnel, the other side of the hill from the village, the tunnel entrance is buried in a deep cutting. Author and Brunel biographer Adrian Vaughan has suggested that the elaborate decoration of the tunnel entrance, which combines an arch of wedge-shaped stones known as 'voussoirs' and intricate corbelling of the space below the parapet, might be an attempt to establish supremacy over another spectacular architectural work that stood nearby, John Rennie's Avoncliff aqueduct.[58] One detail in the tunnel entrance's decoration remains intriguing: the inclusion of the

French (originally Roman) Republican fasces, the bundle of bound birch rods that represent justice and unity. Vaughan speculates that Brunel may be referring to his French roots, or even expressing his frustration at the difficulties he experienced obtaining permission to drive his railway through lands owned by the British gentry. Brunel's politics are slippery. Although relentlessly tough on those he employed, he was not a member of the idle rich, having worked unstintingly since he was a teenager. His family connections might be expected to make him less rather than more sympathetic to the use of French Revolutionary imagery, as his father had come to Britain a royalist refugee from the Terror. Yet in 1848 he indulged in a little revolutionary play-acting with his brother-in-law J. C. Horsley, given added piquancy perhaps by his family history. 'He wished to see Paris in Republican garb,' Horsley wrote to Brunel's son Isambard Jr. 'We were there for some days, and, armed with cards of admission, on which our names were inscribed with the prefix "Citoyen", heard and saw the various celebrities of the hour.'[59]

Myth adheres to Box, as if the navvies who constructed it dug not just into the soil but also into the psyche of the country itself. The best known is that Brunel deliberately aligned the angle of the tunnel so that on his birthday, 9 April, the sun would shine down its length before it climbed above Box Hill. Most commentators now believe the sun is indeed visible through the tunnel on certain days in April, but not, as it happens, on the 9th. However, this is contested by author and academic R. Angus Buchanan, who cites the calculations of Brunel scholar James Richard as establishing the sun would be visible through the tunnel on that day, provided the sky was clear, shortly after dawn.[60] Anyone determined to check on the veracity of these statements and counter-statements would need to contend with the frequent passage of high-speed trains, as well as the unsettled skies typical of the month of the engineer's birth.

The substance of other legends adhering to the tunnel would be equally challenging to establish, mixed as they are with fact just as unlikely. In the 1960s, it has emerged, old mine workings here were the location for a secret emergency governmental headquarters known as Site 3, to be used in the event of the outbreak of war. It was kept in full working order until it was eventually decommissioned in the 1990s. Even this is not enough for the hill's mythologisers, who claim it also contains a 'strategic reserve' of steam trains in case electric and diesel services are disabled by a nuclear attack, as well as a secret rail connection from the main line to RAF Rudloe Manor for the covert delivery of recovered UFOs. None of these notions is more remarkable than the truth: that Victorian engineers created what was then the longest tunnel in the world using nothing more than explosives and the brute strength of animals and men. Visitors from the future might well wonder how such a feat was possible without modern equipment, just as present-day archaeologists puzzle over the construction of the pyramids. The secret in both cases may be simple: human life during these times was cheap. Over 100 men were killed during the construction of Box Tunnel; many more were injured or maimed. When Brunel was shown the names of 131 workers taken for treatment at Bath hospital alone, he is reported to have said, 'I think it is a small list, considering the very heavy works, and the immense amount of powder used.'

As I enter the tunnel on a Bristol-bound train and the landscape suddenly disappears, my own face stares back from the window like a ghost. At such a time it seems right to remember those other ghosts that populate the darkness, the tunnel a grave they dug with their own hands.

LOCATION: BATH
CITY OF OINTMENT, LEPERS AND KINGS

'I went to Bath – Bath, because that city, where
much of England's glorious literature, above all the works
of Fielding, was written, soothes the eye more reliably
than any other city in England, giving the illusion
of reflecting another and more peaceful age.'
Stefan Zweig, *The World of Yesterday* (1942)

To a man as keenly aware of history as Brunel, the arrival of the
line at Bath was of immense significance. The city had long held a
particular place in British cultural life. Its famous waters, promoted
as a remedy for everything from infertility to gout, drew visitors
from throughout Britain and across Europe. In its heyday, Bath
was thronged with artists come to paint the portraits of the great
and good taking the cure. It was also home to notable musicians,
including organist, composer and director of the city's orchestra
William Herschel, later the astronomer-king of Slough. (Our
westward direction of travel takes us backwards through Herschel's
career, to a time when music was his profession and the music of
the spheres a mere hobby, gradually mutating into an obsession.)
Bath was a city of appearances, ideally designed to show off the latest
fashions, its public spaces offering a rare opportunity to mix without
the usual rigid social distinctions, as if the medical problems, both
real and imagined, that afflicted many of its visitors somehow granted

a temporary equality through mutual suffering. This is at least the impression created by Tobias Smollett's satirical portrait of the 18th-century city in his novel *The Expedition of Humphry Clinker.*

> Yesterday morning, at the Pump-room, I saw a broken winded Wapping landlady squeeze through a circle of peers, to salute her brandy-merchant, who stood by the window, propped upon crutches; and a paralytic attorney of Shoe-lane, in shuffling up to the bar, kicked the shins of the chancellor of England, while his lordship, in a cut bob, drank a glass of water at the pump. I cannot account for my being pleased with these incidents, any other way, than by saying they are truly ridiculous in their nature, and serve to heighten the humour in the farce of life, which I am determined to enjoy as long as I can.

But our arrival in Bath is marked by no such fashionable occasion. Instead, we alight on an evening in January 1834, a year and a half before the Great Western Railway was created by an act of parliament on 31 August 1835. It is cold outside, but in the warm fug of the White Lion public house a group of residents have gathered to hear a speaker come to persuade them of the virtues of a line connecting their town to London and Bristol. He is seeking more than their approval; the committee of the railway has failed to raise the £3m they estimate they need to build and equip the line; take-up of shares in Bristol itself has fallen short of their expectations and they are in urgent need of capital. Such persuasion will be a delicate matter; particularly in a city that has built its reputation on being, as the composer Joseph Haydn wrote in a notebook recording his visit, one of the most beautiful in Europe, its half-moon-shaped crescent 'more magnificent than any I had seen in London', 100 fathoms long with 'a Corinthian column at each fathom'.

Smoke, soot, sparks, cinders, noise: before these inconveniences, the residents of Bath could expect crowds of the dreaded navvies, along with the excavations, demolitions and evictions that would inevitably accompany the arrival of trains within the city boundaries. In addition, it was widely understood that the railway would destroy the coaching trade on which much of the prosperity of the town had been built. Many could have been justified in viewing its arrival with as much enthusiasm as the inhabitants of George Eliot's *Middlemarch*, for whom the approach of the railway was equivalent to 'the imminent horrors of cholera'.

Charles Saunders, secretary of the Great Western committee, is the speaker at the meeting in the White Lion. How can he convince his audience of the benefits of allowing such a scar to be gouged in their elegant city? Reading his speech from this distance, his words sound eerily familiar, his arguments remarkably similar to those employed by the line builders and would-be line builders of today.

It has been seen by numerous examples that, wherever communication has been improved, towns have become larger and more prosperous. Bath is an acknowledged place of favourite resort and it is likely the railway will double the number of families residing here. A great many people come to Bath for the purpose of seeking health; the railway will enable them to reach Bath from London in four hours and a half, without any fatigue; for it has been ascertained on the Liverpool and Manchester Railway that there is no fatigue in travelling of this kind.

In fact, railways, as revolutionary new technologies always do, had effects and consequences entirely unforeseen by their developers. In 1834, a railway speculator promises to increase business in and double the size of a provincial city by connecting it to the railway. Some 180 years later, a chancellor of the exchequer promises to link cities in the north of England together by rail and thereby create 'prosperity and jobs' and a 'northern powerhouse' that will 'change the economic geography of the country'. To justify the huge capital investment required, he reaches back to the days of Brunel. 'Of course, there are opponents of the project, just as there were opponents of the original railways. I've discovered that almost everything worth doing in politics is controversial.'[61]

The tactic employed by Saunders proved the right one. The truth was Bath had ceased to be the 'favourite resort' known to Beau Nash and Jane Austen, its shops no longer, as Josiah Wedgwood claimed, 'richer and more extravagant in their shew than London'. By the dawn of the railway age Bath's ascendancy had been lost to more fashionable seaside towns, the 'racket and dissipation ... noise, tumult and hurry' described as characterising the place in Smollett's novel replaced by a somnolent decay that matched the condition of its increasingly elderly visitors. This long and slow decline saw a rise in unemployment, along with Chartist rioting and social unrest giving certain quarters of the town an unhealthy reputation. Nevertheless, Bath's face was still its fortune and Brunel might have been expected to skirt the edge of the city as far as he could to avoid damaging its appearance. Instead, he was determined to make a triumphal entry into the city, his trains the latest attraction in a theatre of spectacles. To this end, the railway would be driven through one of its best-known attractions, Sydney Gardens, opened to the public in 1790, rivalling London's Vauxhall Gardens in the range of diversions they offered. (Jane Austen wrote of them to her sister Cassandra in 1799, telling her how much she was looking forward to visiting them for a firework display.) Their carefully designed topography featured cascades, ornamental grottoes, a labyrinth, a sham castle and swings adapted for both ladies and gentlemen; an artificial landscape enlivened by music, lanterns and illuminations hosting gala nights in summer that attracted as many as 4,000 visitors. In short, the gardens were, as the guidebook *Walks through Bath* explained in 1819, 'another, among the numerous proofs of the great anxiety of the inhabitants to render the amusements of this elegant city, without a parallel in the kingdom'.

By the time Charles Saunders arrived at the White Lion, that 'great anxiety' was growing. The proprietors of the gardens had already allowed a canal to be built through their land some 30 years before, in return for the payment of 2,000 guineas in compensation and the insistence that the canal owners build two iron bridges over the canal to an ornamental 'Chinese' design. It had, most were agreed, added to rather than detracted from the gardens' charms, opening up vistas replete with multiple, elegant reflections. With revenues diminishing, compensation payments again looked attractive; even if the railway would destroy many of the gardens' best-known features, it would add something new, as well as bringing more potential customers to the city. As a guide to the spa towns of Britain wrote in 1840, those 'who have not yet seen the English "Spa of Spas" (as I trust it will soon become again), will proceed thither in numbers as soon as Sir Isambard the magician shall, with his Great Western wand, have brought Bath within three hours of the metropolis'. Once again the engineer is cast as conjurer, one who can alter reality through his occult knowledge of the arts of fire, iron and steam. It is a role he relished. Rather than burying his trains away in an inaccessible cutting, the gardens would be a showcase for their display, the architecture of the line allowing the public a space in which to gather and marvel at this new technology of travel.

Gather they did, despite the fact that the railway brought about no sudden growth in Bath's population or prosperity, arguably undermining several local trades and certainly hastening the discolouration of the city's famous Bath stone. Gather they still do, albeit to a lesser extent; although long since domesticated, trains never seem to lose their potent allure for certain sectors of the population. On a clear blue December day on which I stroll through the gardens, key viewing positions on bridges above and parkland alongside the track are occupied by parents and grandparents chaperoning young children, all straining their necks to see trains streak past on Brunel's iron road.

Charles Saunders's diplomatic mission to Bath achieved what it set out to do, one staging post in the transformation of Britain that was to ensue. A century later another delegation arrived in the city, from a much more distant location. Historically, Bath was no stranger to royalty. Kings, queens and princes had been regular visitors, as well as the nobility of many nations. Seldom had it received foreign potentates whose position was as desperate as the royal couple who stepped from the train at Bath station on 5 August 1936.

His Imperial Majesty Haile Selassie, King of Kings of all Ethiopia, Lord of Lords, along with Empress Menen, the crown prince, Princess Tsehai, Haile Selassie's father Ras Makonnen of Harar, Ras Kassa (the emperor's chief commander and a trusted friend) and Dr Bayen (a secretary and interpreter) took up residence at the Spa Hotel. While the hotel, with its spacious rooms, suited the party well, it was obvious the emperor would need a more permanent base in which to receive visitors and maintain a centre of operations, effectively a court in exile. He had come to Europe seeking asylum but also the backing of the League of Nations in his struggle to regain his country's independence. In October 1935, half a million Italian troops had invaded Abyssinia, as Ethiopia was then known to Europeans, from Eritrea, determined to establish an Italian empire in the Horn of Africa and avenge the shame of their defeat at the hands of King Menelik in the closing years of the 19th century. The Italian nation seemed galvanised in support of the imperial ambitions of their leader; in Rome, housewives supported the war effort by throwing their gold wedding rings into a bonfire at the *Altare della Patria*.

Two months before his arrival in Bath Selassie had addressed the League of Nations. Despite the whistles and catcalls of Italian journalists as he came to the podium to speak, he described the sufferings of his people and the tactics of the invaders, which were in contravention of international law. 'The deadly rain that fell from the aircraft made all those whom it touched fly shrieking with pain,' he told his audience. 'All those who drank the poisoned water or ate the infected food also succumbed in dreadful suffering. In tens of thousands, the victims of the Italian mustard gas fell. It is in order to denounce to the civilised world the tortures inflicted upon the Ethiopian people that I resolved to come to Geneva ... What reply shall I have to take back to my people?'

The truth was that Selassie's appeal put the League in a difficult position. France was eager to strike up an alliance with Italy to resist German aggression on her border. The League had little appetite for inflicting sanctions on Italy and the British government found the presence of the emperor in London, when they were not officially taking sides in the conflict in Abyssinia, an embarrassment. Thus it was he was sent west, down the line from Paddington, to where he would be less visible. At Fairfield House, the Italianate villa the emperor purchased in Bath in the autumn of 1936, I listen to an interview with Rosemary Hooley, who encountered the emperor as a child, her account capturing something of the character of his wanderings before he came to settle in the city.[62]

The War Office rang my father F. O. Morris who was owning and running the Arundel Arms in Lifton, Devon, and asked him whether he would be prepared to shelter Haile Selassie and his entourage – not described, but a lot of people – 'incognito', which was absurd because it was a little Devon village which had probably never seen a coloured person before; and my father, having negotiated a very good figure, said yes of course, and down on the train from London to Lifton station came Haile Selassie with a large entourage. They marched up through the village to everyone's utter astonishment and took up residence in a suite in my father's hotel. It was lovely warm weather. The next day Selassie, accompanied by two parasol bearers and somebody carrying a firearm, went for a walk followed by all the people he had come with including his wife [the Empress Menen] and various handmaidens. They were in their Abyssinian raiment, not European clothes, and everybody in Lifton was absolutely astounded.

A few days later, amid concern that his whereabouts were known, perhaps that agents of the Italian government were on his trail, the emperor and his retinue returned to the station and continued their wandering. However, he did not forget the warm reception he had experienced at the hotel. 'After a bit a black ceremonial horse arrived on the train,' Mrs Hooley recalls, 'as a gift from loyal Abyssinians to my father, who was a keen hunting man, for sheltering Selassie. This huge black horse proved to be an absolutely useless and dangerous hunter.'

Perhaps it appealed to a man whose country had been overrun by the Italian army to establish his government in exile in a Roman city; Mussolini's fascists, after all, believed that through their African adventures they were drawing the borders of a new Roman empire. Despite their insularity, the British public was well schooled in deference to royalty. No doubt the fact that Selassie traced his line back to a union between King Solomon and Queen Makeda of Ethiopia, better known in Europe by the title Queen of Sheba, added to his almost magical status. Fairfield, built in extensive grounds that afforded him privacy, suited the emperor. Its elevated position gave a view, now partially obscured by trees, of hills across the valley, reminding him of his birthplace at Harar, the city where Arthur Rimbaud spent the last years of his life. (What is it about the countryside around Bath that makes exiles recall their homeland? The Austrian Stefan Zweig, whose country had been annexed by a different European dictator, arrived in Bath in 1939 and stayed in a house called Rosemount on Lyncombe Hill, where he installed a piano that had once belonged to Ludwig van Beethoven. He maintained the view was like that of the alpine scenery surrounding his residence in Kapuzinerberg, outside Salzburg.)

Fairfield was large enough to accommodate 20 people, including the empress, seven children, two grandchildren, three Ethiopian

271

Coptic priests, a cook, butler, servants and political advisors. We know from the accounts of children who came to play with the royal offspring that the family ate off gold plates, in silence unless the emperor spoke first. Services were held in a specially appointed chapel. As head of the Coptic Church, Selassie's schedule was wrapped in ritual, the maintenance of which was given the highest priority. At the Feast of Passover he washed the servants' feet. Beyond these few details little information exists about daily life at Fairfield during the emperor's residency. The routine at court in Addis Ababa after the emperor's return is better documented. There, Selassie's day started with a walk in the park, where he fed his pet lions and leopards with choice cuts of veal and beef, as palace spies and informers whispered news into his ear of conspiracies hatched overnight. Selassie's reliance on spoken reports – what he refers to in his autobiography as 'absorbing knowledge by the ear' – as well as being in accordance with tradition may have been the result of his never having attended school. Instead, his education was received from tutors who included a French Jesuit called Monsignor Jarousseau, who, despite their divergent attitudes to religion, had been a friend of Rimbaud in Harar. The atmosphere at court was characterised by fear, rumour and an impenetrable fog of bureaucracy. Position was entirely at the discretion of the emperor and could be removed at any time. The instructions the emperor muttered to his 'Minister of the Pen' in response to the reports he received were deliberately ambiguous and open to interpretation, so that good decisions reflected well on the emperor and bad ones could be blamed on his underlings. Another minister carried his purse, distributing envelopes of money, in response to his whispered commands, to those who came to make their petitions. According to Ryszard Kapuściński's hallucinatory account, the halls of the palace would often echo with wails of disappointment when supplicants opened their envelopes and found they contained only a few meagre coins, rather than the answer to prayer they had hoped for.[63] Rimbaud came up against similar forces when dealing with the officials of Ras Makonnen, Haile Selassie's father, when he attempted to extract money he was owed by King Menelik of Shoa, to whom he had sent a caravan bearing rifles and ammunition. 'One of the nastiest tricks they can play on you in Shoa is to land you with these Orders of Payment at Harar ... Payments here are tortures, disasters, tyrannies, abominable slavery,' he wrote, as he watched the profits he had dreamt of from his expedition trickle away in a succession of duties, taxes, debts and interminable delays.

Rimbaud returned to France in 1891 having delayed his departure week after week in an attempt to settle his affairs to his best advantage. 'I will return with iron limbs, dark skin, fierce eye,' he had prophesied in the poem 'Bad Blood'. 'By my mask I shall be judged to come from a strong race. I will have gold.' Instead, he left Harar in excruciating pain, worried about money, carried for interminable miles through the desert jolted this way and that in a litter, his right knee grotesquely swollen with the cancer that would kill him. The following year Ras Makonnen's wife gave birth to a son, christened Ras Tafari Makonnen, later to be given the regnal name Haile Selassie. By the time he was 13, his father had appointed him *Dejazmach* (literally gatekeeper) in the city, the first of his official roles that would see him become regent and eventually King of Kings, Emperor of Ethiopia. Both Rimbaud and Ras Tafari were in some way formed by the isolated city of Harar, ringed by its high wall built to keep out the jackals and leopards that patrolled its perimeter. Both learnt about masks here; about inscrutability as a means of self-preservation ('the belly of the master is never known', as the Amharic saying has it). Like Ras Tafari, Rimbaud acquired these skills early. His youthful poetry was wilfully obscure, concealing its occult ambition and transgressive sexuality from hostile eyes. In Harar, he

273

recreated himself. Christened 'Abdoh Rinbo' by the local traders, he was described by his contemporaries as an experienced merchant with a serious and somewhat aloof manner, his prematurely grey hair making him look older than his years.

Rumours adhere to his life at Harar, filling in the gaps between established facts. 'Rimbaud's house', a stop on the tourist itinerary, seems to have been built after his death. The claim that he was involved in the slave trade, disputed by more recent authors, persisted down the years; as late as 1976, a critic wrote that Rimbaud's 'biography offers a classic example of the man whose left-wing ideals die with his youth and who lives on to exploit his brothers'.[64] His mistress and servant may well have been slaves. Trusted in business by both European and African trading partners, when rumours of his literary past reached Ethiopia he dismissed it all as 'slops'. His ambition had shifted, from literary immortality to more tangible wealth and respectability on earth. (In a letter home, he imagined having a son who was 'a famous engineer, a man rich and powerful through science' – an imagined figure strangely reminiscent of Brunel, another man born of a French father who made his way in a foreign land.) We cannot know what he would have made of the Rastafarian faith; he couldn't have helped feeling a connection to its object of veneration, whose birth in Harar he missed by only a few months. He was no stranger to that religion's chief sacrament, at least in the form of hashish; as a young man he famously claimed that the way to become a 'seer' (*voyant*) was through 'a long, prodigious and calculated disordering of all the senses'. He enjoyed cordial relations with Haile Selassie's father, Ras Makonnen, despite the challenge of trading with his officials; the strength of their bond is reflected in the fact that the governor of Harar was one of only three people in Ethiopia he wrote to from Marseille in June 1891, a letter giving little hint of the despair he felt at his fate.

Excellency,

How are you? I wish you good health and complete prosperity. May God vouchsafe to you all you desire. May your life flow peacefully.

I write this to you from Marseille, in France. I am in hospital. They cut off my leg six days ago…

In six weeks, he goes on to say, he will be healed. The morphine must be working; he expects to return to Ethiopia in a few months' time. There was one last series of feverish train journeys through France from the family farm at Roche to Paris and on to Marseille, the gateway to Africa he was too sick to step through. Instead, he crossed another threshold into hospital, from where the cancer that had spread through his body ushered him on his final journey.

II

Haile Selassie came to Bath fleeing oppression by an Italian dictator. Some 72 years earlier, the city received an Italian statesman of a very different kind, one who had earned himself the name *Il Duce* years before Mussolini was born. On 25 April 1864, General Giuseppe Garibaldi, liberator of Italy and veteran of numerous campaigns on both sides of the Atlantic, passed through Bath by rail on his way to Cornwall. Such was his fame and the widespread interest taken in him by the people of the city that arrangements were made for his train to make a brief halt at Bath. The plan was he would leave his carriage and stand on the slender iron footbridge that joined the station to the Royal Hotel, from which he could address, or at least wave to, the assembled citizens. The mayor and mayoress headed a procession to the station, joined by officials and a number of eminent local worthies, to welcome the revolutionary hero to the city. Before long, and despite the presence of 50 policemen, they found themselves so pressed by the crowds that they had to retire to the end of the platform. As Garibaldi's train pulled in cannons were fired, flags waved and onlookers surged forward; parasols were crushed, hats lost and dresses torn as both male and female onlookers succumbed to hysteria. Garibaldi was unable to leave his carriage, let alone reach the bridge, and merely gazed, perplexed, from the window; from both sides a forest of hands reached up to touch his, in an effort to connect with the electric current of his glamour. Four years earlier, after his successful conquest of Sicily, he had entered Naples in triumph on board a train; the scenes at Bath station were hardly less tumultuous. As a correspondent for the *Bath Chronicle* recorded, if he had managed to step down and 'trusted himself to [the crowd's] mercies, he would undoubtedly have been injured, for the desire to seize some part of him and to shake him and hug him had become general, and had deprived the struggling concourse of all sense of decorum'.[65] The mayoress managed to hand Garibaldi a nosegay of flowers through the window before she was pulled into his carriage for her own safety. There she remained trapped until the train was ready to leave. Her exit from the train, the *Chronicle* records, was 'dangerous, and but for the assistance of The City Architect she would hardly have escaped serious injuries'. The bridge, on which the revolutionary hero never set foot, remained tantalisingly out of reach on the other side of the tracks, across which boards had been laid for the wounded general to walk on.[66] From that day it became known as the Garibaldi Bridge; it stood as an enigmatic symbol of his passage through the city until it was finally demolished in 1936, the year Haile Selassie took up residence in Bath.

The appearance of an Ethiopian emperor in a provincial English spa town was merely the latest in a long string of extraordinary events that have marked Bath's development. Different versions of its history overlay each other and are endlessly recycled, just as the ancient British settlement built here next to the hot-water spring was succeeded and built over by the Roman, medieval, Georgian, Victorian and 21st-century cities. Bath's foundation myth reaches back in time some 800 years before the birth of Christ, when Lud Hudibras, the eighth king of the Britons, occupied the throne in London. Legend has it that his son and heir, Bladud, contracted leprosy and was banished from the court. (By catching the disease, Bladud forfeited his right to the throne. The king must represent in his own body and being the health of the nation; what would it say of the condition of his kingdom if his digits were falling off or the skin of his face was flaking and beginning to rot?) Before he left London, his mother the queen gave him a ring by which she would know him again if he should ever find a cure. Bladud wandered west and found employment as a swineherd at Keynsham, but infected his herd with leprosy. To keep this from his master's knowledge he drove his herd across the river Avon at a ford, intending to fatten the pigs on the acorns growing in the woods that ran down the slopes of the valley. This was where he came upon the hot springs bubbling out of the ground that mark the position of the present-day city. John Wood, the Elder, the 18th-century architect and builder who, together with his son, was responsible for some of the greatest architectural icons of Georgian Bath, has left a powerful if imaginative account of what happened next. As well as being an architect, Wood was an amateur historian, a Mason and a druid. In his history of the city, published in 1742, he describes the moment the outcast prince and his disfigured herd came upon the springs and were transformed.

The Scum, which the Water naturally emits, mixing with the Leaves of Trees, and decay'd Weeds, had then made the Land about the Springs like a Bog, into which the Pigs directly immerged themselves; and so delighted were they wallowing in their Ouzy Bed, that BLADUD was some Days before he could get his whole Herd away; which he had no sooner Done and got them clean of the Filth, with which they were covered, when he observed the Pigs to have shed their hoary Marks. The Prince, in Astonishment of this, ran back to the Hot-Springs, striped himself naked, plunged himself into the Sedge, and Waters, and wallowed in them, as the Pigs had done; so that in a few Days, his white Scales began to fall off.[67]

Just as the converts of St Birinus stepped from Bapsey Pond at Taplow, or as Christine Keeler emerged from the pool at Cliveden, Bladud emerged from these miraculous waters irrevocably changed; returned from death to life, from obscurity to prominence, his position in history shifted forever. According to legend, he set out immediately to London to present his ring to his mother and be reconciled with his father, reclaiming his inheritance. On his father's death, he became a kind of priest-king or arch-druid, skilled in 'Astrology and the Mathematical Arts', as Wood relates. As ruler, Bladud is credited with being the first to enclose the springs and build the baths 'for the Benefit of the Publick', dedicating them either to the Celtic goddess Sulis (hence the Roman name for Bath, *Aquae Sulis*) or to Minerva. Naturally enough, this ancient king was unfamiliar with the form of wheeled transport central to this book. But he did have ambitions to conquer time and space – in short, he did *fly*, on this Wood is clear, quoting numerous sources, differing in detail but agreeing on his ultimate fate. 'This Prince was a very ingenious Man, and taught Necromancy in his Kingdom; nor left off pursuing his magical Operations, 'till he attempted to fly to the Upper Region of the Air, with Wings he had prepared, and fell down upon the Temple of Apollo ... where he was dashed to Pieces ...' In another account, taken from Geoffrey of Monmouth, Bladud 'applied himself to ingenious Studies, invented and made himself Wings to fly with; but on one of his Flights, unfortunately, fell down upon Salisbury Church and broke his Neck, to the great grief of all his Subjects'. The story of Bladud's flight contains echoes of another: that of Daedalus, whose conquest of the air failed when his son tumbled from the sky, undone by the fact that wax softens in the heat of the sun. (Accounts often hold such simple, physical laws responsible for undoing the most visionary transport plans. Brunel's futuristic atmospheric railway, built between Exeter and Teignmouth in Devon and powered by differential air pressure, was long said to have failed because rats, attracted by the tallow rubbed into the leather to keep it supple, ate the leather flap valves sealing the traction pipes.)

In his account of the history of Bath, Wood gives much credence to the story that either as prince or king, Bladud travelled to Athens to be schooled in Pythagorean magic, from where he brought back 'four eminent Philosophers, to instruct the Britons in all Liberal Sciences'. Wood was obsessed with proving a connection between ancient British monuments and classical mathematics; according to him, the stone circles at the nearby village of Stanton Drew mark the place the four philosophers assembled to teach the people, arranging the stones for educational purposes to 'form a perfect model of the Pythagorean system of the planetary world'. The situation and the soil of Bath, Wood argued, were perfect 'as tho' both had been made by the Magick of King BLADUD ... to answer the ancient British name given to Bath, of, the City of Ointment in the Warm Vale'. None of this would matter except that such half-truths, legends and imaginings, along with Masonic symbols, *are built into the architectural fabric of Bath itself*; the diameter of The Circus at Bath, which Wood designed but did not live to see built, is based on his rough measurement of the stone circle at Stonehenge.

Haile Selassie invested in this mythic territory when he bought Fairfield House for £3,500 in 1936. The decision to acquire a property made financial sense. The royal party could hardly live in hotel suites for the indefinite future; the emperor's funds were limited and called on from many sides. Apart from running his extensive household there were the needs of Ethiopian exiles in Palestine, Kenya and Egypt; the legal fees from interminable lawsuits; and the cost of placing his children in private schools. (At a book launch on the Welsh borders I fall into conversation with a man in his 80s who remembers playing football against the crown prince, Haile Selassie's son, at a school outside Bath, and the black-caped figure who stood on the touchline, silently watching.) 'Our life at Bath was very hard,' the emperor wrote in his autobiography. 'We also encountered great financial difficulties. Some sources of information had spread the rumour that We had taken a great deal of money with Us when leaving the country and they were attempting to make people believe this, but it was a complete lie...' Whether these 'sources' were Ethiopians or Italians, he does not specify. The truth is that the idea the emperor might abandon his country rather than die defending it had outraged many of the Ethiopian nobility, exposing the faultlines in the elaborate networks of loyalties that held the nation together. (It also led to disillusionment among some of his supporters in the West. Marcus Garvey, a John the Baptist figure in the Rastafarian pantheon, who had urged his followers in 1927 to 'look to Africa where a King would be declared, for the day of deliverance is near', wrote that Selassie 'ran away from his country to England, leaving his people to be massacred by the Italians'.[68]) As the royal party rattled towards Djibouti on the train, before the Italians marched into Addis Ababa the city descended into looting and skirmishing, many of its buildings put to the torch by its own people.

Living at Fairfield, attempting to embody through his continuance of ritual the nation and church of which he was the head, Selassie was isolated from the political mainstream, at least until the tide of history turned and made the reconquest of Ethiopia strategically important to the Allies. This period of enforced inaction, along with the feeling that he was being deliberately sidelined by the British government, was undoubtedly frustrating.

The emotion would have been one recognised by Stefan Zweig. 'I never knew one modern devil could destroy a thousand years of Art and Thought,' he wrote to a friend, before leaving London for Bath. He hoped it would provide a refuge where he could think and write, but with the outbreak of the second world war he found himself classed as an enemy alien; restrictions were placed on his travel, a situation not rectified until the following year when he was granted a British passport. For the world-famous writer, who regularly crisscrossed Europe and North America on author tours, such limitations were insufferable. It is striking how many of his stories and novellas begin with mention of stations and trains. 'At the First Junction beyond Dresden, an elderly gentleman entered our compartment ...' (*The Invisible Collection*); '"R", the famous novelist, had been away on a brief holiday in the mountains. Reaching Vienna early in the morning, he bought a newspaper at the station, and when he glanced at the date, was reminded it was his birthday ...' (*Letter from an Unknown Woman*); 'Having just got back to Vienna, after a visit to an out of the way part of the country, I was walking home from the station ...' (*Buchmendel*). Zweig had to ask for special permission to take the train to London to speak at the cremation of his friend Sigmund Freud at Golders Green in 1939, a procedure that angered him so much he chose to miss the memorial to Freud, held some weeks later. From Bath, Zweig wrote to the government suggesting he be allowed to set up a German language newspaper for propaganda purposes. 'From all writers in the German language not one has today a larger public in all languages of the world than myself and … very few could have such an influence in neutral countries on both sides of the ocean,' he declared, without exaggeration. 'Nothing is more painful than to be obliged to be idle in a time when everybody's service is a moral duty.' Words the exiled emperor would doubtless have concurred with.

As a result of his official isolation, many of Haile Selassie's daily contacts beyond his household were with the ordinary citizens of Bath: with tradespeople; with the owner of the local cinema, where he went to watch Pathé newsreels of the African campaigns; with people he met while walking by the river or in the city's parks. This mixing with other social classes would, of course, have been totally impossible in his home country, where even senior officials were forbidden to meet his eye. One local tradesman, a purveyor of leather goods called Ernest Smith, who had supplied various items to the royal household, seems to have become a trusted friend. Harried by rumours beginning to circulate that he could not meet his bills, increasingly worried about his finances, Selassie summoned Smith and asked him to recommend a jeweller to whom he could sell some of his belongings. A few days later, Mr Smith boarded a train to London carrying a bag that contained a precious selection of royal jewellery, including a quantity of diamonds, its contents probably worth more than he would earn in a lifetime. He returned with funds sufficient to secure the royal household until their departure.

Haile Selassie left Bath in January 1941, setting out on his long return journey, firstly to Poole, then flying boat to Egypt and on to Sudan, eventually re-entering Addis in triumph. It appears he didn't forget his stay in Bath. 'On this occasion of Our entry into Our territory and Our reunion with Our people, We also do not forget the great people of Great Britain who accorded Us such a warm and cordial reception,' he said in a speech made on 22 January 'We will never forget Our indebtedness to those people for their deep understanding of Our suffering or of that of Our people and for the encouragement they gave Us at the time of Our distress.'[69] It is said he renamed his residence in Addis 'Fairfield'. A letter on headed notepaper for Ernest Smith arrived after the war, assuring him and members of his family a warm welcome should they ever visit Addis Ababa. What is certain is that he donated Fairfield House and its grounds to the Corporation of Bath, as the plaque next to the front door reads, 'in appreciation of the warm and courteous hospitality of the people' of the city, 'to serve as a home for the aged'. Avon county council ran it as an old people's home for some years, until the regulations governing such institutions rendered the building obsolete. Today, its ground floor hosts a day centre for Bath's Ethnic Minority Senior Citizens Association, while upstairs is given over to a small museum relating to the emperor's life and stay in Bath. Naturally, the house is of immense significance to Rastafarians. Shawn Naphtali Sobers, an academic and filmmaker born in Bath and based at the University of the West of England in Bristol, who researched a documentary about Selassie's time at Fairfield for the BBC, told me that 'for the Rasta community it is probably the most important place outside Ethiopia and Jamaica'. An interested group of both believers and non-believers have formed themselves into the Friends of Fairfield House, with the ultimate intention of taking control of the building from the council and running it themselves, making sure it remains accessible to all those with an interest in its history.

I asked Dr Sobers whether he remembered people being aware of Haile Selassie's connection with the city when he was growing up there as a child.

'Very little; people knew he had lived here but they weren't really sure where', he told me, 'because the house is hidden from the road.

People knew there was this connection ... When I put an ad in the local newspaper I got a flood of letters from people who had memories of him, people who knew him and were really affectionate. As a Rasta myself and also as a journalist and documentary maker, I could have found out anything; I could have found out things I didn't want to hear. Normally, it's only Rastas you hear talking about Haile Selassie. But hearing elderly middle-class and working-class white people from Bath talk about him the same way, in some cases, that you hear Rastas talking about him was a revelation.'

It is 23 July, the emperor's birthday and a holy day in the Rastafarian calendar. In the garden, near where a vegetable plot has been laid out by a volunteer, the nyabinghi drums are already sounding. The chair of the Friends of Fairfield House, Steve Nightingale, has been showing me around, in between overseeing arrangements to accommodate the evening's visitors who include Cherry Beath, the mayor of Bath. In the corridor we bump into Ras Bandele Selassie, the Rastafarian elder who is taking the lead in the evening's celebration. Steve explains to him that I am writing a book that will take in His Imperial Majesty's time at Fairfield. Ras Bandele holds my hand without releasing it, looking searchingly into my eyes. 'Research, research,' he urges, in gentle exhortation. Later, in the garden, I watch as he stands in the centre of a circle of Rastafarians, holding the mayor's hand aloft, reasoning with the congregation, his words emphasised and underlined by the deep throb of the drums.

Like Bladud, the man these people have gathered to commemorate also made a mystical flight, one with a gentler landing, at Palisadoes airport in Kingston, Jamaica, in 1966. His plane was greeted by thousands of worshippers; like Garibaldi at Bath station, he was trapped on board, until Rasta leaders reasoned with the crowds. This, they believed, was the Messiah who Marcus Garvey had foretold would lead his people out of slavery; the Lion of the Tribe of Judah and root of David spoken of in chapter five of the Book of Revelation. That day at the airport, a world religion was born. At home, Haile Selassie presided over a system that kept many of his own populace in a state of feudal near-slavery; in a kingdom of 30 million farmers, 1 per cent of the budget was spent on agriculture and 40 per cent on the army. Abroad he was, and remains, an inspiration to countless thousands; a source of pride and identity that has transformed lives, his words set to music by and infused with the spiritual breath of Bob Marley, helping to spark a cultural renaissance the influence of which has been felt worldwide. It seems fitting he should have spent his interregnum in Bath, a city designed by a druid, its first king an astrologer with the power of flight. If Selassie's coming was the stuff of prophecy, his end was also a matter of portents in the heavens. As one of those who served the emperor in Addis Ababa during the final days of his reign told Ryszard Kapuściński, 'The whole world stood on its head, my friend, because strange signs appeared in the sky. The moon and Jupiter stopping in the seventh and twelfth houses, instead of turning in the direction of the triangle, began ominously to form the figure of the square.'[70] How could one man embody so many different things to so many different people: despot, oppressor, Messiah and spokesman for African liberation? The city of Bath, its beginnings and construction rooted in myth and dream, is probably not the place to try to separate the intertwined strands of history, superstition, politics and belief in which he remains entwined.

LOCATION: BRISTOL

READING BETWEEN THE LINES
OF BRUNEL'S BLANK PAGES

> "'What a thinking steam-ingein this old lady is. And she
> don't know how she does it. Nor does the ingein!'"
>
> Charles Dickens, *Our Mutual Friend* (1865)

I know it is time to leave Bath when, standing in front of the abbey contemplating the famous sculpted stone ladders that transport angels between heaven and earth, I find myself thinking they look like railway tracks.

We are now just one stop from Bristol, where our journey ends. In terms of Brunel's involvement with the Great Western Railway we have read the story backwards, flipping the pages to the place his involvement with the line began. Geography triumphs over chronology; physical reality over insubstantial time, through which, as readers, we are empowered to move at will. His physical presence is everywhere, of course. The suspension bridge he designed but never saw completed embodies notions of the sublime contrasted with the latest industrial technology. His castellated, Tudor revival-style station at Temple Meads still stands, converted to other uses, crumbling gently alongside the building that replaced it; and his iron ship, the SS *Great Britain*, sits newly restored in the Great Western Docks where it was first constructed, towed back from the distant Falkland Islands bay in which it ended its active life.

If Brunel shaped the city during his lifetime, the city is shaping him after his death. Bristol is the capital of the Brunel industry, in all its varied forms, from world-class archives enabling the pursuit of serious scholarship and research to heritage tourism and the sale of souvenirs. His copious papers, including architectural and engineering drawings, diaries, notebooks and correspondence were left to the University of Bristol; they now reside in the Brunel Institute, administered by the SS *Great Britain* Trust and located next to the renovated ship. It is here I have come to see his drawings and diaries first hand, to hold in my gloved fingers the notebooks he would have carried on his person while prospecting the route of the line. The entrance to the institute is through a 'nautical gift shop' where items for sale include Brunel's SS *Great Britain* luxury pens; a chocolate engineer's tool kit, 'for the budding Brunel in your life'; and rolls of dockyard chain parcel tape, illustrated with chain links reminiscent of those in Howlett's famous photograph. A short walk away on the other side of the dry dock is the drawing office where Brunel and his team would have worked on plans for the ship. This building is currently being converted to be the centrepiece of a new museum called 'Being Brunel', which will house a collection of nearly 14,000 items, scheduled to open in 2017. A visitor to the museum will be encouraged to literally step inside Brunel's mind by entering a vast replica of his head, enabling him or her 'to see the world through Brunel's eyes, and experience the rush of thoughts channelling through his brain'.[71] This visceral sense of connection with Brunel and the vestiges of his presence will be encouraged by the display of artefacts with something of the character of religious relics: a horn-handled penknife engraved with the initials 'I. K. B.' that would have travelled in Brunel's pocket and which includes 'a tin opener, blade, saw, hook, spike, drill, corkscrew, metal toothpick, tweezers and a device for removing stones from horses' hooves';[72] and a relic of the engineer's 40-a-day habit in the shape of a half-smoked cigar in his cigar case.

Bristol's engagement with Brunel at every level in its topography, from the visitor centre at the Clifton Suspension Bridge high above the city to the passenger ferries crossing the water to the Great Western Docks, makes it an open-air laboratory in the workings of the 21st-century heritage industry. This history, after all, is a more comfortable one than that which preceded it – the city's long connection with slavery. Walking through streets surrounded by magnificent architecture and public buildings, some of the best-known the result of the altruism of slave merchants like Edward Colston, it is hard not to be reminded again of Frantz Fanon's *The Wretched of the Earth*: 'Europe is literally the creation of the Third World,' he wrote. 'The wealth which smothers her is that which was stolen from the under-developed peoples.' The city has engaged in extensive public discussions about how to acknowledge this troublesome inheritance. At the turn of the millennium, Bristol Museum & Art Gallery staged an exhibition called 'A Respectable Trade? Bristol and Transatlantic Slavery', which was both the city's first substantive response to this aspect of its past, Shawn Sobers assures me, as well as the most attended in the museum's history, until it in turn was eclipsed by a Banksy exhibition in 2009. (Arguably, it is now Banksy rather than Brunel who can claim to be Bristol's most famous adopted son.) Dr Sobers is particularly interested in the way that when history is not acknowledged it is replaced by myth – or, as he puts it when we meet at the university, 'if you leave a silence it gets filled. There are lots of people who want to believe that slaves were kept in the Redcliffe Caves in Bristol. There are tunnels underneath St Mary Redcliffe church, so people say that's where the slaves were held … And the round space at Broadmead, people think that's where they were sold. All these things were talked about when I was growing up and it was hard to know what to believe without doing your own research. Of course, it was the spoils of slavery that were kept in Redcliffe Caves, the sugar and tobacco, not slaves themselves ... But that direct connection, that emotional attachment to people rather than money, meant people wanted to believe the stories. Not everyone's a historian, not everyone knows the facts, but they still know there's something in the fabric of the city that hasn't been acknowledged or resolved.'

This search for resolution haunts the city's dialogue with itself. During 2006, in the run-up to the 200th anniversary of abolition, focus shifted to the question of whether or not Bristol should make a formal apology for its involvement in the murderous triangular trade. A public debate was organised, chaired by academic and philosopher A. C. Grayling and held in the British Empire and Commonwealth Museum, then situated in Brunel's original Temple Meads station building. Arguments ranged back and forth beneath the engineer's famous hammerbeam roof, modelled on the medieval Westminster Hall in London, the iron strengthening its wooden structure the only hint of the sweeping modernity of his design for Paddington station at the other end of the line, completed some 13 years later. On one side were those who held that until an apology (and possibly reparations) had been made, the roots of present-day racism and the enduring psychological damage done by slavery could never be addressed. On the other were those who pointed out that while the wealthy merchant class of Bristol certainly benefited from the trade, the far greater part of the city's inhabitants were living and working in conditions little better than slavery themselves, denied political representation or a stake in the wealth slavery created. Still others argued that attention would be better directed towards the slavery very much present in various parts of the world today. Perhaps a better meeting of minds could have been achieved if a delegation of Brunel's navvies had debated with slaves from a plantation owned by one of Bristol's merchant class, but this could not be arranged. A 'statement of regret', signed by some of the city's business, religious and political institutions, was issued later in the year.

In a more surprising development, still touched with mystery, the Empire and Commonwealth Museum itself closed in 2007, the year of the 200th anniversary of the abolition of the slave trade, after it was discovered that artefacts loaned to it had been sold without their owners' knowledge or permission. Investigations into how such things could have been allowed to happen continue. Having failed to find a new home in London, the museum's collection was donated to Bristol Museum & Art Gallery, where much of it remains in the archives, as if the city had once again swallowed this indigestible part of its history to be addressed at some future date.

The vigour of the debate over slavery is testament not only to the political engagement of Bristol's black community, one of the longest established in Britain, but also to the city's radical tradition, stretching back to the time Brunel lived there in the 1830s and very much alive today. Sometimes the gaps in the archive are more eloquent than words. Brunel experienced revolutionary sentiment at first hand when he volunteered to be a special constable during the Bristol riots in 1831. His account of events in the autumn of that year begins eloquently enough. Having arrived in Bristol on 30 October, he hears there has been some firing 'and that the 14th [Light Dragoons, under the command of Lieutenant Colonel Thomas Brereton] were gone – could hardly believe it – went to the Mansion House [the residence of the mayor in Queen Square] and found it nearly deserted – it had been broken into again and sacked – armed myself with a chair back and found the guard'.[73] Together Brunel and this employee made themselves busy 'getting off the pictures and plate by the roof and through the custom house' next door. We know that Brunel apprehended one rioter but when he handed him over to another special constable, the man was twice released. Brunel recognised the constable responsible for letting him go as one of the rioters he had seen in action on Saturday night, but although he was summoned as a witness he did not provide the man's name to the magistrates.

It is the next and following pages in the diary that are most intriguing. They are completely blank, both in the main body of the diary and in the crowded index at the back of the volume, in both of which it looks as though Brunel blocked out a section under the heading 'Riots' to return to at a later date and never did. Ever the self-conscious author, even in his supposedly private diaries, did he think better of commenting, in view of the huge popular support for those involved in the uprising in Bristol? The disturbances had begun when Sir Charles Wetherell arrived in the city to open the assizes. Wetherell had opposed the Reform bill that proposed to modestly extend the franchise in the House of Lords; only 5 per cent of the inhabitants of Bristol had the right to vote. Two thousand protesters took to the streets to receive him into the city with 'hisses, yells and groans', including the 'female habituées' of the alleys of Temple Street, 'who added shrill execrations to the din'. In the ensuing days the Mansion House, much of Queen Square, several prisons and the Bishop's Palace were put to the torch.

Despite the attack on the house of his friend Christopher Claxton and the havoc they wreaked in the wider city, did Brunel feel some sympathy for the protesters' cause? Many of the rioters were young men of a similar age, though different background, to himself. He may have been affected, as others were, by the death of Lieutenant Colonel Thomas Brereton, who shot himself during his court-martial. Brunel pasted the full report of the court-martial from the *Bristol Mirror* of 14 January 1832 into his diary,[74] as well as the account of the inspection of Brereton's body by the coroner's jury and the testimony on his state of mind from his servants. Brereton stood accused of 'improper ... conduct towards the rioters, in shaking hands and conversing with them, on various occasions during the 29th, 30th and 31st', as well as the more serious charges of withdrawing his soldiers and taking to his bed, allowing the unrest and looting to continue unchecked. When the court-martial received news of his death, the lawyer in charge of the case against Brereton made a statement of regret in which he expressed the hope that the conduct of the case had not driven him to his action.

The following year Brunel was in London, helping his brother-in-law Benjamin Hawes in his campaign to become the member of parliament for the new borough of Lambeth on a radical, reformist ticket. The activity helped him through an uncertain time, when he was stalked by doubts about his career and what sounds, from the letter he appended to Hawes in his diary, like depression. ('I am unhappy – exceedingly so,' he wrote to his brother-in-law. 'The excitement of this election came just in time to conceal it.'[75]) Work on the Clifton Suspension Bridge had been put on hold in the aftermath of the riots. However, as a result of both political pressure within parliament and agitation on the streets of a number of cities throughout the country, the First Reform Act had passed into law. From Brunel's standpoint, the uprising had both halted progress, in the shape of the bridge – the project he was later to call 'my first child, my darling'[76] – and ushered it in, by advancing the cause of long-overdue political reform. Brunel's true feeling about the dramatic events he experienced in Bristol is concealed somewhere in the blank pages of his diary. As always when it comes to his private political opinions he eludes us, too careful perhaps of damaging his business interests to be pinned down.

If Brunel's career looked uncertain for a brief period after the riots, his entrance to the city in July 1843 could hardly have been more triumphant. Brunel was at the controls of the broad-gauge locomotive *Damon*, drawing the train bringing Prince Albert to Bristol for the launch of the SS *Great Britain*. He seems on this occasion to have overcome his reluctance to take charge of the engine, at least for its arrival at Bristol; no doubt the importance of his passenger served to concentrate his mind. As he steamed into Temple Meads along the railway he had personally prospected and every aspect of which he had designed, conveying the most important man in the kingdom into the city through a station that had first taken shape at the end of his pencil, perhaps he was able to put aside the continuing frustration of the Clifton Bridge. Work had once again been halted in February through lack of funds, leaving the great abutments standing on either side of the gorge unconnected, objects of local ridicule. It was easier to cross the Atlantic, it appeared, than the Avon Gorge.

The streets and the dockside were crowded with onlookers, the water with craft small and large, and a further 30,000 people had gathered on Brandon Hill to watch the proceedings. The ship was the largest in the world and the first to be driven by a steam-powered propeller, the technology for which Brunel had refined through working as an engineering consultant for the Royal Navy. Albert made a tour of inspection and banqueted in a pavilion on the dockside, his table decorated with a scale model of the ship. Prussian, Sardinian and American ministers were in attendance, along with Isambard's father, Sir Marc Brunel, who had taken such a major supporting role in the design of the Clifton Bridge. The ship was decorated with the flags of all nations (a custom maintained with the restored ship today, as if it perpetually awaits a relaunch into the ocean). A moment of farce ensued when Mrs Miles, the wife of one of the directors of the steamship company, invited by Prince Albert to launch the ship, missed with her bottle by about 10 feet. Albert immediately took control of the situation, hurling another bottle that exploded against the iron hull, showering those pushing the boat from the dock with champagne and glass fragments. He left shortly afterwards, arriving in London two hours later, declaring himself impressed that he had spent six hours in Bristol and travelled

240 miles all in the course of a day. A day, he might have said, shaped and enabled by the technological genius of one man.

A day, too, on which Brunel's status in the city that has adopted him must have seemed more secure than it had done for some time. Reputation is a fickle thing. In his monumental *Annals of Bristol* published in 1887, John Latimer compares Brunel unfavourably to 'the sober-minded, practical engineers of the North'. By contrast, he was 'an inexperienced theorist, prone to seek for difficulties rather than to evade them, and utterly indifferent to the outlay which his recklessness entailed upon his employers. The evil consequences of his pet crotchet, the "broad gauge" system, on the commerce of Bristol will have to be noticed hereafter.'

Perhaps it is his combination of success and abject failure – underpowered and badly designed locomotives, unfinished bridges, grounded ships, above all his stubborn refusal to recognise the impact of choosing a gauge for his line that made it impossible to integrate with a national network – that explains in part the British public's continued fascination with Brunel. (His stature beyond British shores is a shadow of what it is at home; every country, it seems, produces its own heroic engineers.) We love those who 'stick to their guns' (a military phrase), who are able to pick themselves up after every reversal and encourage us in our turn by their refusal to lose hope. If we really were able to step inside Brunel's mind, as the new museum promises to allow us to do, we might find he had no choice but to pursue his own course; that his way of understanding a problem was to take it back to first principles and rethink it, brooking no interference or distraction from others, in the confidence that if he worked at it hard enough that same mind would find a solution. These were certainly the qualities he brought to the challenge of constructing the line from London to Bristol. The experience of doing so, he wrote to GWR company secretary Charles Saunders, was like 'the sudden adoption of a language familiar enough to the speaker and in itself simple enough but unfortunately understood by nobody but him – every word has to be translated – and so it is with my work'. If the 'work' he is referring to is the iron road we have travelled, it is, he maintains, written in a language of its own, a story that can only be read by following its course.

Brunel was not a machine; his capacious brain was not a computer. He drove himself hard, as if his body was a locomotive: 'a thinking steam-ingein', as Mr Boffin calls Mrs Boffin in Charles Dickens's *Our Mutual Friend*. Nephritis, leading to a stroke, took him at the age of 53. Partly he was killed by tobacco, grown for half his lifetime by slaves; partly, no doubt, by the way he enslaved himself.

As I said at the outset of this book, it was never my intention to write any kind of biography of Brunel, or history of the railway he created; I leave that to the many who have preceded me and on whose shoulders I have stood. Instead I have followed the direction he set for me, the trajectory of my journey dictated by the line he drew between two English cities.

Once the vehicle was moving people climbed aboard; some were invited, others invited themselves. Defeated kings and deposed emperors, displaced exiles and slaves. Musicians, magicians and astronomers. Politicians, painters and polygamists. Murderers, missionaries, chatelaines and suicides. Actresses and showgirls; ambitious fathers and their struggling sons. An average sample, probably, if you turn the soil of this history-sodden kingdom, the way the building of a railway inevitably does.

We are moving back in the other direction, past Bath, towards London. The seats are all taken, the corridors crowded and a hubbub of voices fills the compartment in a multitude of languages. 'Every word has to be translated,' the engineer insists. And as we turn to one another the light vanishes and our train enters the longest tunnel in the world...

ENDNOTES

1. Thomas Carlyle, essay 'Hudson's Statue' in *Latter-day Pamphlets* (1850), p. 266.
2. Cited L. T. C. Rolt, *Isambard Kingdom Brunel* (London: Longmans, Green and Co Ltd, 1990), p. 231.
3. Walter Benjamin 'Surrealism: The Last Snapshot of the European Intelligentsia' (1929), from *Walter Benjamin: Selected Writings, Volume 2, Part 1, 1927–1930* (Cambridge, MA: Harvard University Press), p. 210.
4. Henry James's essay in *The Century* was illustrated by the American artist Joseph Pennell, who contributed a beautifully detailed sketch of top-hatted passengers passing through a gateway marked 'To the Continental Mainline' at Charing Cross station. *The Century: A Popular Quarterly*, Volume 37, Issue 2 (December 1888).
5. One of the most scathing was the Bloomsbury critic Clive Bell, who cited *The Railway Station* as a perfect example of a 'descriptive painting' devoid of 'significant form' or 'aesthetic emotion'. In his book *Art* (1914) he claimed to have spent 'many a weary 40 minutes … disentangling its fascinating incidents and forging for each an imaginary past and an improbable future'.
6. Later editions included black-and-white photographs and adjusted the subtitle to *Points of Interest Seen from the Train, Paddington–Penzance*; a companion guide entitled *Through the Window: Paddington to Killarney via Fishguard & Rosslare* was produced for the route to Ireland.
7. London *Evening News* (24 April 1979).
8. Émile Durkheim, *Suicide: A Study in Sociology* (Illinois: The Free Press, 1897), p. 292.
9. Sanjay Suri, 'The Suicide Station', *Outlook India Magazine* (26 November 2007).
10. The National Archives, Kew, reference AIR 8/356.

11. Directors' Report, August 1837, cited in MacDermot and Clinker, *History of the Great Western Railway, Volume 1* (1927), p. 30.

12. Gibbs' diaries are quoted in Jack Simmons (ed.), *The Birth of the Great Western Railway: Extracts from the Diary and Correspondence of George Henry Gibbs* (Bath, Somerset: Adams & Dart, 1971).

13. DM 162/1/8/1/3/GWR sketchbook 9/folio 1 & 4. GWR sketchbook 9, University of Bristol Collection.

14. MacDermot and Clinker, op. cit., p. 350.

15. 'Poverty is pushing people to steal food' by John Dickens, *Slough and South Bucks Observer* (27 June 2014), p. 3.

16. Henry M. Field, *The Story of the Atlantic Telegraph* (New York: Charles Scribner's Sons, 1892).

17. Kenneth Grahame, *The Romance of the Rail*, in *Pagan Papers* (1893).

18. Brunel Archive, Bristol: DM 1281/1. All underlinings and punctuation are Brunel's own.

19. The difference between time spent in a debtor's prison for a middle-class engineer and businessman like Marc Brunel and for the urban poor was immense, however. In the entrepreneurial age in which Brunel father and son both worked, making, losing and restoring fortunes was a common and relatively respectable aspect of life, inevitably accompanied by inconvenient visits to Marshalsea when debts could not be settled. Marc Brunel's stay was shortened to a few months through his connections in high places, his debt paid off by the government in view of his services to the nation.

20. E. P. Thompson, *The Making of the English Working Class* (London: Victor Gollancz, 1963).

21. 'Slaves and Labourers', *The Saturday Review* (16 January 1864).

22. DM 1306/2/1 folio 33, personal diary kept by Isambard Kingdom Brunel (the locked diary), University of Bristol Brunel Collection.

23. Blakey Vermeule, *The Unreasonable*, NONSITE.ORG issue 10, 13 September 2013, http://nonsite.org/the-tank/writing-against-time

24. Merlin Holland and Rupert Hart-Davis, *The Complete Letters of Oscar Wilde* (London: Henry Holt & Company, 2000), p. 484.

25. All quotations of Spencer's notebooks and letters are taken from Adrian Glew (ed.) *Stanley Spencer: Letters and Writings* (London: Tate Publishing, 2001), by permission of the Tate Trustees.

26. Ibid., Notebook, 6 December 1947.

27. Gilbert Spencer, *Stanley Spencer* (London: Victor Gollancz, 1961).

28. Op. cit., Notebook/Diary 1915–1918, p. 58.

29. Cited in letter from Viscount Astor to Thomas Gibson, reproduced in Carolyn Leder, *Stanley Spencer: the Astor Collection* (London: Thomas Gibson Publishing, 1976), p. 7.

30. Op. cit., *Stanley Spencer: Letters and Writings*, pp. 232–4.

31. Extract from the journals of Brion Gysin, cited in J. Geiger, *Nothing Is True – Everything Is Permitted: The Life of Brion Gysin* (New York: The Disinformation Company, 2005), p. 160.

32. Interview with Gysin included in the documentary *FlicKer* (2007) by Nic Sheehan.

33. Charles Darwin, *The Expression of the Emotions in Man and Animals* (London: John Murray, 1872), p. 219.

34. Havelock Ellis, *Studies in the Psychology of Sex, Volume 1: The Evolution of Modesty; The Phenomena of Sexual Periodicity; Auto-Eroticism* (1910), cited in Shelley Trower, *Senses of Vibration: A History of the Pleasure and Pain of Sound* (London: Continuum, 2012), p. 130.

35. Stefan Zweig, *Journey into the Past* (London: Pushkin Press, 2009).

36. David Bissell, 'Vibrating Materialities: Mobility–Body–Technology Relations' (London: Royal Geographical Society, 2009).

37. Translated as *Arrival of the Train at La Ciotat Station*, first shown in Lyon in January 1896.

38. Michael Clune, *Writing Against Time*, NONSITE.ORG issue 10, 13 September 2013 http://nonsite.org/the-tank/writing-against-time

39. Edward Thomas, *A Literary Pilgrim in England* (London: Methuen & Co. Ltd, 1917).

40. Frantz Fanon, *The Wretched of the Earth* (New York: Grove Press, 1963), p. 26.

41. *Station News*, Thames Valley Edition, Issue 2 (autumn/winter 2014).

42. DM 1306/2/1 folio 28, personal diary kept by Isambard Kingdom Brunel (the locked diary), University of Bristol Brunel Collection.

43. Isambard Brunel Jr, *The Life of Isambard Kingdom Brunel, Civil Engineer* (1870), pp. 511–13.

44. Ibid.

45. *Illustrated London News* (21 January 1871), p. 66.

46. Ben Marsden, *Re-Reading Isambard Kingdom Brunel: Engineering Literature in the Early Nineteenth Century*, in *Uncommon Contexts: Encounters Between Science and Literature, 1800–1914* (London: Pickering & Chatto, 2013), pp. 534–60.

47. Pocket notebook DM 1758/6/6/, University of Bristol Brunel Collection.

48. Kenneth Grahame, 'Oxford Through a Boy's Eyes', *Country Life*, Vol. 23, No. 12 (1932).

49. Richard Morris, 'Comment: Farewell, Cousin to the Crystal Palace', *British Archaeology*, No. 38 (October 1998).

50. 'A Mere Don', *Aspects of Modern Oxford* (London: Seeley and Company Ltd, 1894).

51. A selection is reproduced in Kenneth Grahame and David Gooderson, *My Dearest Mouse: the Wind in the Willows Letters* (London: Pavilion Books, 1988).

52. Dr Richard Beeching was the author of *The Reshaping of British Railways*, better known as the Beeching Report, published in March 1963, which recommended the closure of almost a third of the British network and over 2,000 stations.

53. Arthur Bryant, *The Spirit of Conservatism* (London: 1929), cited in Patrick Wright, *On Living in an Old Country* (Oxford: OUP, 2009).

54. H. V. Morton, *In Search of England* (London: Methuen, 1927), pp. 1–3.

55. *Let's Imagine: A Branch Line Railway with John Betjeman,* broadcast 29 March 1963.

56. Richard Jefferies, 'My Old Village' in *Field and Hedgerow* (London: Longmans Green and Co., 1889).

57. Richard Jefferies, *After London: or, Wild England* (London: Duckworth & Co., 1885).

58. Adrian Vaughan, *The Intemperate Engineer: Isambard Kingdom Brunel in His Own Words* (Shepperton, Surrey: Ian Allan Publishing, 2010), pp. 31ff.

59. Op. cit., *The Life of Isambard Kingdom Brunel, Civil Engineer.*

60. Angus R. Buchanan, *Brunel: The Life and Times of Isambard Kingdom Brunel* (London: Bloomsbury Continuum, 2007), p. 269, note 48.

61. Speech made by George Osborne, 23 June 2014, reported on ITV news.

62. The interview was made by researcher and oral historian Kayley Porter and is part of the archive being built up at Fairfield House.

63. Ryszard Kapuściński, *The Emperor* (New York: Harcourt Brace Jovanovich, 1983).

64. Nick Osmond (ed.), *Arthur Rimbaud: Illuminations – Colour Plates* (London: The Athlone Press, 1976), p. 49.

65. A fuller account of this incident can be read in Andrew Swift's excellent book *The Ringing Grooves of Change: Brunel and the Coming of the Railway to Bath* (Bath, Somerset: Akeman Press, 2006), chapter 19.

66. Garibaldi had been wounded two years before at the Battle of Aspromonte in 1862.

67. The description is from John Wood, *AN ESSAY TOWARDS A DESCRIPTION OF THE CITY OF BATH: In TWO PARTS. Wherein Its ANTIQUITY is Ascertained: Its SITUATION, MINERAL WATERS, and BRITISH WORKS Described: the ANTIENT WORKS in Its NEIGHBOURHOOD, the GODS, PLACES OF WORSHIP, RELIGION and LEARNING of the BRITONS Occasionally Consider'd: the RISE of the BRITISH DRUIDS Demonstrated: the DEVESTATIONS Commited by the ROMANS at BATH, Their ENCAMPING on the HOT-WATERS, and Their Turning Their CAMP into a CITY Fully Set Forth: and the WORKS of the SAXONS, and Their SUCCESSORS Briefly Related.*

68. Marcus Garvey, 'The Failure of Haile Selassie as Emperor', *The Black Man* (March/April 1937).

69. His memories of British politicians and officials and the many slights and snubs he received in the early years of his residence in England were less warm, leading to a turning away from alliance with Britain and towards the United States after he returned to power.

70. Op. cit., *The Emperor*, p. 133.

71. *What is Being Brunel?* The SS *Great Britain* website, http://www.ssgreatbritain.org/node/472/what-being-brunel

72. Article 'Isambard Kingdom Brunel Artefacts to go on Display', *Western Morning News* (27 August 2014).

73. DM 1306/2/3/1 private diary March 1830 to September 1832, University of Bristol Brunel Collection.

74. Ibid.

75. DM 1306/2/1/ folio 0, personal diary kept by Isambard Kingdom Brunel (the locked diary), University of Bristol Brunel Collection.

76. DM 1306/2/3/2 folio 167, private diary September 1832 to 3 March 1840.

77. DM 1758/11/15 typed copy of a letter from Isambard Kingdom Brunel to Charles Alexander Saunders, 3 December 1837, University of Bristol Brunel Collection.

ACKNOWLEDGEMENTS

Station to Station grew out of my time as Writer on the Train for rail operator First Great Western. I would particularly like to thank Sue Evans and James Davis at First for their support, as well as the other members of staff who have shown kindness and tolerance to me on my way.

I am indebted to everyone who suggested avenues to explore, provided inspiration through their work, acted as early readers or stepped in at opportune moments to steady the ship, among them Charlotte Attlee, Joseph Attlee, Rachel Barbaressi, Martyn Bull, Alex Butterworth, my agent Catherine Clarke and my editor Lindsay Davies, Stanley Donwood (magician of Bath), Chris Dorsett, Peter Furtado, Alexandra Harris, Andrew Kelly, Patrick Keiller, Roman Krznaric, Laura MacCulloch, Ramuntcho Matta, Fabrizio Nevola, Roger Sealey, Shawn Sobers, Volker Straub, Shelley Trower and Wes Williams.

Thanks are due to Adrian Glew at the Tate Archive, for his generous encouragement regarding Stanley Spencer, as well as Vanessa Garden at Tate Publishing; Eleni Papavasileiou for her knowledge and enthusiasm at the Brunel Institute, which was much appreciated; Elaine Arthurs at the Library and Archive at the Steam Museum in Swindon, which is also where I met Jack Hayward; Jonathan Oates at the Ealing Local History Centre; Ann Danks at the Stanley Spencer Gallery; Kayley Porter and Steve Nightingale at Fairfield House in Bath.

To the members of Orphan Train and everyone at Lizieres: Aloha! Thanks always.

Digital exploration of the line, which in turn fed into print, was made possible through funding from REACT in Bristol; special thanks to Jo Landsdowne, Jon Dovey and Clare Reddington. I am also grateful for support from the Author's Foundation during the early stages of this project.

PHOTOGRAPH CREDITS

INDEX

(page numbers in italic type refer to photographs)